JOHN
WAYNE
SPEAKS

"THE ULTIMATE JOHN WAYNE QUOTE BOOK"

JOHN WAYNE SPEAKS

Written, researched, and compiled by

Mark Orwoll

ST. MARTIN'S
GRIFFIN
NEW YORK

First published in the United States by St. Martin's Griffin,
an imprint of St. Martin's Publishing Group

JOHN WAYNE SPEAKS. Copyright © 2021 by Mark Orwoll.
All rights reserved. Printed in the United States of America.
For information, address St. Martin's Publishing Group,
120 Broadway, New York, NY 10271

www.stmartins.com

Library of Congress Cataloging-in-Publication Data

Names: Wayne, John, 1907–1979, author I Orwoll, Mark, editor,
    compiler.
Title: John Wayne speaks : the ultimate John Wayne quote book /
    written, researched, and compiled by Mark Orwoll.
Description: First edition. I New York : St. Martin's Griffin, 2021. I
Identifiers: LCCN 2021021934 I ISBN 9781250815835 (paper over
    board) I ISBN 9781250815842 (ebook)
Subjects: LCSH: Wayne, John, 1907–1979—Quotations. I
    Quotations, American.
Classification: LCC PN2287.W36 A25 2021 I DDC 791.4302/8092
    [B]—dc23
LC record available at https://lccn.loc.gov/2021021934

Our books may be purchased in bulk for promotional,
educational, or business use. Please contact your local bookseller
or the Macmillan Corporate and Premium Sales Department at
1-800-221-7945, extension 5442, or by email
at MacmillanSpecialMarkets@macmillan.com.

First Edition: 2021

10 9 8 7 6 5 4 3 2 1

This book is dedicated to the
memory of my parents,
Sylfest Peter Orwoll, Jr., and
Frances Patricia Giffin Orwoll,
who taught me that words matter.

CONTENTS

PREFACE

This book is not meant to be an academic tome, but it *is* meant to be as accurate as possible.

All quotations are accompanied by a superscript number, which refers to the film source for each quote, as listed by number in appendix B. Films in that appendix are ordered chronologically, based on the U.S. premiere and/or general release dates. Release dates are sourced from the American Film Institute's AFI Catalog, Fred Landesman's exhaustive and well-researched *The John Wayne Filmography,* the Internet Movie Database (IMDb.com), and, when various dates are cited, a consensus of these and other references.

The categorization of quotes is the author's choosing. Quotes within each category are listed in chronological order, from the earliest film to the most recent. The author relied on actual screen credits for production notes and cast lists wherever possible, and confirmed them (and occasionally added to them) with information from Landesman, IMDb, and AFI.

As for the number of John Wayne films included in this book, 173 is an informed total, though not universally agreed on. Many references simply use "more than 170." The Internet Movie Database lists 140 Wayne films, but doesn't include most of the many silent films in which Wayne was an extra or had only a walk-on role. Landesman places the total at 171 (169 features and two shorts), which includes *The Sweetheart of Sigma Chi* (1933), a film in which Wayne's only scene was edited out of the final print, and for that reason, I have not included that film here. Landesman's list also includes *Hollywood Handicap,* but that was a short made for the Thalia Club, a private group, and not meant for public showings, so I have not included it here. Further, I have included four films that do not appear in the Landesman list: *A Home-Made Man* (1927) and *The Draw-Back* (1927), in both of which Wayne is identifiable; *Seeing Stars* (1928) (a researcher identified an uncredited Wayne after obtaining stills of this "lost" film, according to author Scott Eyman in *John Wayne: The Life and Legend*); and *Cancel My Reservation* (1972), a Bob Hope comedy in which Wayne has an uncredited cameo appearance as himself.

Details such as these, mostly found in the appendices of this book, are meant not to steal the editorial spotlight, but are presented here simply as background to support the main function of this book: to celebrate the memorable movie quotes of John Wayne.

—M.O.

INTRODUCTION

Why I Watched Every
John Wayne Movie

I watched every John Wayne movie because I couldn't track down a quote: "Shoot low. They might be crawlin'."

I love that quote, and just assumed it was from a Wayne movie because it's so . . . *right*. I went to the John Wayne official website and found a long list of quotes (a couple of which were actually spoken by him, too). But not the "shoot low" quote. Turns out, that was the motto of singing cowboy Monte Hale, who made a series of B Westerns for Republic Pictures in the 1940s and '50s. But it led me to wonder how many other supposed John Wayne quotes were either misattributed, inaccurate, or just plain made up.

And so I began my cinematic odyssey: to watch every John Wayne film and to transcribe as accurately as possible the most memorable bits of dialogue, the mumbled soliloquies, and the playful banter with his costars, in hope of creating a catalogue of authenticated verbatim lines. I would then break the quotes down into various categories (romance, duty, threats, etc.) and credit each of them to a specific film, so it could be traced back to the source for verification. I would list the title of each movie, its director, screenwriters, production notes, and original writing sources—taken directly from the screen credits. It would be the ultimate compendium of cowboy quotes, the sine qua non of the star's sayings, the final word on what Hollywood put into John Wayne's mouth and how he spat it out.

"But for God's sake, man," you must be asking yourself, *"why would a fully formed adult put himself through that*?!"

About a quarter of the way through watching his 173 films, I found myself thinking the same thing. Trouble is, you get that far into any major project, you're reluctant to waste all the time you've already invested by quitting.

So I admitted to myself what I knew to be true: I had become the reluctant Boswell to John Wayne's Dr. Johnson. And there was no turning back.

My first mistake was to begin with those films I already knew were legendary: *Stagecoach, The Quiet Man, The Shootist,* and the like. But I shortly realized I had a long slog ahead of me, and the movies I was watching, in no particular order, lacked any context regarding Wayne's career. How did his 1930s Saturday-matinee Westerns stack up against his World War II flicks of the 1940s and '50s? Did he improve as an actor as he got older, or was he just mailing it in with his later films? Did the quotes get juicier and more frequent with the advancing years? And so I decided to go back to the beginning, to his first role as a principal actor, *The Big Trail* (1930). (Later I would watch his earlier bit parts and walk-ons in silent films in the late 1920s, but, for obvious reasons, there were no quotes from those films.)

The Big Trail is a largely unsung masterpiece. Granted, Wayne was far from polished. His persona comes off as a bit shy, somewhat uncertain. But from the outset, John Wayne was a beautiful specimen—big, broad-shouldered, as handsome as the Marlboro Man. And boy, could he sit on a horse! Merely to watch him on the screen was to be assured that *here* was a movie star. And the film itself, in which Wayne plays a wagon-train scout, is a legitimate spectacle, with sprawling scenery and hundreds of extras. It must have seemed certain to producers as well as the moviegoing public that a great career was in the offing.

But then . . . but then . . .

The Big Trail proved not to be the vehicle to screen stardom one might have predicted for the young actor, owing at least in part to the recent crash of the stock market, the onset of the Depression, and the resulting inability of some movie theaters to pay for the abundance of films they once offered. So Wayne, still a working stiff and not yet a movie star, continued accepting bit parts and secondary roles in third-rate films, as he had for years in silent movies leading up to *The Big Trail*. Some of those roles are incomprehensibly awful, as in *The Deceiver* (1931), in which Wayne portrays a corpus delicti. But it was also in the early 1930s that Wayne found his footing as a cowboy star in a series of cheapie Westerns made on Poverty Row, the industry's nickname for Hollywood's low-budget studios.

There is a small coterie of film watchers who love John Wayne's early oaters, but they're not to everyone's tastes. The plots are usually the same throughout—the good guy is perceived to be a bad guy until he can prove that he really is a good guy, and possibly kiss a plain girl somewhere in between. Either that or the innocent settlers are about to be bamboozled by a tough pistolero or a fancy city slicker until Wayne enters the scene and puts the villain in his place, usually after a speedy horse chase. (An interesting note about these early Waynesters: Although there was a fair amount of fisticuffs, it was far exceeded by chases on horseback over dusty trails.)

I was intrigued by how the Monogram/Lone Star (and later, some of the Republic) productions are "sort of" set in the 1800s, yet feature cars, telephones, and women with bobbed hair and Depression-era fashions. The culture clash of the settings in these early movies continues to astound, with cowboys on cattle drives going into towns where people are dressed in their modern-day finest, where newsreel crews are filming desperado shoot-outs, where passenger buses are robbed by horse-riding outlaw gangs. City men wearing three-piece suits and snap-brim fedoras waltz into old-school ranches like something that stumbled out of a time machine. So what year is it, anyway?! In a handful of those films, there are only oblique glimpses of motorized vehicles, as if from a parallel universe in which crime and evildoing and jazz music have corrupted the citizens, while in the Wayne Utopia of the nostalgic West, farmers and ranchers and even the kids get around by horseback or buggy, and the good folks dress in the duds of an honest telegraph operator or schoolmarm or general-store clerk, and turn giddy when the weekly stage arrives from the territorial capital. The people of, let's say, New Hope Valley live under a bell jar, which, as it must, develops a crack through which the dystopian world seeps like a miasma. You don't need white hats to tell the good guys. Honest ranchwear trumps double-breasted suits. Gingham is good, glimmering gowns are ungodly. Therein lies the crux of the plotlines of the majority of Wayne's 1930s Westerns.

I couldn't wait to finish watching the Lone Star productions (1933–35), most of which were directed by (and many also written by) Robert N. Bradbury. These quickies were Wayne's bread and butter in the early days, and he must have learned from them, because he shows a considerable improvement in later years over his stiff performances in these B movies. That being said, some Wayne fans simply go gaga over the innocence and big-sky backgrounds of these movies. But I caution you: They are an acquired taste, like red-eye, sarsaparilla, or tainted water from a bad desert spring.

For me, a collector of quotable dialogue, the thirties-era scripts hold little notable that passed through Duke's lips. He was the strong, silent type of Western lore, a rock against which other characters bounce their crazy quotes. More often than not in those early films, the lines from George "Gabby" Hayes, Walter Brennan, and other costars shine brighter than anything from Wayne himself.

And talk about costars! John Wayne's career is indebted to the high quality of his screen cohorts. George Hayes (fourteen movies with John Wayne, between 1933 and 1944) was a recurring player. He could portray a sheriff, a bartender, a drunk, a cranky old-timer, a stern patriarch, or whatever else the script called for. But he was always at his most delightful playing a crusty old coot saying things like, "Consarn it!" Yakima Canutt (an amazing thirty-two John Wayne movies, mostly uncredited, and many as a stunt double for Wayne, between 1930 and 1959) was another standby. He often played the bad guy, but he came across as such a naturally sweet man you couldn't hate him. A special mention should also be made of the largely unheralded and usually uncredited Chuck Roberson, another stuntman who doubled for Duke, fell off horses and rooftops, and/or played ruffians, desperadoes, henchmen, and other delightful bit characters in thirty-two John Wayne films, from 1943 to 1976. Other sidemen who livened up those pictures include Strother Martin (six films, from 1959 to 1975); Ben Johnson (seven films, from 1944 to 1973); Grant Withers (eight films, from 1943 to 1950); Harry Carey, Jr. (eight films, from 1948 to 1971); Patrick Wayne, John's son (ten films, from 1950 to 1971); Bruce Cabot (eleven films, from 1947 to 1971); Ward

Bond (thirteen films, from 1929 to 1959); Earl Dwire (seventeen films, from 1933 to 1936); Jack Pennick (seventeen films, from 1930 to 1962, mostly uncredited); Hank Worden (eighteen films, from 1939 to 1973); and the omnipresent Paul Fix (twenty-five films, from 1931 to 1973), who appeared on average in one of every seven John Wayne movies.

These costars were often given a movie's best lines. Much of Wayne's dialogue is in response to what someone else utters. He once even said, "I don't act. I react." But that opened the door for some unforgettable lines from his top colleagues:

Jim Toney (*The Lonely Trail*): If Texas gals is anything like the menfolk, my boy, the only use she's got for your heart is to cut it out and make jerky.

Hattie Noel (*Lady for a Night*): Dere ain't no bustle, honey! Dat's me!

George "Gabby" Hayes (*In Old Oklahoma*): Dan'l's the thinkin'est man I ever knowed.

Paul Fix (*Tycoon*): In the cool of the evening, the guy arrives and starts giving orders!

Walter Brennan (*Red River*): Never liked seein' strangers. Guess it's 'cause no stranger ever good-newsed me.

Maureen O'Hara (*The Quiet Man*): If you passed the pub as fast as you passed the chapel, you'd be better off, ya little squint.

Victor McLaglen (*The Quiet Man*): He'll regret it to his dying day—if ever he lives that long.

Claude Akins (*The Sea Chase*): In the fo'c'sle, they're saying a ship may belong to her captain, but the lifeboats belong to her crew.

Victor McLaglen (*The Quiet Man*): It was good morning you said to her, but it was good night you had on your mind!

Ward Bond (*Hondo*): There's times when water is . . . good.

Anthony Quinn (*Back to Bataan*): A guy's got to have something to live for before he can ask others to die.

Edmond O'Brien (*The Man Who Shot Liberty Valance*): Just give me a beer! A beer's not drinking!

Rod Taylor (*The Train Robbers*): Time was I could get drunk for a week, maybe two. Now I go on a bender for six, seven days, I get the blind staggers so bad I gotta get me to my bed. Yep, a man can't hold his liquor, that's the first sign [of getting older].

Slim Pickens (*The Cowboys*): Wil, if yer neck was any stiffer, you couldn't even bend over to pull yer boots on!

Roscoe Lee Browne (*The Cowboys*): I could swallow each of you whole without choking! All I need do is butter your heads and pin your ears back!

Yes, those costars, sidekicks, bit players, walk-ons, and other below-the-title cast members formed a supportive cadre of acting talent that served Wayne well to the end of his career.

Like many actors during the Depression, Wayne would sign a multipicture contract with one studio, then accept an even more lucrative offer from a competitor when the first contract ran out. His choice of studios, however, wasn't always inspired. The string of pictures he made for Universal in the late 1930s, for instance, was ill conceived. Wayne was often placed in urban roles that would have been better suited to Paul Muni, a young Humphrey Bogart, James Cagney, or some other Warner Bros.–style tough-guy actor. The 1930s certainly gave John Wayne the foundation of a long career, but, in retrospect, it was not the Duke's shining decade.

After researching seventy-two John Wayne movies released from 1930 through 1939 (not to mention his roles in eighteen silents and early talkies in the 1920s), I was fatigued by the John Wayne of that era. I longed for the John Wayne of the forties and fifties, the bigger-than-life war hero and cavalryman who was torn by inner conflict but who never shirked his duty. Those simplistic cowboys he portrayed in the early pictures are, in the main, just plain boring for a modern-day viewer. Of course, the biggest disappointment of those first six or seven dozen movies was that they didn't have to be so dopey, with such formulaic plots. To watch the quickies that followed his star turn in *The Big Trail* over the next nine years is an exercise in what-might-have-been. Or perhaps not really, because what-might-have-been eventually morphed into what *was*.

The 1930s ended with Wayne's reintroduction as an authentic star of the big screen, thanks to John Ford's much-esteemed *Stagecoach,* in which the actor plays the Ringo Kid. Wayne's entrance in his first scene is Hollywood star-making at its most glorious, with Duke every inch the John Wayne who would become a Hollywood icon. To think of the 1930s beginning and ending with such memorable performances, and with some seventy largely forgettable roles stuffed in between, marks one of the greatest wastes of acting talent in the history of the movies. To see what we got in those days instead of what we might have had is a source of actual physical pain for me.

A new John Wayne emerged after *Stagecoach,* though still not the fully fledged Wayne of later years. Gone were the Western duds and the fifty-eight-minute matinee B movies; instead came meatier roles, more urbane and complex, framed as more modern characters. But the trade-off was that Wayne was not the star of all these films from 1939 through 1942. If anyone expected Hollywood to redeem itself and use Wayne in roles he was best suited for, a bucket of cold water awaited. His first films of the 1940s were problematic, as if the studios still couldn't figure out exactly what to do with this big beautiful man.

Sure, his face still adorned the one-sheets and window cards in the theater lobbies, but he often received second or third billing, and his characters sometimes came off as afterthoughts. His role in *Reunion in France,* for example, is far less important than that of the leading lady, Joan Crawford. The same is true of 1942's *Reap the Wild Wind,* in which Ray Milland and Paulette Goddard steal the show; *Seven Sinners* (1940), with a scenery-chewing, over-the-top Marlene Dietrich; and John Ford's somber *The Long Voyage Home* (1940), an ensemble performance by a delightful cast of veteran B-listers like Thomas Mitchell, Barry Fitzgerald, Joe Sawyer, Ward Bond, and John Qualen. Maybe Wayne was keeping himself out of the limelight purposely, learning real acting skills from Hollywood's finest performers and directors. Or maybe, as it seems to me, Hollywood simply didn't have a plan for John Wayne once he hitched his horse and doffed his ten-gallon sombrero. Earnest mountaineer? City slicker with an eye for the big con? Romantic leading man? Norwegian mariner? In the years just before and shortly after America entered the Second World War, Duke played them all.

The 1940s, though, set the stage for the following decade, during which Wayne would routinely be voted into the list of Top 10 actors in Hollywood. And that wasn't just because of his rah-rah semi-propaganda World War II movies. I was surprised to discover that John Wayne didn't appear in many WWII-themed movies during the actual war— only six, in fact (*The Long Voyage Home, Flying Tigers,*

Reunion in France, The Fighting Seabees, Back to Bataan, and *They Were Expendable*). He would go on to make seven more WWII films in the years after.

No, what cemented Wayne's climb to stardom in those years was a newfound gravitas. His squint, by then, was more effective in front of the camera than his once long-and-lean six-foot-four frame. By the mid-forties Wayne was not the handsome stud of *The Big Trail* or even *Stagecoach.* He was only thirty-eight years old in 1945, but he was already becoming stouter. His hairline was receding. Conversely, his face exuded honesty and determination from every pore. The wrinkle lines of his forehead, the sad eyes, the hard set to the jaw, they all combined to create the bust of John Wayne that we envision when his name is mentioned. Middle age came early to John Wayne, but it suited him well.

Those years were crucial to Wayne's reputation and his place in the cultural firmament. The construction of that iconic John Wayne image owes much, perhaps everything, to director John Ford and the so-called Cavalry Trilogy from that period: *Fort Apache* (1948), *She Wore a Yellow Ribbon* (1949), and *Rio Grande* (1950). Although the films are not connected by plot or character, there is much that binds them into a unified, much-venerated triptych. Wayne aficionados revere these films for the wide-open Monument Valley scenery, the men-of-action plotlines, the grim realities of military life on the Western frontier, and the mature acting of Wayne himself. Sprinkle that with superb cinematography, compelling scripts, and the man's-man direction of Ford, and the Hollywood legend-making is nearly complete.

Considering that celebrated trilogy of 1948–50, it's no wonder that the fifties were the pinnacle of Wayne's stardom. During that decade he starred in twenty films, including some of his very best (*Hondo, The Quiet Man, The*

Searchers, Rio Bravo) as well as one of his worst (*The Conqueror*). But Hollywood now knew without a doubt what to do with John Wayne—and what John Wayne could do on the big screen. Gone was the patchwork quilt of roles of the previous ten years. Forevermore he would be a hero, a man alone, living by his code of honor, whether on horseback in Monument Valley or wearing the uniform of World War II. Now his acting persona was fixed: steely-eyed, determined, slow to anger but fast with a punch. He perfected the slow, quizzical double take. His hip-cocked stance, rolling gait, and laconic drawl with its peculiar emphases were solidified, a ready-made gift for Frank Gorshin, Rich Little, and other celebrity impressionists in the coming years. Even his dress became iconic, with the oversize, loosely knotted neckerchiefs, the red or dark-pink costume flares, and the battered cowboy hat with the front brim turned up. The public gorged on it. Wayne was on fire. Jimmy Stewart? Marlon Brando? Elizabeth Taylor? James Dean? Marilyn Monroe? Don't even bother. John Wayne was the No. 1 box-office star in 1950, '51, and '54, and in the Top 10 every other year except 1958. Duke Wayne had been elevated to the pantheon of great movie stars of the decade.

The sixties, though, was another matter. Whereas middle age came to John Wayne unusually soon, old age came even faster. As early as 1962 (when he was only fifty-five), in *How the West Was Won,* Wayne was hoarse, paunchy, wrinkled, and balding. He began to be cast as a character actor in big ensemble films, as in *The Longest Day* (1962), *How the West Was Won* (1962), *The Greatest Story Ever Told* (1965), and *Cast a Giant Shadow* (1966). An unexpected comic element was introduced into the story lines of his starring pictures, as in *North to Alaska* (1960), *Donovan's Reef* (1963), and *The Sons of Katie Elder* (1965), all of which feature a less-than-appropriate, supposedly humorous fistfight complete with wacky sound effects. His films became repetitive. *El Dorado* (1967) was little more than a rewrite of *Rio Bravo* (1959). His Noble Character threatened to devolve into a kitschy caricature.

But make no mistake, Wayne made plenty of good, even great films in the 1960s. Chief among them was *The Man Who Shot Liberty Valance*. One could easily argue that James Stewart was the film's lead actor, but John Wayne, as the seen-it-all gunslinger with a heart of gold, had the better role by far. It was the film in which Wayne used the word "pilgrim" to describe a newcomer—and apart from *McLintock!*, released one year later, is the only feature film I've found in which Wayne uses that word. Another praiseworthy effort from those years was *True Grit* (1969), which introduced the world to Rooster Cogburn, a role in which John Wayne was at his crazy best—blustering, loud, ballsy, unapologetic.

But there was also *The Green Berets* (1968). It was the wrong movie for the wrong time, at least in terms of a showbiz career, because it forever identified Wayne as a conservative, militaristic warmonger among a generation of (largely antiwar) filmgoers. Wayne had been a conservative long before that film, but so had any number of well-known actors—Jimmy Stewart, Glenn Ford, Gary Cooper, Fred Astaire, Gene Autry, and Bob Hope among them. Yet none of those famous actors became as divisive on the American political scene as did John Wayne following *The Green Berets*. In the movie, Wayne plays Colonel Mike Kirby, U.S. Army Special Forces, who makes it a point to persuade an antiwar American journalist (David Janssen) that the Vietnam War is a just cause. Because Wayne's own production company, Batjac, produced the movie, he was able to actively inject his conservative views in a way that might not have been possible if he were under the thumb of a studio.

Although it did well at the box office, the movie was a PR disaster for Wayne. A majority of people under the age of forty, and plenty of older people besides, found his views to be archconservative, militaristic, and defiantly out of step with the progressive 1960s zeitgeist and the growing antiwar movement. John Wayne was no longer America's Hero, the man who saw us safely through World War II while opening the American West to covered-wagon settlers. No, in the minds of many, he had become the hateful Nixon crony who wanted only to wipe out the Vietcong and spit on hippies.

In the history of movies, one cannot separate public perception from Hollywood performance. The chronicles of the studios are rife with such examples, from Fatty Arbuckle to Charlie Sheen. And in 1968, John Wayne was on the outs with a sizable chunk of the American public—reviled, a pathetic has-been, the get-off-my-lawn old fart who hated the longhairs and their peacenik point of view.

There would forever be a taint on Wayne's reputation as a result of that film and his public outspokenness. Even people who might otherwise appreciate the scripts and acting of John Wayne's numerous great films were reluctant to embrace them because of the actor's politics. But as the Vietnam War approached its conclusion, and the public passions shifted in other directions, many film lovers, including young baby boomers, either discovered Wayne's movies for the first time or renewed their interest in his performances.

The 1970s was John Wayne's final decade as an actor, a decade in which he made eleven films in seven years. One of them (*Cancel My Reservation*) entailed a brief cameo in a Bob Hope comedy. Two of them (*McQ* and *Brannigan*) are egregiously bad, with Wayne miscast as a modern-day detective. A couple of the others are merely forgettable. But he made three very good ones (*Rio Lobo, Big Jake,* and *Rooster Cogburn*) and two that are arguably great.

The Cowboys (1972), in which Wayne's paternalistic rancher relies on a gang of schoolboys to drive his cattle to market, is unabashedly sentimental, but superbly acted by all, including the young players and especially Roscoe Lee Browne as the camp cook and the film's moral compass.

But the crowning achievement of Wayne's work in that decade is the final film of his career, *The Shootist* (1976). Wayne, as an aging gunslinger with a terminal illness, hits all the marks of his finest works across fifty years of moviemaking. He is a man of honor despite a dark past. His words are few but chosen with care. His performance is in full flower—not just as "John Wayne," but as an actor. Wayne was already in declining health when he made *The Shootist.* There's comfort in knowing, decades later, that this would be his last work; the film, in context, brings his career to a fitting completion, from the birth of a new star in 1930's *The Big Trail* to the closing chapter of a man's long and adventurous life in *The Shootist.*

As Wayne's rancher in *The Cowboys* says, "Well, it's not how yer buried. It's how they remember ya." When it comes to John Wayne, it's the best of his work that we'll remember—his devotion to duty, his loyalty to family and friends, his determination, and the code he lived by.

The CODE

Honor, Loyalty, Life Lessons, and Being True to Yourself

No other actor in history is more closely connected with his own code of honor than John Wayne. Fair play. Common decency. The right to do as one pleases short of harming others. Staying true to one's word. Honoring a handshake agreement. Standing up for your saddlemates. The code, as practiced by Wayne in his finest films, is the definition of How to Behave. The code is no less than the code of honor America sees for itself. When we think of John Wayne as a forthright rugged individualist, a man of supreme honor, an icon of the American ideal, it's because of the code.

. . .

We all git off on the wrong trail once in a while.[24]

. . .

Where I come from, we don't shoot horses when they get ornery. We tame 'em.[36]

. . .

Well, talkin' ain't my strong point, especially where I'm a stranger.[36]

. . .

Well, I've always been a lucky sort of a cuss playing a lone hand.[36]

. . .

No man can stop the progress of the West![41]

. . .

Don't worry about me. I've always been a lucky sort of a cuss.[44]

. . .

I'm not interested. I don't play my cards that way.[65]

. . .

Chasin' outlaws, a fella can always expect trouble.[66]

. . .

I don't believe in signs.[83]

. . .

Well, there's just some things a man can't run away from.[85]

. . .

Well, I guess you can't break out of prison and into society in the same week.[85]

. . .

Dead men make no peace treaties.[90]

. . .

I can't go around poppin' people all my life.[91]

. . .

We got a sayin' down in Texas. It takes a good fire to burn down the weeds, let the flowers grow.[91]

. . .

There's no land anywhere worth a hoot till it's flowed with good honest sweat.[92]

. . .

The heavier the man, the deeper his boot track.[97]

. . .

And remember, if you have to shoot, aim low. We don't want to kill anybody.[100]

. . .

If you think you're in trouble, pour on the coal and head for home.[102]

* * *

You know me! Never tip your mitt till the deal's closed.[103]

* * *

Oil boss: What's the big idea?

Daniel F. Somers (John Wayne): You really didn't wanna catch that little fella, did ya?

Oil boss: I oughta break his neck! And yours too!

Somers: Now, just a minute. I got no steady side in this fight. When he had a gun and you didn't, that was takin' unfair advantage.

Oil boss: So what?!

Somers: So when you took out after him with seventy-five pounds which *he* ain't got, that was takin' a little advantage too.[106]

* * *

Ya never see a rainbow unless the storm's over and fair weather's ahead. And if ya follow a rainbow, ya sometimes find a pot of gold.[106]

* * *

Wanderin' around in the woods at night ain't exactly safe.[106]

* * *

Colonel Thursday, I gave my word to Cochise. No man is gonna make a liar out of me, sir.[116]

* * *

I don't like quitters. Especially when they're not good enough to finish what they start.[117]

* * *

Don't ever trust anybody till you know 'em.[117]

* * *

Never apologize, mister. It's a sign of weakness.[120]

* * *

You know, everybody gets outta line once in a while.[122]

. . .

Let him alone. He's got a right to dislike me.[122]

. . .

But he must learn that a man's word to anything, even his own destruction, must be honored.[123]

. . .

In this racket, you believe one percent of the bright rumors and two hundred percent of the dark ones, and you'll win most of your bets.[125]

. . .

I pretended like I wanted to make this pinch myself. It's unusual, of course. But that's what I kept pretending. The real reason was I wanted to hit you one punch. Just one full-thrown right hand! But now I find I can't do it. Because you're too small. That's the difference between you people and us, I guess. We don't hit the little guy. We believe in fair play and all that sorta thing. So you get a pass.[127]

. . .

Father, Ring Lardner once said, "The race is not always to the swift, nor the battle to the strong—but that's the way to bet."[128]

. . .

People learn by gettin' bit.[130]

. . .

A long time ago I made me a rule. I let people do what they wanna do.[130]

. . .

A man oughta do what he thinks is best.[130]

. . .

Once in a while, a fella's got to lie if it'll make it easier on someone else.[130]

. . .

Mister, when I give my word, I keep it![130]

* * *

Angie Lowe: You think truth is the most important thing!
Hondo Lane (John Wayne): It's the measure of a man![130]

* * *

Don't confuse sincerity of purpose with success.[132]

* * *

I figure a man's only good for one oath at a time.[135]

* * *

Don't pity me. I never pitied anybody, so I don't want any.[136]

* * *

Everybody has to take a few punches. Ya flop and then ya get up again.[138]

* * *

We'll compromise. You live your way, I'll live mine.[138]

* * *

Only by understanding can the world hope to progress.[140]

* * *

"Sorry" don't get it done, Dude.[141]

* * *

I'm gonna tell you somethin', Flaca, and I want you to listen tight. It may sound like I'm talkin' about me, but I'm not. I'm talkin' about you. As a matter of fact, I'm talkin' about all people everywhere. When I come down here to Texas, I was lookin' for somethin'. I didn't know what. Seems like you add up my life and I spent it all either stompin' other men or in some cases gettin' stomped. Had me some money, and had me some medals. But none of it seemed a lifetime worth the pain of the mother that bore me. It's like I was empty. Well, I'm not empty anymore. That's what's important. To feel useful in this old world. Hit a lick against what's wrong. Or to say a word for what's right, even though you get walloped for sayin' that word.

Now I may sound like a Bible-beater yellin' up a revival at a river-crossing camp meeting. But that don't change the truth none. There's right and there's wrong. Ya gotta do one or the other. Ya do the one, and you're living. Ya do the other and ya may be walkin' around, but you're dead as a beaver hat.[143]

· · ·

When there's trouble, I come from any direction as sudden and surprising as I can.[143]

· · ·

I'm an easy forgiver. At times.[143]

· · ·

You don't get lard less'n you boil a hog.[143]

· · ·

A fella gets sore, that's all. Works it off, that's all.[144]

· · ·

What I can't stand is when people look down on others who aren't doing them any harm.[144]

· · ·

I've got what you might consider a weakness. I'm honest.[145]

· · ·

I been trying to explain to you that I ain't your friend. But I wouldn't want anyone to accuse me of not havin' a heart.[145]

· · ·

Compliments are always welcome, no matter what the source.[145]

· · ·

Capt. Jake Cutter (John Wayne): And then I say back to myself, you can't let him run. Ya swore an oath when they put that badge on ya.

Paul Regret: And that's important to you?

Cutter: I said I swore an oath.[145]

· · ·

Words are what men live by—words they say and mean.[145]

. . .

And I say that a man has the right to resign only if he's wrong, not if he's right.[149]

. . .

Sit down in a boat.[150]

. . .

You have to be a man first before you're a gentleman.[151]

. . .

I give ya my solemn word.[151]

. . .

Everybody's entitled to their own opinion.[151]

. . .

Toni Alfredo: What's wrong with a make-believe world?
Matt Masters (John Wayne): It's for weak people, to hide in. [152]

. . .

Omens! Hexes! Voodoos! It's all bunkum![152]

. . .

That's one thing I don't want, Billy—trouble.[155]

. . .

I'm paid to risk my neck. And I'll decide where and when I'll do it . . . And this isn't it.[158]

. . .

Next time you shoot somebody, don't go near 'em till you're sure they're dead.[158]

. . .

I never shot nobody I didn't have to.[161]

. . .

Ya can't serve papers on a rat, baby sister. Ya gotta kill him or let him be.[161]

. . .

Baby sister, I was born game and I intend to go out that way.[161]

. . .

A fella's gotta think about himself once in a while, baby sister.[161]

. . .

Lookin' back is a bad habit.[161]

. . .

Well, things usually change for the better.[163]

. . .

No sir, no sir, I ain't—ain't butted into anybody's business since I was eighteen years old, at which time it almost got me killed. Ain't gonna start that again.[165]

. . .

A man shouldn't butt into anything that ain't his own affair.[165]

. . .

Michael, there's two reasons to kill: survival and meat. And we need meat.[165]

. . .

I hate secrets. Never knew one to be kept.[165]

. . .

"Little Jake" McCandles: I'm scared.
Jacob McCandles (John Wayne): So am I. But don't let them know it.[165]

. . .

In my day, a man'd stay with ya on a handshake.[166]

. . .

I don't hold jail against ya, but I hate a liar.[166]

. . .

I pay a full day's wages, expect a full day's work.[166]

. . .

Tryin' don't get it done![166]

. . .

It's a hard life.[166]

. . .

I hate to have to tell you this, Ben, but whether you like it or not, you're a man, and you're stuck with it. You're gonna find yourself standin' your ground and fightin' when you oughta run, speakin' out when you oughta keep your mouth shut, doin' things that seem wrong to a lot of people, but you'll do 'em all the same. . . . You're gonna spend the rest of your life gettin' up one more time when you're knocked down, so you better start gettin' used to it.[168]

· · ·

You call the tune, you pay the piper. Meaning, you don't like the treatment, don't rob the banks.[169]

· · ·

Without any schoolin', you're up against it in this country, sister.[172]

· · ·

I ride hard and alone. I eat light and sleep on the ground.[172]

· · ·

I won't be wronged, I won't be insulted, and I won't be laid a hand on. I don't do these things to other people, and I require the same from them.[173]

· · ·

I can't abide a skulker. You wanna see me? Knock on my door, like a man.[173]

· · ·

Mrs. Rogers: Mr. Books, you are a notorious individual, utterly lacking in character or decency. You're an assassin.

J. B. Books (John Wayne): It's according to which end of the gun you're on.[173]

· · ·

My soul is what I've already made of it.[173]

· · ·

[I] don't believe I ever killed a man who didn't deserve it.[173]

* * *

Don't dive in until you know how deep it is.[173]

* * *

A man should be allowed his human dignity.[173]

* * *

WIMMINFOLK

Females—Why They Think the Way They Think and Do the Things They Do, and Why Everything Is Usually a Man's Fault

John Wayne's relationship with his female costars is complicated. Sure, he always has an eye for the turn of a lissome ankle or the stalwart nature of a handsome frontierswoman. But in the early days, when Wayne was a matinee star of cheapie Westerns, you could be forgiven if you felt like he'd rather kiss his horse than a purdy gal. And in his later years, from the late fifties onward, he was more avuncular than lecherous when it came to females. But one thing's for sure: He never learns to hold his tongue in front of his distaff counterparts—often to his detriment.

. . .

"[She's] charming"? That usually means fat and over forty![27]

. . .

My women understand me. They take one look and know they can expect nothing.[27]

. . .

But I thought we had an understanding between us. We weren't going to account to each other or ask questions. When one of us was ready to shout quits, why, that was going to be that.[27]

. . .

Well, you don't exactly figure that Ziegfeld would celebrate if he run across you when he was lookin' for front-row babes, do ya?[34]

. . .

(*When you're obviously not wanted*)
Well, this is a fine way to welcome a man. . . . [56]

. . .

(*How to avoid a romantic entanglement*)
Well, don't tip your hat. Don't even *talk* to 'em![63]

. . .

(*How to avoid sex*)
Well, if you'll excuse me, Mary, I think I'll hit the hay. I'm kind of tired.[66]

. . .

Why, Tom! This ain't for you. Besides, somebody's gotta stay here and take care of the womenfolks.[67]

. . .

I never saw a woman yet who could do a man's work.[70]

. . .

Kinda looks like you're the one that's on the warpath, miss![70]

. . .

Tom Fillmore: Dare, I don't quite understand you. Why don't you get married and settle down? Why, you're running around like a maverick without a brand on.

Dare Rudd (John Wayne): Well, I don't like branding. It hurts in the wrong place.[80]

. . .

I know a girl like you back home, only she doesn't get invited out much.[95]

. . .

How insignificant is man when confronted with the divine mystery of birth—and the courage of a woman like that. I don't suppose that means anything to you![101]

. . .

I usually kiss 'em goodbye and leave 'em crying.[103]

. . .

She ain't my type. Too suspicious. She's wacky.[105]

. . .

(*On marriage*)
They just make out they like it 'cause they're ashamed to admit they made a mistake.[105]

. . .

Honey, this is strictly from Brooklyn, but why don't you dance with the guy that brung ya?[107]

. . .

Take Baby Snooks out and buy her a Popsicle.[107]

. . .

I never feel sorry for anything that happens to a woman.[108]

. . .

You might as well know right now that no woman is gonna get me hog-tied and branded.[109]

. . .

Quirt Evans (John Wayne): This'll sound like I'm buttin' into your business—and I am! And you oughta give me a watch with a gold case for doin' it. You dim-witted nail-bender, marry that girl!

Nelson: Marry her? Why, I assure you my intentions . . . Well, she knows how I feel.

Evans: How would *she* know? Stop yammerin' about shoein' horses. That's no way to talk to a girl. Talk to her about *her*. And marry her! And do it quick![114]

. . .

Does a lot of foofaraw and nonsense have to go with it? I'm not gonna stand for a lot of dressin' up and a batch of jabberin' people lookin' at me just 'cause I'm gettin' married.[114]

. . .

It's a tenderfoot wagon. Man and his woman, they come from New Jerusalem. They made the tanks all right, but the water was a little low. Mr. Tenderfoot ain't got sense enough to dig out the sand, sit back, and wait for that sump hole to fill up. No, sir. Besides, he don't take kindly to usin' a shovel. He puts in a stick of dynamite to start the water runnin'. So he stuck in his dynamite, only the fool's lucky he didn't blow himself up doin' it. But he didn't. He just put Terrapin Tanks outta business forever. Cracked the granite floor of that sump hole and busted down her sides, and the tanks are dry. And they'll stay dry! They can have cloudbursts in this country from now till I get religion. Them tanks'll never hold another drop of water. The fool tenderfoot's dead, I guess. But he's gonna keep right on killin' people just the same. They'll come here bankin' on water. Five or six years, there'll be a dozen skeletons around them busted tanks. But that ain't bitin' me half as hard as what he went and done next. He went and let his stock nose around and lick up that alkali slop below the tanks. Drove 'em plain loco. And they took off up the canyon, huntin' water, with him right after 'em. That's four days ago, and he ain't back yet. So we don't need to waste no time speculatin' on his case or feelin' sorry for him. That wouldn't've been so bad. But he left his woman alone in that wagon. Yes, she's there, right now. She had a little water, so it wasn't so bad until yesterday. Then it gives out. Been pretty hard on her in there, all alone. She's a nice little woman, too. Twenty-eight or thirty, I'd guess. Too blasted good for the cuss she married. But still that ain't the worst of it. No, sir. Not by a long shot. She's gonna have a baby. She's gonna have it now.[118]

. . .

You'll build a fire under someone. But not me.[128]

* * *

Miss, I've met a lot of belligerent people in my time. You're in the first division![128]

* * *

Alice Singleton: Tell me about myself. . . .

Steve Williams (John Wayne): Four years at finishing school, one year at the New School for Social Research, no love life, because you're afraid of it. One of the generation of young old maids.[128]

* * *

Oh, why don't you get outta here and find yourself a man. . . . [128]

* * *

Anne Williams McCormick: Hello, Steve.

Steve Williams (John Wayne) (*hesitantly*): Hello, Anne.

Anne: You look a little startled. I guess five years *is* a long time.

Steve: Not long enough.

Anne: Aren't you going to ask a former wife to take a seat?

Steve: Go ahead. You've taken everything else.[128]

* * *

Women always figure every man comes along wants 'em.[130]

* * *

People I know, a man and his wife, got along real well, for twenty years. And then one day she up and blew a hole in him big enough to drive a stagecoach through. She got mad.[130]

* * *

Angie Lowe: Well, everyone needs someone.

Hondo Lane (John Wayne): Yes, ma'am, most everyone. Too bad, isn't it?[130]

* * *

I forgot to mention a highly probable reason why I've never married. I like to run my own ship![132]

* * *

She is a woman, Jamuga—much woman. Should her perfidy be less than that of other women?[134]

• • •

A couple o' men and a dame are a strain on any civilization.[138]

• • •

A woman throws a harpoon into ya and ya go where she pulls.[138]

• • •

Okichi (Japanese geisha): When wife in street, she walk behind husband, yes?

Townsend Harris (John Wayne): Rarely.

Okichi: Where walk?

Harris: By his side.

Okichi: By his side?!

Harris: Or a little in front. . . .

Okichi: Husband permit this?

Harris: Sometimes he can't help himself.

Okichi: In Japan, different husbands!

Harris (*smiling*): No! In America, different wives![140]

• • •

A wonderful thing about Alaska is that matrimony hasn't hit up here yet. Let's keep it a free country.[144]

• • •

Sure, he struck it. But a lot o' good it'll do him—sittin' on a pile o' gold, moanin' for his two-timin' fiancée.[144]

• • •

Ah, wimmin! I never met one yet that was half as reliable as a horse![144]

• • •

You have a real snooty look, missy. And I don't like dames that have snooty looks![144]

• • •

(*How to get rid of a roomful of hookers*)

Well, good night, ladies! Here ya are. . . . For being such nice girls and showing your legs. And good dispositions! March 'em out, Irving! And Irving, tell the management I'm through shopping for the night![144]

. . .

It's my only politics: anti-wife. Any woman who devotes herself to making one man miserable instead of a lot of men happy don't get my vote.[144]

. . .

Come on, come on, there's nothing to fear. She's half human![144]

. . .

I thought we were invited to a picnic! Not an uprising of nutty wives . . . with war paint! Which I am not interested in attending! So my friend and I bid you goodbye! And am sorry that you find us unfit to sit on your lousy grass![144]

. . .

Angel (*at picnic*): Are you going to take part in any of the games?

Sam McCord (John Wayne): If they have a wife-strangling contest, I might join that.[144]

. . .

Women! Peculiar![144]

. . .

Where there are two men and one girl on top of a mountain, it's trouble, and I don't think it's smart to import it. . . . [144]

. . .

There's one thing you gotta learn about women: They're all liars. And if they ain't liars, they're worse! Laying for ya with wedding music. Take that little dame from Oregon. All I was doin' was tyin' her shoelaces and she starts beatin' me over the head with a preacher. Or that little thing from Minnesota, who tried to marry me while I was so drunk I didn't know what I was doin'. If it hadn't been for the parson's mercy, I'd've been hooked good! For good! Ya just can't trust women. No matter how honest they act, they all wanna be wives.[144]

• • •

Looks like country boys ain't the only ones that get lied to by gals.[145]

• • •

Me and my wife used to fight like a couple of wildcats with only one tree between us. But sooner or later, missy, you'll find out that it doesn't make a tinker's damn who's got the upper hand. A few years roll by and ya kinda settle down to bein' at ease with each other. Then life gets worth living.[145]

• • •

Well, Pompey, looks like we got ourselves a ladies' man.[146]

• • •

Now what the hell did I say . . . ?![147]

• • •

Michael Patrick "Guns" Donovan (John Wayne): What started it was this knothead tried to push a hoochie-coochie dancer off on me in Panama.

Dr. William Dedham: Gilhooley? Well, what's wrong with that?

Donovan: Nothing—except a marriage license and a wedding ring through my nose went with it![150]

• • •

Amelia Sarah Dedham: Say, I've got a wonderful idea! How would you like to spend Christmas at my house?

Michael Patrick "Guns" Donovan (John Wayne): You mean, that'd be better than putting a Christmas tree up in a saloon?[150]

• • •

When in doubt, tell the truth. She wouldn't expect that from you anyway.[151]

...

I think we better join the ladies—before they get curious.[151]

...

You women are always raising hell about one thing when it's something else you're really sore about. Don't you think it's about time you told me what put the burr under your saddle about me?[151]

...

G. W. McLintock (John Wayne): Remember the year I rode in that event? I wore your garters to hold up my sleeves? We had a bet—and I won it!

Katherine McLintock: George Washington McLintock! You are a very crude man!

G. W. McLintock: Well, I guess so, but that was a very rough horse! Like to jarred my insides loose. . . . But it was worth it!

Katherine McLintock (*embarrassed*): Oh![151]

...

I guess this is the only engagement that ever started off of a spanking![151]

...

Drago: And I'm sorry, Katherine. That "Kate" just slipped out from times when I remember you as being nice people.

Katherine McLintock (*to G.W.*): Are you going to stand there with that stupid look on your face while the hired help insults your wife?

G. W. McLintock (John Wayne): He's just ignorant. He doesn't know any better than to tell the truth. And I can't help this stupid look. I started acquiring it as you gained in social prominence![151]

...

Oh, bellyache and fight all you want, it won't do ya any good. You been digging those spurs into me for two years. Now you're gonna get your comeuppance.[151]

* * *

Well, she thinks that Cuthbert H. Humphrey is panting for her like a bull buffalo at the first green-up of spring. But what Cuthbert is panting for is *my money*![151]

* * *

Capt. Rockwell Torrey (John Wayne): Ever hear the name "Cunliffe"?

Maggie Haynes: It's one of those expensive New England names, isn't it?

Torrey: Well, she was a Cunliffe, Jere's mother. I met her at a Navy ball, 1917. She was beautiful. I don't know why she married me; I was just an ensign.

Haynes: I bet you were something when you were an ensign.

Torrey: Fell over my feet most of the time. But when I came back from the war, I had a son, and the Cunliffes had great plans for me. I was to resign my commission in the Navy, and do something useful . . . the stock market. They sat around with teacups on their laps, and ticker tape coming out of their ears, and I said no. It was quite a scene. Then, Athalie—that was her name, Athalie— said, "Rockwell, I will not become a camp follower. Whenever you are not busy boating with the Navy, feel free to come visit us." And that's the way it was. I visited. Then I was assigned to duty in the Philippines, and that ended it.

Haynes: You left out one small detail. You were terribly in love with her.[154]

* * *

Women have no generosity, Lord God! They hate to pay up. A man will never work for a woman unless he's got clapboard for brains.[161]

· · ·

Mattie Ross: You never told me you had a wife.

Rooster Cogburn (John Wayne): Oh, well, I didn't have her long. My friends was a pack of river rats and she didn't crave their society, so she up and left me and went back to her first husband, who was clerkin' in a hardware store in Paducah. "Goodbye, Reuben," she says, "the love of decency does not abide in you!" That's a dee-vorced woman talkin' for ya, about decency. Well, I told her. I said, "Goodbye, Nola, and I hope that nail-sellin' bastard makes you happy this time!"[161]

· · ·

She's a purdy girl. A little young, but purdy.[162]

· · ·

I taught you what to do when the snow comes. How to survive in a blizzard. And I taught you how to deal with men. But women . . . Nobody knows what's on a woman's mind.[162]

· · ·

Ann Langdon: You said that you were once married, Mr. Thomas?

Col. John Henry Thomas (John Wayne): Yes, ma'am. But lucky for me, she left me.[162]

· · ·

She was so busy being a lady that she forgot to be a woman.[162]

· · ·

When I wanna go huntin' and fishin', I go huntin' and fishin', and she didn't like that.[162]

· · ·

She's happy now, I guess. She's living in Philadelphia with her cat, giving piano lessons.[162]

· · ·

There was a girl once. Back in Texas. Long time ago. And I knew the best thing for me to do was to turn my back. Let her marry a man that'd make her happy.[163]

⸱⸱⸱

Shasta Delaney: Did I kill him?
Col. Cord McNally (John Wayne): Not entirely. But ya sure helped.[164]

⸱⸱⸱

Comfortable?! I been called a lot of things, but . . . comfortable?![164]

⸱⸱⸱

Your mind is as changeable as the weather![168]

⸱⸱⸱

Now you do your crochetin' or fingernail fixin' or whatever it is that women do, but you stay out of my way![172]

⸱⸱⸱

If they ever give 'em the vote, God help us.[172]

⸱⸱⸱

Out in the Territory, we prize a dead shot more than we do a lady's charms.[172]

⸱⸱⸱

Out here, we value a spirited woman almost as much as a spirited horse. . . . Not quite, but almost.[172]

⸱⸱⸱

Ma'am, you are an almighty trial. This is a man's work. And dangerous![172]

⸱⸱⸱

Why do women always wanna change a man?![172]

⸱⸱⸱

Well, teacher, don't you start pressin' yer dress for my graduation, 'cause I intend to stay in my own lower class. Indefinitely![172]

⸱⸱⸱

I ain't forgot the naggin', schemin' ways of a woman. Yer figgerin' to take a bottle outta my hand and put a cake of soap in it! Prob'ly a Bible for a gun in the other. Well, it ain't gonna work. No bit and harness fer me. I am what I am. That's what I am.[172]

• • •

J. B. Books (John Wayne): Damn!
Mrs. Rogers: John Bernard, you swear too much.
Books: The hell I do![173]

• • •

BIG SKIES and
OPEN PRAIRIES

Nature, and Man's Place in It

Mother Nature surely ranks high among John Wayne's most important costars. From the chaparral-covered hills of a Hollywood movie ranch to the magnificence of Monument Valley, the settings of Wayne's Westerns are part and parcel of the Duke's mythos, nearly inseparable from the roles he plays. His characters are often at their most eloquent when talking about the fertile land, the refreshing waters, the majesty of the mountains, and the cool clean air that surrounds it all.

• • •

It's everything a Missourian's heart could crave. There's two snowcapped mountain ranges with peaks lost in the sky. And between them ranges, men, is a great valley. Lakes and streams everywhere. Fish, you ask, and game? There's salmon swimming up them rivers thicker than blackbirds in a cane patch.[24]

• • •

I love it. Especially now that it's spring, and everything's so happy. Why, there's trees out there, big tall pines, just a-reachin' and a-reachin' as if they wanted to climb right through the gates of heaven. And there's brooks, too, where the water's smilin' all day long. But the part I like best is the night. Lyin' out there beneath a blanket of stars, with that ol' moon smilin' down on ya. And every time ya look up, there she is, sorta guardin' over ya, like a mother mindin' their young. Sometimes it's so beautiful that I just lie there, listenin'. Birds singin', brooks laughin', and the wind sorta croonin' through the forest, like some great organ. Oh, I've always loved it.[24]

. . .

There's something strange about it. It's like places I've seen when I dreamed what real peace and quiet might be. I've spent most of my life out of doors, in the woods, on rivers and lakes. I've seen lots of places like this before, but none of them got me like this. I wish I could say it like I feel it. That fellow Romeo would know just what to say![75]

. . .

Look, men. Let's stop arguin' and kiddin' ourselves. We're all in the same boat. And we're all gonna sink—unless we stick together. Every one of us has been served with a dispossess notice. Not by Uncle Sam or a bank or some mortgage company, but by a little ol' gal we've been kickin' in the teeth. Mother Nature.[92]

. . .

Maybe I am a green hand at this sort of thing, but remember I told you about the blue lake at the foot of the snowy mountains? Well, there's a cabin near that lake. And close beside it is a forest of firs with branches that reach right up to the sky. There's horses, cattle. The air's so clean you can wash your face in it. I own that cabin. Course it's nothing like this. It's a small cabin. But it's got a nice fireplace. The roof doesn't leak.[109]

. . .

(*On the Pacific Ocean*)
Big, isn't it? I been hearin' about it since I was a little fella.
Say it runs all the way to Asia.[109]

· · ·

Ya can't say it except in Mescalero. It means morning. But
that isn't what it means either. It means more than just
that. Indian words mean the sound and feel of a word,
like "crack o' dawn" or "first bronze light makes the buttes
stand out against the great desert." Or the first sound ya
hear of a brook spillin' over some rocks with trout jumpin'.
It's like when ya get up in the first light, just you and her,
and ya go out of a wickiup, where it smells kinda smoky
and private, just you and her, and kinda safe with just
the two of ya, and stand outside and feel the bite of the
first wind comin' down from the High Divide, promises
snowfall. Yeah, ya can't say it in English, but that was her
name.[130]

· · ·

Sump'n I oughta tell you. I guess now's as good a time
as any. You're gonna have every young buck west of the
Missouri around here tryin' to marry you. Mostly because
you're a handsome filly. But partly because I own everything in this country from here to there. They'll think you're
gonna inherit it. Well, you're not. I'm gonna leave most of it
to . . . Well, to the nation, really. For a park. Where no lum-
bermen'll cut down all the trees for houses with leaky roofs.
Nobody'll kill all the beaver for hats for dudes. Nor murder
the buffalo for robes.[151]

· · ·

Hey, sister! Better be careful movin' around out there!
Everything that grows in this country'll either bite ya, stab
ya, or stick ya![172]

· · ·

I wanna go out in the world again and see the trees and the lakes and the hills and the sky. And I don't fancy seeing it alone. I've been full of alone lately. . . .[173]

. . .

My church has been the mountains and solitude. No doors at all.[173]

. . .

NATIVE AMERICANS

Indigenous Philosophies and Proud Enemies

John Wayne's Western heroes are often friendly with Native Americans—and just as often ready, if not eager, to kill them. Looking at some of his movie roles from a twenty-first-century perspective, one can find little admirable in much of what Wayne says about Indians. But behind nearly every comment is an often unspoken sentiment of profound respect.

...

Y'see, the Indians are my friends. They taught me all I know about the woods. They taught me how to follow a trail by watching the leaves. And how to cut your mark on a tree so you won't get lost in the forest. And they taught me how to bury in in the snow so you won't freeze to death in a storm. And they taught me how to make a fire without even a flint. And they taught me how to make the best bow and arrows, too.[24]

...

Feed 'em well and treat 'em right, and we'll have no trouble.[24]

...

I'll go out and palaver with 'em.[24]

...

Those red devils![41]

...

I was raised around the Indians, and I seen 'em pushed and squeezed enough as it is. And if my offerin' 'em half of what already belongs to 'em is fantastic, well, then, that's what I am, whatever it is.[106]

* * *

The Sioux once raided into Apache territory. Old-timers told me you could follow the line of their retreat by the bones of their dead.[116]

* * *

If you saw them, they weren't Apaches.[116]

* * *

No troop or squadron or regiment is gonna keep the Apaches on this reservation unless they wanna stay here. Five years ago we made a treaty with Cochise. He and his Chiricahuas and some of the other Apache bands came on the reservation. They wanted to live here in peace—and did, for two years. And then Meacham here was sent by the Indian rings, the dirtiest, most corrupt political group in our history. And then it began. Whiskey but no beef. Trinkets instead of blankets. The women degraded, the children sickly, and the men turning into drunken animals. So Cochise did the only thing a decent man could do: He left, took most of his people and crossed the Rio Bravo into Mexico.[116]

* * *

We broke that treaty. Us whites. There's no word in the Apache language for "lie." And they been lied to.[130]

* * *

Yep, the end of a way of life. Too bad. It's a good way.[130]

* * *

Angie Lowe: Anyway, I don't believe a dog can smell Indians. I mean, as different from anyone else. You and me, for instance.

Hondo Lane (John Wayne): Well, they can. As a matter of fact, Indians can smell white people.

Lowe: I don't believe it.

Lane: Well, it's true. I'm part Indian, and I can smell ya when I'm downwind of you.[130]

...

Human rides a horse until it dies. Then he goes on afoot. Comanch' comes along and gets that horse up, rides him twenty more miles. Then eats him.[135]

...

An Indian specialty is not bein' seen.[145]

...

Paul Regret: Tame Indians! Ha! How do you tell the difference? How do you know these from the wild ones?

Capt. Jake Cutter (John Wayne): Well, it's pretty hard to explain to a city fella. But now you take . . . like that snake there at your feet. Don't shoot him! He's a gopher snake. He's a friend. Eats mice and rats. We'll put him in the shade. Ya see those darker markings? Cross-patch overlay? Makes him *look* like a rattler. But you can see a thousand like that one. And when you see your first rattlesnake, you'll know the difference.

Regret: You still haven't told me how you tell a Comanche from a tame Indian.

Cutter: It's just like your first rattler. One look and you'll know.[145]

...

The first thing I learned about Indian fighting was to wait for daylight.[151]

...

Agard, if you knew anything about Indians, you'd know they're doing their level best to put up with our so-called benevolent patronage, in spite of the nincompoops that've been put in charge of it.[151]

· · ·

We stood off five hundred Plains Indians for nine days.[151]

· · ·

The Comanche say, "We are an old people, and a proud people. When the white man first came among us, we were as many as the grasses of the prairie. Now we are few, but we are still proud, for if a man loses pride in manhood, he is nothing. You tell us now that if we will let you send us away to this place called Fort Sill, you will feed us and care for us. Let us tell you this: It is a Comanche law that no chief ever eats unless first he sees that the pots are full of meat in the lodges of the widows and orphans. It is the Comanche way of life. This that the white man calls 'charity' is a fine thing for widows and orphans, but no warrior can accept it. For if he does, he is no longer a man. And when he is no longer a man, he is nothing, and better off dead. You say to the Comanche, 'You are widows and orphans. You are not men.' And we, the Comanche, say we would rather be dead. It will not be a remembered fight when you kill us, because we are few now and have few weapons. But we will fight, and we will die Comanche."[151]

· · ·

Gov. Cuthbert H. Humphrey: Am I to gather the Comanche defy the government of the United States?

G. W. McLintock (John Wayne): Yes, you may gather that the Comanche defy the United States government—or at least, this commission.[151]

· · ·

Puma: Oh, McLintock! You are important chief amongst these white people! Sway them! Have them give us few guns to make the fight worthwhile. Let us have one last remembered fight for end of Comanche!

G. W. McLintock (John Wayne): I almost wish I could arrange that, Puma. *A halanay cha.*

Puma: *A halanay cha.*[151]

• • •

I've seen plenty of Indian scalps on Indian belts.[161]

• • •

John Chisum (John Wayne): It was a gamble, all right. And it was wild. But there was land here for the taking—and the keeping—if you were willing to fight. Rustlers. Disease. The land itself. Indians. One Indian in particular. Comanche chief named White Buffalo. The bravest man I ever knew.

Sallie Chisum: Dead now?

John Chisum: Might as well be. He's penned up on a piece of desert the government calls a reservation. It was the end of *his* way of life. Pretty good way, too.

Sallie Chisum: You sound as if you're sorry for him. Your enemy.

John Chisum: Well, I respect him. We're brothers. As close as your father and I were. Maybe even closer.[163]

• • •

J. D. Cahill (John Wayne) (*looking at a friend's broken leg*): We're gonna have to straighten it and splint it.

(*Lightfoot screams in pain*)

Cahill: I thought an Indian didn't show pain. Especially a bona fide Comanche war chief!

Lightfoot: Who in the hell ever told you that?! A damn white man?

Cahill: This is gonna hurt. (*Hands him a cigar*) Here's sump'n to bite on.

Lightfoot (*smiling*): Well, thank you, J.D. I . . . (*Screams*)[169]

• • •

WHIPPERSNAPPERS

Baby Raising, Smart-Aleck Young'uns, and Too-Big-for-Their-Britches Whelps

Lighthearted banter is bound to ensue whenever Wayne has to deal with young people. Unexpectedly tender at times, he is bewildered by babies, can't quite comprehend children, and simply has no patience with teenagers and young adults, especially the know-it-all sort. You get the sense that if human beings came into this world as fully formed grown-ups, John Wayne wouldn't have minded a bit.

• • •

A week without a bath?! Well, that's all right for a growin' boy that ain't supposed to bathe between water holes. Or in town on Saturday night, sparkin' his gal. But a baby? I'll lay my silver spurs the doc's wrong.[118]

• • •

Cut out the Mex lingo around the kid, willya, Pete? First thing ya know, he'll be talkin' it. We gotta raise him with good ol' American habla, like his ma.[118]

• • •

[I'd] teach him good horse sense and respect, say yes, sir, when he's spoke to . . . [118]

• • •

• • •

Capt. Nathan Brittles (John Wayne): Did anyone ever take down your britches and tan your hide?!

Young lieutenant: Why, no, sir. That is, yes, sir. My father, sir, with a strap.

Brittles: Well, I'm just old enough to *be* your father, bub. Take the point![120]

• • •

Well, haul off and kiss her back, blast you! We haven't got all day![120]

• • •

Knock off the skylarkin'![122]

• • •

Ya mean ya been to two universities and ya still can't find the words to say ya been outta line?[122]

• • •

(*Sarcastically*) I'm the nicest father a little girl ever had. Show the lady how the welts are healing where I beat you.[128]

• • •

Why don't you quit trying to carry the world around on your shoulders? You're only eleven years old. Wait till you're twelve.[128]

• • •

What do you know about love? I think love is watching your child go off to school for the first time alone, or sitting beside a sick kid's bed waiting for the doctor, praying it isn't polio, or that cold chill you get when you hear the screech of brakes, and know your kid's outside on the street someplace, and a lot of other things you can't get out of books, 'cause nobody knows how to write 'em down.[128]

• • •

Well, you just gotta stop lookin' at me like I was George Washington, Babe Ruth, and Florence Nightingale all rolled into one.[128]

• • •

If it was me, I'd let him sleep. Youngsters grow sleepin'.[130]

. . .

Johnny Lowe: I can't swim.

Hondo Lane (John Wayne): You can't *what*?

Johnny: I can't swim.

Lane: How old are you?

Johnny: Six.

(*Hondo picks up the boy by his shoulders and belt loops and heaves him into the river*)

Angie Lowe (*running to her son's rescue*): Help him! He can't swim!

Lane: Time he learned. Everybody should swim. (*Calling out to the boy*) Just reach out in front of ya and grab a handful of water! Pull it back towards ya! Not too fast! That's the way *I* learned.[130]

. . .

Pretty hard to change what you learn in your youth—and believe.[132]

. . .

Don't call me uncle. I ain't your uncle. No need to call me sir, either. Nor Grandpa. Nor Methuselah. I can whup you to a frazzle.[135]

. . .

Every size they get to seems to be the most lovable.[143]

. . .

Kind of a shame kids have to grow up into people.[143]

. . .

Well, I guess I been taking care of ya for so long that I forgot you can take care of yourself.[144]

. . .

Spring comes to the bush veldt and the young bucks start butting their heads together.[147]

.   . . .

Hey, I'll bring ya before the mast! I'll throw ya in the brig, ya little mutineer![150]

. . .

Boy: Oh boy! In a real bed instead of that hot old cot he makes me sleep on.

Michael Patrick "Guns" Donovan (John Wayne): What do you got to complain about?! I'm sleeping in a hammock, ya fresh kid! I oughta belt ya![150]

. . .

(*On seeing his grown daughter after several years' absence*)
I guess I'm gonna have to stop callin' you Tomboy.[151]

. . .

Get yourself cleaned up. Go ask that girl for a dance.[151]

. . .

You learned a lot of words back East, Becky. I wish to God they'd've taught you some meanings.[151]

. . .

Drago: Boss, what does "reactionary" mean?

G. W. McLintock (John Wayne): Me, I guess. He says that anyone that wanted to sell at a profit was a reactionary.

Drago (*defensively*): Was we reactionaries back in them days when you was sellin' beef cattle for six cents a pound on the hoof?

McLintock: Well, no use arguin' with him. College boy![151]

. . .

(*To a girl's mother*)
Some things a man just can't do. She has to learn from a woman. From her mother. She needs you.[152]

. . .

Well, I spanked her when she was bad, loved her when she was good. I'm just there, like night and day.[152]

. . .

Well, I'm flying under false colors, Miss Haynes. I don't know my son. I've been divorced for many years, and he's been raised by his mother and family. I didn't even know he was in the Navy.[154]

. . .

Capt. Rockwell Torrey (John Wayne): He's my son.
Commander Powell: Well! I'd like to meet him, Rock.
Torrey: No you wouldn't.[154]

. . .

I'll tell ya what happened. Ya left a boy out there to do a man's job![158]

. . .

Mattie Ross: I'll walk over there by myself.
Rooster Cogburn (John Wayne): You scared of the dark?
Mattie: I've never been scared of the dark.
Cogburn: Well, if I had a big horse pistol like that, I wouldn't be scared of no "boogerman."
Mattie: I'm not scared of no "boogerman."[161]

. . .

Mattie Ross: All right. One understanding: that we leave for the territory this afternoon to get Tom Chaney.
Rooster Cogburn (John Wayne): Well, *you're* not goin'.
Mattie: You've misjudged me.
Cogburn: I can't go up against Ned Pepper's gang and try and take care of a baby all at the same time!
Mattie: I'm not a baby!
Cogburn: You'll slow me down! There's no hot grub or warm beds out there!
Mattie: I've slept out at night before. Papa took me coon hunting last summer.
Cogburn: Well, this ain't no coon hunt, and it's no place for a shirt-tailed kid!
Mattie: That's what they said about coon hunting.

Cogburn: First night out, you'd be calling, "Mama! Mama!"[161]

. . .

I oughta paddle your rump![161]

. . .

Mattie Ross: Did you have any children?

Rooster Cogburn (John Wayne): There was a boy. Nola taken him with her. He never liked me anyway. A clumsier child you'll never see than Horace; I bet he broke forty cups.[161]

. . .

By God, she reminds me of me![161]

. . .

Well, son, since you don't have any respect for your elders, it's time somebody taught you some respect for your betters![165]

. . .

You can call me Father, you can call me Jacob, you can call me Jake, you can call me a dirty son of a bitch. But if you ever call me Daddy again, I'll finish this fight.[165]

. . .

(*After punching his son for nearly killing himself in a motorcycle crash*)
That's for scaring me out of ten years of my life—which I can't spare![165]

. . .

(*Sons punch him in the face*)
Well, boys, you know that's no way to treat your old daddy.[165]

. . .

There ain't a kid in that school over fifteen. They're between hay and grass. I need men.[166]

. . .

Now this is the way it's gonna be. I'm a man, and you're boys. Not cowmen, not by a damn sight. Nothin' but cow*boys,* just

like the word says. And I'm gonna remind you of it every
day and night.[166]

. . .

Wil Andersen (John Wayne): You all right, boy?
Fats: Yes, sir. My name's Clyde Potter. They call me Fats.
Andersen: Tendin' toward the gut myself.[166]

. . .

Wil Andersen (John Wayne): Yeah, thirty years older than
    you are. Had my back broke once, and my hip twice.
    And on my worst day I could beat the hell out of you.
Younger man (*smiling and shaking his head*): I don't think so.
Andersen: You will. (*Swings and knocks him down*)[166]

. . .

My oldest boy, be close to forty now, middle-aged, if he'd've
lived. Two of 'em. Went bad on me . . . or I went bad on
them. I don't know. I can't figure it out. . . .[166]

. . .

I'm proud of ya . . . all of ya. Every man wants his children
to be better'n he was. You are.[166]

. . .

I don't need 'em standin' up to me. I need 'em standin'
alongside of me![168]

. . .

(*They hear a baby crying*)
Lane (John Wayne): We're not stayin'.
Jesse: How the hell come?
Lane: You ever bury a baby, Jesse?
Jesse: No.
Lane: Neither have I. And I don't plan to. Not over gold.
    Let's move![168]

. . .

J. D. Cahill (John Wayne) (*smiling and tipping his hat to
    Indian woman*): Ma'am.

Indian woman: Morning, gentlemen.

(*Cahill looks at his teenage son expectantly*)

Cahill: Daniel . . . ?

Daniel: I don't tip my hat to a squaw! Ain't no squaw's gonna . . .

(*Cahill whaps Daniel in the face with his hat, knocking him off his horse and into the mud*)

Cahill (*to Indian woman*): Sorry, ma'am. Slight negligence in his upbringing.[169]

• • •

All I had was three brothers, and we were always bangin' knuckles.[170]

• • •

Every young man feels the need to let the badger loose now and again.[173]

• • •

IT'S NOT a THREAT.
IT'S a PROMISE.

Warnings, Insults,
Intimidation,
and Ultimatums

You don't want John Wayne mad at you. No way will that end well. And he doesn't need to say anything to show his frustration, dismissiveness, or outright anger. He can express those emotions, and their potential ramifications for the unlucky recipient, without saying a word. But even a man of action reverts to language now and then. And what language!

· · ·

If ever I find those hellhounds, I'll sure make 'em hunt their holes.[24]

· · ·

(*Wagon boss Red Flack threatens to replace wagon-train scout Breck Coleman, who suspects Flack of murder*)

Red Flack: We're taking on a new scout.

Breck Coleman (John Wayne): Guess again, Flack! I started with this outfit and I'll be with it at the finish.

Flack: Who says so?

Coleman: I'm just tellin' ya! I got two reasons. One is I told Wellmore I'd scout the train through. And the other is a little personal business I aim to transact at the end of the trail. See if ya can figure out what *that* is, Flack![24]

. . .

I'm going to make a break for it, Buck. Don't come after me.[29]

. . .

John Walton: No whelp from the Turner litter can marry my daughter, unless it's over my dead body.

Clint Turner (John Wayne): That'd be one way of doing it.[29]

. . .

I think you better get off the lot while you're still in one piece.[32]

. . .

All I can wish for [him] is a rough horse, a cactus saddle, and a long journey![37]

. . .

All right, you had your fun. Now you're gonna pay like a true caballero.[48]

. . .

Make it fast, Slippery. This is your last draw.[49]

. . .

Hangin' or shootin's too good for you, Gentry.[53]

. . .

And you can also tell 'im that if he'd had the nerve to come himself instead've sending you renegades that I'd've shoved that offer right down his throat![60]

. . .

Snakes like you usually die of their own poison.[60]

. . .

(*About a bald man*)
Well, that's the first forehead I ever saw that ran clear to the back of the neck.[63]

. . .

You must be the joker in this deck.[64]

. . .

Your cyclones are all whirlwinds, fella![64]

. . .

Let's cut out the compliments and get down to business. What do you want me for?[65]

. . .

Hey, where do you think you're goin'?! Get back over there with the herd, ya muttonhead.[66]

. . .

Just a bunch of tough gorillas, eh?[70]

. . .

Keep yer wig on, grandpa, I'll tell ya all about it later.[82]

. . .

C'mon, Bain, get off your high horse. I'm wise to your racket.[84]

. . .

Take it easy. You don't know the kinda people yer dealing with, mister.[89]

. . .

I don't want no trouble with you, mister. Just leave me be. I'm minding my own business, you mind yours.[91]

. . .

All right, mister. You asked for it.[91]

. . .

I'll tell ya, ya pack o' coyotes. A man born in this country is an American, don't forget that. It's *his* right to go where he pleases and *my* business to . . . (*Punch!*)[91]

. . .

Yeah, I know the breed. String-hollered and spavined, squeeze the blood out of a turnip.[91]

. . .

The next one o' you polecats throws anything's gonna get a law busted right in his face.[91]

. . .

First time I ever had two kinds of bird with one meal—
turkey to eat and buzzard to look at.[91]

. . .

Remember what I said. I'll be lookin' to see you gone.[97]

. . .

Shut up about her, or I'll tear the jaw out of your face.[99]

. . .

Let's say that your version of how it happened shows a great
deal of imagination.[101]

. . .

You got your halo on crooked, pal.[102]

. . .

You picked your side of the fence. Stay there.[106]

. . .

Sandy Poli: Papa says you are a gun-totin', high-bindin' tin-
    horn gambler.
John Devlin (John Wayne): Well, Papa shouldn't talk like
    that in front of the children.[111]

. . .

Ya gonna be neighborly or not?[114]

. . .

Stickin' your head in this bucket will shut you up.[114]

. . .

Haven't you got some real important business to attend
to—someplace else?![114]

. . .

Vaquero: Others have thought as you, señor. Others have
    tried.
Thomas Dunson (John Wayne): And you've always been
    good enough to stop 'em?
Vaquero: Amigo, it is my work.
Dunson: Pretty unhealthy job.
(*They draw; vaquero dies*)[117]

. . .

(*In a fight, to an onlooker*)
How about you? You want some of it?[117]

. . .

You should've let 'em kill me, because I'm gonna kill you.
I'll catch up with ya. I don't know when, but I'll catch
up. Every time you turn around, expect to see me. 'Cause
one time you'll turn around and I'll be there. And I'll kill
ya. . . .[117]

. . .

You're soft! Won't anything make a man outta ya?[117]

. . .

Thomas Dunson (John Wayne): You started all this.
Cowboy (*remorsefully*): Yeah. Yeah, I did. I know it, and I'd
  do anything . . .
Dunson: The tally is three or four hundred head short. And
  ya killed Dan Latimer.
Cowboy: Sure, sure I did. I know that too. I know it, I know
  it, and I'd give . . . I'd give my right arm . . .
Dunson (*brandishing bullwhip*): Stealin' sugar like a kid.
  Well, they whip kids to teach 'em better. Laredo, Keeler,
  tie him to that wagon wheel.
Cowboy: No, no they won't. Nobody's gonna tie me to no
  wagon wheel. No, sir.
Dunson: Then you'll take it without a wheel to lean against.
Cowboy: Oh, Mr. Dunson, I was wrong. Awful wrong. But
  nobody's gonna whip me.
Dunson: Turn around, Bunk. Turn around or you'll get it in
  the eye.
Cowboy (*going for gun*): Don't do it, Mr. Dunson, I tell ya
  don't do it!
(*Matthew Garth, looking on, shoots the cowboy*)[117]

. . .

Get down offa them horses. I don't favor lookin' up to the likes of you.[117]

. . .

I'm sorry I called ya a chili-dippin' horse thief back there.[118]

. . .

If I ever hear that you hurt her, I'll come back and kill ya.[119]

. . .

John Breen (John Wayne): We haven't settled anything, have we?

Blake Randolph: I honestly didn't think we would.

Breen: We could. Mighty easy. I don't threaten good.[121]

. . .

Will Danaher: I'll count three, and if you're not out of the house by then, I'll loose the dogs on you.

Sean Thornton (John Wayne): If you say "three," mister, you'll never hear the man count "ten."[126]

. . .

That breaks all bargains. You can take yer sister back. It's *your* custom, not mine. No fortune, no marriage. We call it quits.[126]

. . .

Well, my countersuggestion is that you'd look real cute with a lump on your head![127]

. . .

Hoodlum: I don't let it go by when some joker slugs me when I ain't lookin'.

Jim McLain (John Wayne): You should keep lookin'.[127]

. . .

Football fan: I don't know how you did it, Steve, but those boys look pretty good out there.

Steve Williams (John Wayne) (*in disgust*): They couldn't even beat a high-school debating team.[128]

. . .

Now, gentlemen, let's dispense with the rosy glasses of childish optimism and look at this thing calmly. You've flipped your lids![128]

. . .

I'll shoot the first one of ya who leaves the camp area. I'll aim for your legs, but I may miss and hit ya in the back of the head! Either way, serves ya right. Does everybody understand me?[129]

. . .

I wouldn't touch that dog, son. He don't take to pettin'.[130]

. . .

I know what ya are, but there's a lady present.[130]

. . .

You're not foolin' this old China hand! Not today. No, sir. Not today, gentlemen![133]

. . .

Come on, blanket-head.[135]

. . .

Ethan Edwards (John Wayne): What you saw wasn't Lucy.
Brad: But it was, I tell you!
Edwards: What you saw was a buck wearin' Lucy's dress. I found Lucy back in the canyon. Wrapped her in my coat, buried her with my own hands. Thought it best to keep it from ya.
Brad: Did they . . . ? Was she . . . ?
Edwards: What do you want me to do, draw you a picture?! Spell it out?! Don't ever ask me! Long as you live, don't ever ask me more.[135]

. . .

Martin Pawley: I hope you die!
Ethan Edwards (John Wayne): That'll be the day.[135]

. . .

All right, let's start over. But you pull a gun on me again, and one of us will be a dead friend.[138]

. . .

I got enough trouble! Cut out the bellyachin'![138]

. . .

You Bible-spoutin' phony! I'm gonna shove this down your throat.[138]

. . .

We don't like tinhorns around here, mister.[141]

. . .

You want that gun, pick it up. I wish you would.[141]

. . .

That's the second time you hit me. Don't ever do it again.[141]

. . .

Open your mouth again and we'll carry you out.[141]

. . .

Let's get this straight. *You* don't like? I don't like a lot of things. I don't like your men sittin' on the road bottling up this town. I don't like your men watching us, trying to catch us with our backs turned. And I don't like it when a friend of mine offers to help and twenty minutes later he's dead! And I don't like you, Burdette, because you set it up.[141]

. . .

You're not as smart as your brother, Joe. He sees Stumpy here sittin' around the corner, locked in with you. And if that isn't plain enough, I'll tell you why. If any trouble starts around this jail, before anybody can get to you, you're gonna get accidentally shot.[141]

. . .

Stop if I say stop. Or I'll stop ya.[141]

. . .

Kirby, you tangle with me and I'll have your hide.[142]

. . .

Don't push me too far, Kendall.[142]

. . .

You better slack off of me, mister.[143]

. . .

I wouldn't believe you on a stack of Bibles![144]

. . .

I wouldn't try any city-slicker stuff on this poor ol' country boy.[145]

. . .

Paul Regret: My friend, you're a very brave man.

Capt. Jake Cutter (John Wayne): And pretty soon you're gonna catch on I ain't your friend.[145]

. . .

I'm gonna take particular delight in seeing you hang.[145]

. . .

Mon-soor, you may not live long enough to hang![145]

. . .

It would break my heart if I had to put a bullet in your back.[145]

. . .

Paul Regret: Cap'n Jake, can you give me one good reason why you don't marry that woman?

Capt. Jake Cutter (John Wayne): Why don't you mind your own business? (*Pause*) I haven't got one good reason . . . that'd make sense to you. Every time I quit to get married, that miserable, low-down, silver-tongue Houston would start bendin' my ear about how Texas needs every man and every gun, what with this Comanche and renegade trouble. But duty and patriotism doesn't make sense to you. You think I'm simpleminded.

Regret: Yes, I do think you're simpleminded.

Cutter: Well, don't make a point of saying that too often. . . . And once more'll be too often![145]

. . .

Whoa, take 'er easy there, pilgrim.[146]

. . .

You talk too much. Think too much.[146]

. . .

Man: You looking for trouble, Doniphon?

Tom Doniphon (John Wayne): You aiming to help me find some?[146]

• • •

(*Reese and Floyd are trying to incite a lynch mob after Stoddard kills Liberty Valance*)

Tom Doniphon (John Wayne): Can't a man have a drink around this town in peace?

(*Throws Floyd through the saloon doors and onto the street*)

Reese: No one's bothering you, Doniphon.

Doniphon: *You* are.

(*Reese starts to draw his pistol, but Doniphon knocks him to the floor*)

Doniphon: Marshal! What are you gettin' paid for? Drag this scum out of here.[146]

• • •

A coupla more cracks like that and you won't have to get a racing car to break your neck. . . . [147]

• • •

Aw, you have no milk of human kindness![151]

• • •

Douglas, I come close to killin' you a coupla times when we were younger. Saddens me I didn't.[151]

• • •

(*McLintock wants his old Chinese cook to retire, but the cook is unwilling*)

G. W. McLintock (John Wayne): Well, you old Cantonese reprobate, how 'bout it?

Ching: You fire me?! I kill myself!

McLintock: I'm not talkin' about firing ya; I'm *retiring* ya! You've been rustlin' food for us for thirty years! We're gonna put you out to pasture. All you'll have to do is give advice, be one of the family!

Ching: I kill myself!

McLintock (*growing frustrated*): I may save you the trouble.

Drago: Hey, Ching, you kill yourself, I'll cut off your pigtail and y'ain't never gonna get to heaven!

Ching (*considering the offer*): I be one of the family?

McLintock: I give you my solemn word.

Ching: Pretty crummy family! Drink too muches! Get in fight! Yell all the time!

McLintock (*gestures at Drago*): Cut off his pigtail!

Ching: All right, all right, I be one of the family![151]

. . .

Remember, I'm a bad loser.[151]

. . .

I'm gonna use good judgment. I haven't lost my temper in forty years. But pilgrim, you caused a lot of trouble this morning. Might've got somebody killed. And somebody oughta belt you in the mouth. But I won't . . . I won't . . . The hell I won't! (*Punches man in mouth*)[151]

. . .

I don't wanna start laying the law down your first day back home, but I'll have no more such talk.[151]

. . .

The important thing is you don't draw that hog leg or this'll be worse than Dodge City on Saturday night.[151]

. . .

Now . . . we'll *all calm down*![151]

. . .

Don't say it's a fine morning, or I'll shoot ya![151]

. . .

You're gonna get yourself killed someday, stickin' yer neck out. I can hardly wait.[156]

. . .

(*After punching out three bad guys who stole his pistol, John Wayne turns to their boss*)

The shells in here belong to him. You tell him he can come and get 'em . . . anytime.[157]

• • •

Lomax: How much is there and what did you do with it?

Taw Jackson (John Wayne): A hundred thousand. I hid it.

Lomax: Where?

Jackson: I'll let you know in about six months.

Lomax: Six months? I want it now!

Jackson: Now, it wouldn't be smart to start flashing gold dust around right after a robbery, would it?

Lomax: What am I supposed to do in the meantime, huh?

Jackson: Well, for one thing, you better make damned sure I stay alive.

Lomax: That's a twenty-four-hour-a-day job!

Jackson: That's *your* problem, partner.[157]

• • •

Milt: You've got a lot of faith in me, don't ya, Nelse?

Nelse McLeod: Faith can move mountains, Milt. But it can't beat a faster draw. There's only three men I know with his kind of speed. One's dead. The other's me. And the third is Cole Thornton.

Cole Thornton (John Wayne): There's a fourth.

McLeod: Which one are you?

Thornton: I'm Thornton.[158]

• • •

I'm lookin' at a tin star with a drunk pinned on it.[158]

• • •

If this bunch is all you've got, don't tangle with Hara, 'cause they don't look tough enough to me to stomp a stringy jack-rabbit.[158]

• • •

A fella as ugly as you are probably couldn't get to first base without a fire.[160]

. . .

Rooster Cogburn (John Wayne): Who are you?

Mattie Ross: Mattie Ross. My family has four hundred and eighty acres of good bottomland near Dardanelle in Yell County. My mother's home looking after my baby sister and my brother, little Frank.

Cogburn: Well, then why don't you go home and leave me alone?! They'll need help with the churnin'.[161]

. . .

Mister Rat! I have a writ here says you're to stop eatin' Chen Lee's cornmeal forthwith. Now, it's a rat writ, writ for a rat, and this is lawful service of the same. See? Doesn't pay any attention to me. (*Shoots rat*)[161]

. . .

Would you mind repeatin' that, jaybird?[161]

. . .

Rooster Cogburn (John Wayne): Well, maybe I'll just catch this Chaney by myself and take *all* the money. . . .

LaBoeuf: You might deliver him, but I'd see to it you didn't collect a thing for it.

Cogburn: Well, how'd you go about that?

LaBoeuf: I'd dispute your claim! I'd muddy up the water!

Cogburn (*quietly*): You do that and I'll kill ya.

LaBoeuf: I wouldn't count too much on bein' able to shade somebody I didn't know, fella.

Cogburn: I ain't never seen nobody from Texas I couldn't shade. LaBoeuf, you get crossways of me and you'll think a thousand bricks had fell on ya! You'll wish you was back at the Alamo with Travis![161]

. . .

(*To a clumsy person*)
You look like a hog on ice![161]

. . .

LaBoeuf: You're lucky to be where water's so handy. I've seen the time I've drank out of a filthy hoofprint—and was glad to get it.

Rooster Cogburn (John Wayne): If ever I meet one of you Texas waddies who ain't drunk water from a hoofprint, I think I'll . . . I'll shake their hand or buy 'em a Daniel Webster see-gar. (*Points to LaBoeuf's long-haired horse*) How long you boys down there been mounted on sheep?[161]

. . .

Chuck yer guns out and follow 'em with your hands high, and nobody'll get hurt![161]

. . .

Rooster Cogburn (John Wayne): When's the last time you saw Ned Pepper?

Bad hombre: I don't remember any Ned Pepper.

Cogburn: Short feisty fella. Nervous and quick. Got a messed-up lower lip.

Bad hombre: That don't bring nobody to mind.

Other bad hombre: A funny lip?

Cogburn: Wasn't always like that. I shot him in it.

Other bad hombre: In the lower lip?! What was ya aimin' at?

Cogburn: His upper lip.[161]

. . .

Bad guy: Well, I always like to help the law as long as it don't harm my friends.

Rooster Cogburn (John Wayne): Pretty good idea. 'Cause otherwise I'll turn you in back at Fort Smith. By that time that leg o' yours'll be swellin' up tighter'n Dick's hatband, mortified, and they'll have to cut it off! And then if you live, I'll get ya three or four years in the federal penitentiary.[161]

. . .

. . .

Rooster Cogburn (John Wayne): What outfit were you with during the war?

LaBoeuf: Shreveport, with Kirby Smith.

Cogburn: Oh, I mean what side were you on?

LaBoeuf: I served with General Kirby Smith. And I don't have to hang my head when I say it, either. Go ahead and make another joke about it. You want to make me look foolish in the girl's eyes, anyway.

Cogburn: You don't need me for that.

LaBoeuf: I don't like the way you make conversation.

Cogburn: And I don't like your conversation about Captain Quantrill.

LaBoeuf: Captain? Captain of *what*? Bunch of thieves?

Cogburn: Young fella, if you're looking for trouble, I'll accommodate you. Otherwise, leave it alone.[161]

. . .

(*LaBoeuf is spanking Mattie Ross with a switch*)

Mattie Ross (*to Rooster*): Are you gonna let him do this?

Rooster Cogburn (John Wayne): I don't believe I will. Drop that switch, LaBoeuf. Put it down, I said! You're enjoying it too much.

LaBoeuf: You'll find that I go ahead with what I start.

Cogburn (*drawing and cocking his pistol*): You do and it'll be the biggest mistake *you* ever made, you Texas brushpopper![161]

. . .

I mean to kill you in one minute, Ned, or see you hanged in Fort Smith at Judge Parker's convenience. Which will it be?[161]

. . .

Fill your hand, you son of a bitch![161]

. . .

Giles: Wait a minute! I didn't do anything!

Col. John Henry Thomas (John Wayne): You should've. (*Punches man in face*)[162]

· · ·

We've lost five hundred horses between here and the border. And I don't think that's very funny. We lose any more and somebody's gonna be damned uncomfortable.[162]

· · ·

Well, it's your game. How do you wanna play it?[162]

· · ·

Ex–Confederate captain: Let's understand each other, Thomas. Your Indian friend rode outta here last night with no explanation. He hasn't returned. One false move on your part, and my men won't miss.

Col. John Henry Thomas (John Wayne): Friend, your men have been missing me for years. And as far as that Indian boy is concerned, his father was Bold Eagle, one of the bravest warriors who ever rode a horse. And on top of that, he's my adopted son. And I haven't done this much explaining in years. Don't press me, Captain.[162]

· · ·

Mrs. Langdon: Why'd you have to shoot the man?

Col. John Henry Thomas (John Wayne): Conversation kinda dried up, ma'am.[162]

· · ·

We won't be hard to find. We'll be right handy.[162]

· · ·

We may have to be neighbors, but I don't have to be neighborly.[163]

· · ·

John Simpson Chisum (John Wayne): Well, I don't favor talking to vermin, but I'll talk to you just this once. You're not just getting started. The line's been drawn. What Billy did balanced the books so far. But if one of your men cross my land or even touch one of my cows, or do anything to that store, I'm not going to the sheriff, the governor, or the president of the United States. I'm coming to see *you*.

Lawrence Murphy: Mr. Chisum, that sounds like a threat.

Chisum: Wrong word. (*Punches man in nose*) Fact![163]

. . .

(*A horse thief wants to ransom stolen horses*)

Horse thief: Did you bring some gold with you?

John Simpson Chisum (John Wayne): Nope.

Horse thief: Silver?

Chisum: Just lead. (*Pulls gun and shoots horse thief*)[163]

. . .

Morton: You gonna shoot us, ain't you, Mr. Chisum?

John Simpson Chisum (John Wayne): I thought about it. Then I thought about something Henry Tunstall once said. He watched a man walk to the gallows, saw him hang. He said it was ghastly. Well, I've seen men hang, and that's the word. "Ghastly." You two are going to hang.[163]

. . .

Sergeant, there's one thing I oughta tell ya. If ya lay a hand on White Buffalo again, I'll kill ya.[163]

. . .

He's a gutless wonder. . . .[163]

. . .

Sergeant Major, you louse this up and you won't live to know it.[164]

. . .

Sheriff: I should've taken you this morning.

Cord McNally (John Wayne): You should've *tried*.[164]

. . .

Sergeant Major, you better wipe that smile off your face or I'll do it for ya.[164]

. . .

(*To a bad-guy hostage*)

Ketcham, we promised you in a trade. But we didn't say anything about what condition you'd be in![164]

. . .

John Fain: Boy mean anything to you?

Jacob McCandles (John Wayne): Never laid eyes on him. But I'm being paid to bring *him* back alive or *you* dead. Each and every one of you. Now, I'd rather bring the boy back. That's easier. But when it comes right down to it, don't matter to me. I'll earn my pay one way or the other. Now, how about you? Are you the big chief or one of the little Indians?

Fain (*slyly*): Oh, just a little Indian. Just a messenger boy.[165]

. . .

Hotel desk clerk: I thought you were dead.

Jacob McCandles (John Wayne): Dead?! The next person who says that, I'm gonna shoot, so help me.[165]

. . .

Ya follow him, I'll hunt ya down and kill ya, every mother's son of ya.[165]

. . .

(*To a kidnapper*)

Well, I hope that boy don't catch cold. That would cause me great annoyance and displeasure.[165]

. . .

Man with gun: Well, friend, that's it. No hard feelings.

Jacob McCandles (John Wayne): The hell there ain't. (*Shoots man with a hidden shotgun*)[165]

. . .

James McCandles: They'll kill little Jake, for sure.

Jacob McCandles (John Wayne): Not if we kill them first.[165]

. . .

Now *you* understand. Anything goes wrong, anything at all, your fault, my fault, nobody's fault, it don't matter. I'm gonna blow your head off. It's as simple as that. No matter what else happens, no matter who gets killed, I'm gonna blow your head off.[165]

. . .

Ya look like the vermin-ridden son of a bitch ya are.[166]

. . .

Well, here's my word: Get the hell off my spread. Now![166]

. . .

In my regiment, Mr. Nightlinger, I was known as old Iron Pants. You might keep that in mind.[166]

. . .

I wouldn't make a habit callin' me that, son.[166]

. . .

Where'd you find these two peckerwoods?![168]

. . .

Anybody starts crossin' that river before we're out of sight, baptize 'em.[168]

. . .

J. D. Cahill (John Wayne): You with 'em, Lightfoot? Or just passin' through?

Lightfoot: If I told you once, J.D., I've told you a dozen times. My name is *Chief* Lightfoot, and I'm a bona fide war chief of the Comanche Nation. And you and I both . . .

Cahill: You didn't answer my question! I'll make it plain. Do I have to shoot you or not?[169]

. . .

Oh, shut up, Simser. If a buzzard bites you, he'd never eat meat again.[169]

. . .

You put a slug in the meaty part of my left shoulder! You knowed damn well I been shot there twice before! You knowed![169]

. . .

Mister, I ain't got a bigoted bone in my body. You don't drop that ax, I'll blast you to hell as quick as I would a white man.[169]

· · ·

His name is Lightfoot. And I wouldn't call him "breed" to his face, if I was you. Not if you want to reach maturity.[169]

· · ·

Well, there's no prodding around. I'm willing to die tryin' to keep 'em. The question is, are you willin' to die tryin' to take 'em? Now, I'm cold and hungry and wet and tired and short-tempered, so get on with it.[169]

· · ·

Radical (*under arrest*): Hey, McQ. What is this asinine police crap?! This is an illegal arrest, man. This is unconstitutional and you damn well know it! Well, this whole damn place is comin' down, you know that? You pigs are gonna be out of work, but don't worry about it. We'll put ya on welfare. That's all your stinking job is anyway. Come on, pig! Shoot me! Pull your pistol and blow me up right here. What's the matter? No guts? Chicken? Huh?
(*Lon McQ kicks the radical in his private parts*)
Police officer (*entering, looking at beaten-up radical*): What happened?
Lon McQ (John Wayne): He bumped into a chair.[170]

· · ·

If this is a shine, I'm coming back and ironing your face.[170]

· · ·

I wouldn't—unless you wanna sing soprano.[171]

· · ·

(*After kicking down door*)
Knock, knock.[171]

· · ·

Listen, you riffraff. You know who I am and what I'll do![172]

· · ·

Damn yer murderin' hides! Meet yer maker![172]

◦ ◦ ◦

It's payday, boys! Come and get it![172]

◦ ◦ ◦

Now clamp your hands on your heads and get off them horses![172]

◦ ◦ ◦

Dobkins, you are a prying, pip-squeaking ass.[173]

◦ ◦ ◦

Mister, you better find another line of work. This one sure don't fit your pistol.[173]

◦ ◦ ◦

Well, now, pardon me all to hell![173]

◦ ◦ ◦

MOVE 'EM OUT!

Going Forward—Because of Orders, to Inspire Others, or Because It's Your Destiny

One of the enduring images of John Wayne is as a battle-hardened cavalry officer, sitting wearily on horseback in front of a squad of mounted troopers, lazily flicking his hand in the air and shouting, "Forward, yo-oh!" But there are many other occasions when it is time to make trails, and Wayne is always ready with a short-and-sweet phrase to motivate his associates—or his enemies—in the right direction.

. . .

I'm afraid you boys got yer brands mixed. Now vamoose![38]

. . .

Now, supposin' you folks move south. And keep movin'![53]

. . .

Now, just start out and keep goin'![63]

. . .

Come on, boys! Once we're through the pass, the goin's easy![101]

. . .

If ya really wanna help, stay outta the way![106]

. . .

Let 'em roll![106]

. . .

I got places to go and country to put behind me.[114]

* * *

Force left, ho-oh![116]

* * *

Forward, ho-oh![116]

* * *

Forward by fours, ho-oh![116]

* * *

Most of you men have come back to Texas from the war. Ya came back to nothing. You found your homes gone, your cattle scattered, and your land stolen by carpetbaggers. Now there's no money and no work because there's no market for beef in the South. But there is in Missouri. So we're goin' to Missouri.[117]

* * *

Take 'em to Missouri, Matt![117]

* * *

Prepare to mount. Mount. Forward, yo-oh![120]

* * *

Saddle up! Saddle up![122]

* * *

Move out! Keep your distance![122]

* * *

Column of twos, Captain. . . .[123]

* * *

Follow me![123]

* * *

Wagons forward, yo-oh![130]

* * *

Powder your nose, baby. We're gettin' outta here![133]

* * *

Chief, full ahead. Let's get this grand old lady to Hong Kong![133]

* * *

Well, c'mon, if you're goin' with us![135]

. . .

Let's go home, Debbie.[135]

. . .

Pour on the coal and head for home![137]

. . .

Stop howling and get out of here![138]

. . .

Yo-oh![142]

. . .

With all due respect, ma'am, I'm gonna get the hell outta here.[142]

. . .

When we move out, give your people, the wounded, a lotta liquor.[142]

. . .

Let's go, parson![143]

. . .

Follow the lieutenant, gentlemen.[148]

. . .

I just remembered I have a date.[151]

. . .

Let's go! Yeeaahh!![151]

. . .

Home! And don't spare the horses.[151]

. . .

Well, sister, the time has come for me to ride hard and fast.[161]

. . .

Move 'em out![166]

. . .

Slap some bacon on a biscuit and let's go! We're burnin' daylight![166]

. . .

You've worn out your welcome. Scat![173]

. . .

I'VE GOT a JOB to DO

Determination, Decisiveness, and Duty

An abiding theme of the best John Wayne movies is the actor's sense of honor, which in turn leads him to make difficult choices and to pursue them, no matter the obstacles ahead. If Wayne says he's going to do something, God help the man who stands in his way. Rarely does he care if completing a task is even the right thing to do, because once he makes his decision, finishing that job is the only *thing to do.*

· · ·

It's a job I've got to finish.[24]

· · ·

I never quit a job in the middle of the road.[24]

· · ·

We can't turn back. We're blazin' a trail that started in England. Not even the storms of the sea could turn back those first settlers. And they carried it on further. They blazed it on through the wilderness of Kentucky. Famine, hunger, not even massacres could stop them. And now we've picked up the trail again. And nothing can stop us! Not even the snows of winter nor the peaks of the highest mountains. We're building a nation! So we've got to suffer. No great trail was ever blazed without hardship. And ya gotta fight! That's life. And when ya stop fightin', that's death. What are ya gonna do, lay down and die?! Not in a thousand years! You're going on with me![24]

* * *

Ah, do your part, men. Why, with the telegraph line in, this wilderness will become a living part of the colonies. It'll mean expansion. New people coming in. Farms. Prosperity. And the end of gun rule.[41]

* * *

Sorry, boys, this is a one-man job. I'm goin' alone.[44]

* * *

We'll keep diggin' and blastin' until we get every one of them.[53]

* * *

For twelve years I've lived with but one thought in my mind: to get the men who killed my parents and stole my younger brother. If he's still alive, I'm gonna find him.[66]

* * *

I'm asking for single men only. And men who will stick. Who will join me here?[66]

* * *

Well, boys, the cat's out of the bag. I might as well come clean with you. I ordered you to load for a trip to St. Louis, but instead we're starting on one of the toughest grinds that's ever been tried. We're going to Los Angeles! The load is for a ship out there. The last ship to be loaded before the strike. And four hours ago the SEP started a special train from the Eagle Aviation to try and beat our time. If they get there first, they load the boat instead. Boys, there's a million-dollar contract at stake. This is a million-dollar race! You might as well know this, too: I'm doing this on my own. If the old man knew what was going on tonight, we'd never leave this yard. I personally guaranteed delivery. If we fail, I go out on my neck. And so will you! Now get this: It isn't gonna be easy. It's gonna be a heartbreaking, backbreaking haul! Two thousand miles through snow and sleet. Over icy, slippery pavements. Down dangerous grades. Danger at every turn of the wheel! Why, Harrison tried to tell me I couldn't get a bunch of men together who could do it. Whaddaya say?[76]

. . .

I'm afraid people around here spend too much time thinking.[80]

. . .

I better take care of this. I may not be as tactful, but I'll get results.[87]

. . .

My grandmother . . . She came out here in sixty-one, by covered wagon. There were Indians back then, and dangers and famine to meet. A little dust couldn't run her out. She could take it. She was a pioneer.[92]

. . .

Are you crazy, mister? You think you're talking to a sharecropper? We're farmers! We own our own land! Like our fathers and our grandfathers. You can't shove us around to match pretty pins on your maps! We're not swivel-chair farmers. And we're not licked yet![92]

. . .

I came here to do a job, Julie. I'm doing it.[96]

. . .

Maybe some of us won't come back. If there's anybody here that isn't set for that kind of action, now's the time to speak up. What we're doin' tonight is gonna be warnin' to any crooks headed this way that the pickin's here are plenty tough![100]

. . .

Ya gotta dig deep to get anything worthwhile.[106]

. . .

Well, what Mr. Gardner says is so—about us being a small detachment of dirt farmers. These are the men who came in with the land rush, and stuck through the dust and the drought. Most of them ain't oilmen, but they'll make a go of things, I figure, because this is their chance to take a chance. To have something for themselves.[106]

. . .

Stick to your jobs. Keep workin' as long as ya can![106]

. . .

For years, I've been taking your fatherly advice, and it's never been very good. From here on in, I'm a one-man band.[112]

. . .

Have you ever heard of some fellas who first came over to this country? You know what they found? They found a howling wilderness, with summers too hot and winters freezing. And they also found some unpleasant little characters who painted their faces. You think these pioneers filled out Form X277 and sent in a report saying the Indians were a little unreasonable? Did they have insurance for their old age, for their crops, for their homes? They did not! They looked at the land and the forests and the rivers. They looked at their wives, their kids, and their houses. And then they looked up at the sky, and they said, "Thanks, God. We'll take it from here."[113]

. . .

My land. We're here and we're gonna stay here. Give me ten years and I'll have that brand on the gates of the greatest ranch in Texas. The big house'll be down by the river, and the corrals and the barns behind it. It'll be a good place to live in. Ten years and I'll have the Red River D on more cattle than you've looked at anywhere. I'll have that brand on enough beef to feed the whole country. Good beef for hungry people. Beef to make 'em strong, make 'em grow. It takes work. It takes sweat. It takes time. Lots of time. It takes years.[117]

. . .

I want you all to know what you're up against. You probably already know. But I want to make sure you do. We've got a thousand miles to go. Ten miles a day'll be good. Fifteen'll be luck. It'll be dry country, dry wells when we get to 'em. There'll be wind and rain. There's gonna be Indian territory. How bad, I don't know. And when we get to Missouri there'll be border gangs. There's gonna be a fight all the way. But we'll get there. And nobody has to come along. I'll still have a job for ya when we get back. But remember this: Every man who signs on for this drive agrees to finish it. There'll be no quittin' along the way. Not by me and not by you. There's no hard feelings if you don't want to go. But just let me know now.[117]

. . .

If I can't teach ya one way, I'll teach ya another. But I'm gonna get the job done.[122]

. . .

At Chapultepec, my father—your grandfather—shot for cowardice the son of a United States senator. That was his duty. I will do mine. You've chosen my way of life. I hope you have the guts to endure it. But put out of your mind any romantic ideas that it's a way of glory. It's a life of suffering and of hardship—and uncompromising devotion to your oath and your duty.[123]

. . .

This is where we separate the men from the boys![125]

. . .

I didn't do ya any favor, Griff. I'm sorry about Cowboy. I know how tough it is to make a decision like that. You're gonna wind up staggering into your bunk every night with your hip pockets dragging. Then you'll lay there and look at the ceiling while your stomach turns over and ya hope to God ya called every shot right during the day. The next morning you'll wake up, wish you were a flight lieutenant again, so all you'd have to do is what the man told ya. And you'll get bad-tempered and snarly just like me. You'll probably wind up just like me. Climbing into an aircraft with your hip pockets dragging, to go back to some desk job. Brother, I didn't do you any favor.[125]

. . .

I may fail, but I can't quit.[132]

. . .

There are moments for wisdom, Jamuga; then I listen to you. There are moments for action; then I listen to my blood. I feel this Tartar woman is for me. My blood says, take her.[134]

. . .

(*Reverend Clayton says a prayer at the funeral of the victims of the Indian raid*)
Ethan Edwards (John Wayne): Put an amen to it!
Rev. Clayton: I ain't finished yet.
Edwards: There's no more time for praying! Amen![135]

. . .

Rev. Clayton: You wanna quit, Ethan?
Ethan Edwards (John Wayne): That'll be the day.[135]

. . .

Well, Reverend, that tears it! From now on you stay out of this. All of ya! I don't want ya with me. I don't need ya for what I gotta do. . . .[135]

. . .

Don't believe in surrenders. Nope. I still got my saber, Reverend. Didn't turn it into no plowshare, neither.[135]

. . .

Ethan Edwards (John Wayne): Our turnin' back don't mean nothin', not in the long run. She's alive, she's safe. For a while, they'll keep her to raise her as one of their own until . . . till she's of an age to . . .

Martin Pawley: Don't you think there's a chance we still might find her?

Edwards: Indian'll chase a thing till he thinks he's chased it enough. Then he quits. Same way when he runs. Seems like he never learns there's such a thing as a critter'll just keep comin' on. So we'll find 'em in the end, I promise you. We'll find 'em. Just as sure as the turnin' of the earth.[135]

. . .

Stay broke and keep moving. It's the story of our lives.[136]

. . .

I said, stand up! You're not gonna go to bed in the desert. You're gonna stand up and walk like a human being. Like a woman![138]

. . .

In an operation like this, everything is stretched. Even our necks.[142]

. . .

Tom Doniphon (John Wayne) (*reading sign*): "Ransom Stoddard, Attorney-at-Law." You're a persistent cuss, pilgrim. You really aim to hang that up outside somewhere?

Ransom Stoddard: That's why I painted it.

Doniphon: Well, take some advice, pilgrim. You put that thing up, you'll have to defend it with a gun. And you ain't exactly the type.[146]

. . .

Think you can make it, pilgrim?[146]

. . .

Lt. Col. Benjamin Vandervoort (John Wayne): Are you posi-
tive that ankle's broken?

Medic: Compound fracture, sir.

Vandervoort: Well, put the boot back on and lace it up.
Tight!

Medic: Don't get mad at me, Colonel. I didn't break it.

Vandervoort: No. And you're not gonna have to walk on it,
either. . . .

Medic: Colonel, don't tell me you're gonna try and . . .

Vandervoort: Aw, knock it off, Doc, and do as you're told.[148]

. . .

No, dammit. We came here to take Sainte-Mère-Église.
We're gonna take it and hold it![148]

. . .

One thing I'm sure of. We're gonna hold this town till the
linkup does come—whenever it is. Today. Tomorrow. Till
hell freezes over. (*Indicates dead soldiers*) For their sake, if
for no other reason.[148]

. . .

God willing, we'll do what we came here to do.[148]

. . .

Lomax: Well, I guess you don't know about his new toy—a
little iron-plated thing he calls the War Wagon.

Taw Jackson (John Wayne): It takes an average shipment of
fifty thousand in gold from Emmett to the railhead in El
Paso forty-three and a half miles away.

Lomax: There *are* a few guards. . . .

Jackson: Thirty-three of 'em. Twenty-eight outriders and five
in the coach. Each man is armed with a Henry repeating
rifle, two Colts, and two hundred rounds of ammunition.

Lomax: What's this all got to do with me?

Jackson: We're going to take that wagon.[157]

＊＊＊

Lomax: Don't let anything happen to ya.
Taw Jackson (John Wayne): Not likely.[157]

＊＊＊

That's no grade. I've freighted iron stoves up harder grades'n this.[161]

＊＊＊

I aim to do what I come here to do! Saddle the horses![161]

＊＊＊

(*After winning a battle against Confederate troops*)
Union Army Col. John Henry Thomas (John Wayne): Major, I've just received word that Lee surrendered to Grant three days ago.
Confederate Army Maj. Sanders: Yes, sir.
Thomas: You knew it?
Sanders: We received the news yesterday.
Thomas: I don't think you understand, Major. The war is over.
Sanders: No, sir.
Thomas: Are you telling me that you intend to keep fighting?
Sanders: Haven't we just proven it?
Thomas: But why?
Sanders: Because this is our land, and you're on it.
Thomas: We're all Americans.
Sanders: Yes, sir. That's always been the saddest part of it.
Thomas: Good day, sir.
Sanders: Colonel, thank you for your courtesy.[162]

＊＊＊

Ya got your town back.[164]

＊＊＊

There's a little eight-year-old boy, somewhere out there. Scared, lonely, and probably wonderin' what's happened to his world. We came here to find him and take him home. Alive, if possible. That's what I intend to do.[165]

. . .

Bring a bedroll, couple of good ropes, horse if ya got one. You'll get the best food in the territory, no rest, damn little sleep. And fifty big silver dollars—if we make it to Belle Fourche. Now, you'll show up at my place first Monday after school's out at five A.M. And come with grit teeth, 'cause gentlemen, that's when school really begins.[166]

. . .

If you don't stand your watch, somebody goes short of sleep. Carry your weight, boy.[166]

. . .

Yes, Daniel, that's a truth you can bank on in Denver. If they're up here, I'll find 'em.[169]

. . .

That fella don't quit easy, does he?[171]

. . .

Sister, I ain't never had a fight I didn't finish standin' up! We'll finish this one. Maybe not standin' up—but we'll finish it. The way we planned it.[172]

. . .

HOW to WOO a GAL

Spoonin', Romance, and
Being Nice to the Ladies

In complete contrast to the He-Man Woman-Haters Club tone of the quotes in the earlier "Wimminfolk" chapter, John Wayne can also be a ladies' man. Granted, that doesn't happen often, and when it does, the words that come out of his mouth are sometimes as awkward as the first steps of a newborn colt. But he does his best, and now and then rises to poetic heights—when he isn't tripping over his own tongue.

· · ·

(*After kissing a woman without consent*)
It was thisaway, ma'am: I thought you were someone else![24]

· · ·

You know, you can get used to havin' somebody not like ya. When they're not around, ya miss 'em not likin' ya. That's why I reckon I'm gonna be lonesome, but I'll be thinkin' of you. Goodbye.[24]

· · ·

Listen, girl, if anything happened to you, it'd be like throwin' my heart to the wolves.[24]

· · ·

Ruth Cameron: He's saying that I'm your squaw!

Breck Coleman (John Wayne): Seems like that's what he's drivin' at.

Cameron: Well, you tell him that you don't want me for your squaw!

Coleman: I've never told Black Elk a lie yet. He knows my tongue is straight.

Cameron: What do you mean?

Coleman: Well, it wouldn't be true if I told him I didn't want you. It happens I do.

Cameron: And you've no better taste than to tell me that before all these savages?!

Coleman: I'd tell you that in front of the whole world![24]

* * *

Aw, you don't owe me anything, señorita, but I certainly would like to know ya better.[48]

* * *

It's not a man I'm looking for. It's a woman. A young woman. She's just about your age.[58]

* * *

Well, now ya got me all flustered.[62]

* * *

I kinda liked you when you were mad at me.[62]

* * *

You just get yourself all dolled up, and we'll go out and buy you a *real* present.[63]

* * *

There's a lotta things about a fella's heart that a doctor doesn't know anything about.[64]

* * *

Don't you remember old times, Virginia? What we thought of each other? The things we'd planned? Can't we start again, now that the war is over?[72]

You know, Tom says I oughta settle down, maybe pick me out a nice girl, and get married. And since you're not already spoken for, I guess I'll just marry you.[80]

. . .

Don't forget to worry about me. . . .[81]

. . .

I think it's time you and I had some serious conversation.[82]

. . .

I'm kind to animals, and help old ladies across the street.[83]

. . .

You got no folks, and neither have I. And well, maybe I'm takin' a lot for granted, but I watched you with that baby. Another woman's baby. You looked, well . . . Well, I still got a ranch across the border. And it's a nice place, a real nice place. Trees and grass and water. There's a cabin, half built. A man could live there. And a woman. Will you go?[85]

. . .

But ya see, I got her figured out this way. If you like someone, and you don't tell 'em right off, why, maybe all that time you wasted, she liked you too. So, well, all that time's wasted, ain't it?[91]

. . .

I figured that if you was to take me over to her and give me an introduce, and then I could tell her who I was, and that I ain't never murdered nobody, and you could go somewhere and sit on a fence till I was through.[91]

. . .

Well, I ain't got no job right now, but I figure to get one. Outside of a snort of hooch now and then, I got no bad habits.[91]

. . .

I was a little hasty a couple of weeks ago, askin' ya to marry me. It was sump'n I shoulda told ya first . . . I shoulda told ya first that I love ya. That's what I really came over for tonight. Oh, there I go again. There's sump'n I shoulda done before that! (*Kisses the girl*)[91]

. . .

You don't know what lovely country is until you've seen Texas. In the springtime. The range is covered with lupine—bright, blue. Blue as your eyes. Well, almost as blue.[91]

. . .

Remember the first time I met ya, when ya kept lookin' around for my keeper 'cause ya thought I was too crazy to be all by myself? Well, ya better start lookin' around again, 'cause I'm gonna say sump'n crazier'n that. I know yer married to him, and I got no right to say this, but . . . I still love ya! You don't love him! Ya never did! I got a ranch in Texas. I wanna turn this wagon west and drive you 'n' me down there. Will you go with me? Willya?[91]

. . .

Forget it. I'm not going to try and sales-talk ya on staying. I'll even help ya pack.[92]

. . .

We'd be a lot better off, Leni, without so much understanding. We get all tangled up in other people's feelings, the duties and obligations. We know where our happiness lies! Why don't we take it?![92]

. . .

It's time we started to think about ourselves for a change and not others. Grab this chance to be free, Leni. It'll never come again.[92]

. . .

Look deep into my honest blue eyes. No, gray. My honest gray eyes. Can you doubt me?[94]

. . .

You got me pickin' wild orchids. That's a new low.[94]

. . .

Bijou Blanche: What were you thinking of . . . ?

Dan Brent (John Wayne): If you keep lookin' at me like that, I'm liable to tell ya.[94]

. . .

(*Lynn and Sabra are stuck on the top of a Ferris wheel at night*)

Sabra Cameron: Well, at least we're alone up here.

Lynn Hollister (John Wayne): Not quite. But we will be, as soon as I give that star a Sunday punch for winking at you.[95]

. . .

Lynn Hollister (John Wayne): You know, you'd be lovely if you had brown hair.

Sabra Cameron: I *have* brown hair.

Hollister (*smiling, leaning in for a kiss*): Yeah . . .[95]

. . .

Missed you? I can't work, can't think, can't even read a report but what there on the page you're smiling at me.[96]

. . .

Been tryin' to figure out what it was I liked about you. Come to find out it's the easy style you unload a full-up wagon.[97]

. . .

Tell her I got a marryin' notion—if she'll ask me real nice.[97]

. . .

Look, sugar, you don't know how lucky you are. A handsome duck like me, fancy duds from Paris, and sparklers enough to light up all Tennessee.[98]

. . .

You're in my blood, Loxi. Same as the sea. And I'm comin' back for ya.[99]

. . .

There's my cabin on the hill. Beautiful view from there. Come on, I'll show you around.[100]

. . .

I imagine that dress is supposed to have a chilling effect.
Well, if it is, it isn't working, 'cause you'd look good to me,
baby, in a burlap bag.[100]

. . .

Ya sure had me skippin' rope tonight. I thought you were
the royal magoo. Now you turn out to be just a hunky.[103]

. . .

I'm your kind of a guy, see? And you're my kind of a gal. We
were cut from the same chunk.[103]

. . .

You should've heard that hyena, blistering his tongue trying to keep me away from you![103]

. . .

You all right? Ya sure ya ain't busted no place?[105]

. . .

I don't sit on people every day.[105]

. . .

Ya like beer, doncha?[105]

. . .

Molly J. Truesdale: You know, I think it's nice for two people to just sit and talk, don't you?
Duke Hudkins (John Wayne): Yeah . . . if they have sump'n
to talk about.[105]

. . .

When I take a girl places it's kinda unusual she don't have
a good time.[105]

. . .

Don't ever leave me, Molly. Don't *ever* leave me![105]

. . .

(*On falling in love*)
I'm drunk! I'm drunk! I haven't had a drink all day and
I'm drunk![105]

. . .

A swell chiffonier. Plenty of drawer space. Room for all your little, um, things.[105]

. . .

I was just tryin' to kiss ya. . . .[105]

. . .

Hope you don't mind sleeping on the same desert with me![105]

. . .

Molly J. Truesdale (*nodding toward a horse*): Aren't you going to put a rope on him?

Duke Hudkins (John Wayne): How'd ya like me to put a rope on you?

Truesdale: Well, I'm not a horse!

Hudkins: What's the difference?[105]

. . .

You got everything![105]

. . .

If I wanted to get hooked, I'd let you hook me. I don't know of nobody that . . . But I don't *wanna* get hooked![105]

. . .

The moon sure is purdy tonight. Don't you feel like talkin'?[106]

. . .

Any way you want it, that's the way I want it.[106]

. . .

Constance Chesley: I thought I'd caught you being human for once. Don't you have anything under that thick hide of yours except cylinders and a carburetor?!

Lt. Cmdr. Wedge Donovan (John Wayne) (*leering, raising his eyebrows*): A spark plug, maybe. . . .[107]

. . .

There's probably nothing there but a trading post. We'll be stuck up there with nothing to do but . . . make love.[111]

. . .

What would ya say, Sandy, if I told ya ya look just as good to me without money as ya did with it?[111]

. . .

Well, I'd like to tell ya that I think you're an all right gal, but you wouldn't wanna hear that, would ya?[111]

. . .

You're a shapely hussy.[114]

. . .

You fill out that dress just right.[114]

. . .

Your cooking's got me grained up and ready for market.[114]

. . .

That is the way little girls with blue eyes get themselves kissed![115]

. . .

If I made a wish, you'd be in it, for sure.[115]

. . .

She's a nice girl. She reminds me of you.[120]

. . .

Ma'am, you're uncommon gracious. And I'd sure admire to meet you properly. May I come a-callin'?[121]

. . .

Yer downright discouragin' to romance, ma'am. Couldn't ya act just a little frightened? Sorta save my pride?[121]

. . .

Hooker: Lonesome?

Sgt. John Stryker (John Wayne): Drift! (*To waiter*) Whiskey.

Waiter: Two?

Hooker: Please . . . ?

Stryker (*reluctantly*): Okay.

Hooker: Thanks. A drink'll be good. I'm tired. It's been a rough day.

Stryker: Knock it off!

Hooker: I'm sorry, Sergeant. (*Wayne pays the waiter*) Sixty-five cents for a drink! It's too much! They cheat servicemen! You could drink cheaper at my house.

Stryker: Don't throw your arm out of joint.

Hooker: Well, thanks for the drink, Sergeant. Good luck. I didn't mean to make too much buzzing in your ear.

Stryker: It's all right. Finish your drink. I didn't mean to sound so tough.

Hooker: I know. You're just unhappy. Me too. My name's Mary.

Stryker: The long arm of coincidence, or something.

Hooker: Her name too, eh?

Stryker (*nodding*): That invitation still hold?[122]

. . .

Kathleen Yorke: Aren't you gonna kiss me goodbye?

Lt. Col. Kirby Yorke (John Wayne): I never want to kiss you goodbye, Kathleen.[123]

. . .

I've been numb for four years tryin' to figure out what happened to us. We had something, but I guess I kicked it around. Why don't we pick up the pieces and start over?[124]

. . .

Glad I didn't marry one of those burst-into-tears dames![125]

. . .

(*Arriving home*)
There's a strange man in the house! Anybody wanna kiss him?[125]

. . .

(*Seeing Mary Kate Danaher for the first time*)
Hey, is that real? She couldn't be![126]

. . .

. . .

Sean Thornton (John Wayne): Some things a man doesn't get over so easy.

Mary Kate Danaher: Like what, supposin'?

Thornton: Like the sight of a girl comin' through the fields, with the sun on her hair, kneeling in church, with a face like a saint.

Danaher: Saint, indeed!

Thornton: And now, coming to a man's house to clean it for him.

Danaher: Well, that was just by way of bein' a good Christian act.

Thornton: I know it was, Mary Kate Danaher. And it was nice of ya.

Danaher: Not at all.[126]

. . .

Say, what is this?! We're gonna get married! Aren't we?[126]

. . .

Can you ride a bike? Well, what are we waitin' for?![126]

. . .

There'll be no locks or bolts between us, Mary Kate, except those in your own mercenary little heart![126]

. . .

Sure I'm smug! The greatest girl in the world is stuck on me![127]

. . .

I'm having great difficulty keeping my hands off you.[127]

. . .

Don't you worry about love, 'cause a girl built like you is gonna collide head-on with it one of these days.[128]

. . .

Steve Williams (John Wayne): Care for a cigarette?

Alice Singleton: No, thank you.

Williams: They're the kind all the doctors smoke.[128]

. . .

You're a good cook, ma'am. A woman should be a good cook. I'm a good cook myself.[130]

. . .

Ya baked today. I can smell fresh bread on ya. Sometime today ya cooked with salt pork. I smell that on ya, too. Ya smell all over like soap. Took a bath. And on top of that, ya smell all over like a woman. I could find you in the dark. . . .[130]

. . .

Her hair was black as ten feet down. Didja ever see a crow's wing, how black and gleaming it is? That's the way her hair shined.[130]

. . .

I don't guess people's hearts got anything to do with a calendar.[130]

. . .

Varlabania. When the Indians wind up their squaw-seekin' ceremony, they only say one word: "*varlabania.*" It means forever. Forever.[130]

. . .

Did anyone ever tell you that you're beautiful when you're angry?[132]

. . .

Dance, Tartar woman. Dance for Temujin. Know this, woman: I take you for wife.[134]

. . .

You're beautiful in your wrath.[134]

. . .

For good or ill, she is my destiny.[134]

. . .

You're pretty well stuffed yourself.[137]

. . .

Lady, you sure are the Peruvian doughnuts! I wouldn't mind having you for a wingman![137]

. . .

C'mon, get in, you silly Siberian cupcake.[137]

. . .

Col. Jim Shannon (John Wayne): You were made for it.
Olga Orlief: Made for what?
Shannon: Love![137]

. . .

If you're through with your fainting-Bertha tricks, we can move on.[138]

. . .

I should've remembered, you're pretty good in a barroom fight.[138]

. . .

I always forgive a lady one murder.[138]

. . .

Come back, you maniac![138]

. . .

Joe January (John Wayne): You were never more beautiful.
Dita: To you?
January: Yeah, to me.[138]

. . .

Dita: You never kissed me like that before.
Joe January (John Wayne): I always meant to.[138]

. . .

Does a man need an occasion to show his wife how much he loves her? Besides, just being married to you makes every day an occasion. Shall we dance?[139]

. . .

Screen wife: Oh, Leonard, I'm so happy it frightens me.
Leonard (John Wayne): Frightens you? Nonsense.
Screen wife: Even after five years, it seems as if we're still on our honeymoon.
Leonard: Our honeymoon will go on forever, and forever, and forever.

Screen wife: Yes, darling. Forever.

Leonard: And forever, and forever . . . [139]

* * *

Feathers: These tights. Why didn't you want me to wear them?

John T. Chance (John Wayne): Because I didn't want anybody but me to see you in them.[141]

* * *

If I give ya back yer clothes will ya promise not to run away again?[142]

* * *

You're tired. You've helped a lot. Thanks for it. Poor way of being grateful after what I've put you through.[142]

* * *

Thank God I won't be the cause of hurting ya anymore. Because it happens I'm in love with you.[142]

* * *

I hope you can drive a mule.[143]

* * *

Sit down, missy! I still have one unoccupied knee![144]

* * *

You're good medicine.[144]

* * *

I guess a fella gets sore, and . . . well, what's the matter? Haven't ya ever had a fella fight over ya before?! I guess I got sore, that's all.[144]

* * *

(*To woman behind locked door*)

Aw, c'mon. Open up. I'll play ya a game of red dog. Casino! I'll spot ya ten points.[144]

* * *

I guess I can see about a room at the hotel for ya, for a parting gift.[144]

* * *

Move over and quit bawlin'![144]

. . .

You know, you look mighty purdy when ya get mad.[146]

. . .

Any more color and you'd be purdier than that cactus rose.[146]

. . .

You went around with your nose turned up at everybody and everything until I made a human being outta ya.[150]

. . .

Half the people in the world are women. Why does it have to be you who stirs me?[151]

. . .

Yes, Mrs. McLintock. Indeed, Mrs. McLintock. Of course, Mrs. McLintock.[151]

. . .

We could wash the mud off of each other. We used to have quite good times doing that sort of thing. . . .[151]

. . .

You are going to tell me why you picked up, packed up, and walked out on me![151]

. . .

Because all the gold in the United States Treasury, and all the harp music in heaven, can't equal what happens between a man and a woman.[151]

. . .

You're a woman, Toni. I got eyes. I can see.[152]

. . .

You're a good cook, Maggie. You look lovely in the candle-light.[154]

. . .

I'm reading a lot into your being here. Am I right?[160]

. . .

It's very simple: You'll do![160]

. . .

I'll say this—you're better than a hot brick to keep a man warm.[164]

. . .

(*On finding a strange woman in his bed*)
Hey, you, how'd you get here?[164]

. . .

Martha McCandles: You've changed, Jacob.
Jacob McCandles (John Wayne): Not you. You're as young and lovely as ever.[165]

. . .

Kate Collingwood: I'll think about ya afore I go to bed at night.
Wil Andersen (John Wayne): You do and you won't sleep.[166]

. . .

Stringy women like you live a long time.[166]

. . .

Yer sisters've seen all their husbands put under. More'n likely you will too. And I don't wanna see you end up somebody's fry cook.[166]

. . .

I want you to kinda stick out in the right places, so that anyone a long ways off sees you, there'll be no doubt yer a woman.[168]

. . .

(*To a sopping wet Ann-Margret*)
Mrs. Lowe, that shirt shrinks up any more, you're gonna be in trouble.[168]

. . .

Eula Goodnight: Well, go with God.
Rooster Cogburn (John Wayne): God, you, and the boy, ma'am. I'm takin' you to Bagby's Trading Post. You'll be safe there. Gather your belongings.
Goodnight: We're not going anywhere, sir. I must stay here and continue my father's work. I will be both preacher and teacher now.

Cogburn: I admire your sand, sister, but you should know that this is no place for a woman alone.

Goodnight: I will look after myself, and have done so very well all my life, thank you.

Cogburn: I won't allow it.

Goodnight: Well, you do not have any say in the matter, sir.

Cogburn: I have a lot to say, sister. I am the federal marshal for this territory, responsible for the citizens' safety. Now you will pack and come along with me quietly, or I'll arrest ya and take ya anyway.

Goodnight: To whom do you think you are talking, Marshal?

Cogburn: *You* is to whom I think I am talking, sister!

Goodnight: It's true you are bigger than I am, but physically, that is all.

Cogburn: I think in this situation, that is enough.

Goodnight: You mean you are willing to use brute force?

Cogburn: That is *exactly* what I mean.

Goodnight: Oh . . . yes . . . well . . .[172]

. . .

It ain't that I don't like ya. It's how ya talk.[172]

. . .

I figgered ya for a Yankee, but ya look more like a prairie bird—bony and tough![172]

. . .

I don't mind scrawny women. My first wife had bones stickin' out all over her.[172]

. . .

You got more backbone than femaleness. That's a fact.[172]

. . .

Well, ma'am, I don't know much about thoroughbreds—horses *or* women. Them that I did know I never liked. They're too nervous and spooky. They scare me! But you're one high-bred filly that don't. Course, I don't know what yer talkin' about half the time, but that don't matter. Bein' around you pleases me.[172]

• • •

Mrs. Rogers, you have a fine color when you're on the scrap.[173]

• • •

Maybe you're afraid of too many things. Sometimes widows are. But I'm sure there's plenty of starch in your corset.[173]

• • •

A man's emotions can tangle him all up sometimes.[173]

• • •

You're such a real lady on the outside, and you're full of vim and vinegar on the inside. I just never met anybody like you.[173]

• • •

In SERVICE to HIS COUNTRY

Patriotism, War, and Life in Uniform

John Wayne played many nonmilitary roles throughout his career, yet we often think of him as a soldier of one sort or another. Cavalry officer. Naval officer. Army officer. His characteristics in those films are as uniform as, well, his uniforms: concern for the welfare of his men, realistic about the disadvantages he faces, determined to succeed or die trying, and proud to fight for his country. Although Wayne never served in the military in real life, he nonetheless came to embody the very best, the never-say-die conviction, the spirit of brotherhood, the humor, and the perseverance of America's fighting men and women.

· · ·

We'll sew up this valley so tight a cricket can't get in without our say-so.[90]

· · ·

Listen, Dale, this is your first time up. Don't try to win this war all by yourself.[102]

· · ·

Capt. Jim Gordon (John Wayne): Should've stayed in college where he came from. But he begged for a chance. Begged for it like some kid wantin' to go to the circus. And I gave it to him.

Nurse Brooke Elliott: What happened?

Gordon: Aw, he didn't watch his tail. And outnumbered, as usual.

Elliott: He did bring his ship back. . . .

Gordon: Yeah . . . he did. But tomorrow or the next day there'll be somebody else in it, with three of 'em on *his* tail. Or six! Or ten![102]

· · ·

(*Flying Tigers pilot Woody Jason has just crash-landed after flying an unauthorized mission*)

Capt. Jim Gordon (John Wayne): Where do you think you are, with some broken-down flying circus?

Woody Jason: Aw, it would've been a cinch; I was ridin' the murder spot right above those Japolas. If I'd had ammunition, I'd have blown them clear out of China!

Gordon: And you washed out a good ship!

Jason: Hey, you talk like that crate is more important than *me*.

Gordon: I can't afford to lose either planes *or* pilots.

Jason: Look, Pappy, it's like I told you down at the barracks. All I get out of this is the dough, so you can't blame me for trying. In a skeet match, the guy who knocks down the most pigeons wins the cup.

Gordon: I can't have grandstanders trying to hog the whole show. Results here are based on cooperation and understanding. Discipline in the air is strict, because that's the only way an outfit like this can operate!

Jason: All right. I'll admit I was wrong. I made a mistake.

Gordon: Okay. . . . In this kind of warfare a fella likes to feel he's flying with somebody he can trust.

Jason: What do I care what they like?! It's every man for himself, isn't it?

Gordon: Not these days! When you look back over your shoulder and see a Jap sittin' on your tail, in a ship that you can't outmaneuver, *then* you'll know what I'm talking about.[102]

. . .

Capt. Jim Gordon (John Wayne): Sit down, Hap. I made a change. Tex Norton'll lead Flight B instead of you.

Hap Davis: Oh, that's okay, Jim. I'd rather be up there in my old spot anyway, protecting your tail feather.

Gordon: Oh, it isn't that, Hap. I gotta hand you one on the chin, but I'd rather it came from me than from somebody else.

Davis: Go ahead, Jim. . . .

Gordon: You're through flying.

Davis: The doc said I'd live to be a hundred.

Gordon: If you stay on the ground.

Davis: Oh. . . . I see. . . . Okay. Was there anything else?

Gordon: No. Wait a minute! I can't send a man up that doesn't know whether he's flying upside down or not! Take a look at that physical; your depth perception's a mile off! I know you've been gunning 'em since they were box kites with broomsticks for rudders. But you gotta believe me, I'm doin' this for you! You've been close-winging in formations, overshooting your landings . . .

Davis (*upset*): You don't have to say any more! (*Hap calms down*) I'm sorry. I was kinda figuring on going back to the States anyway. Maybe get me a chicken ranch or somethin'. I hear there's a lotta dough in eggs.

Gordon: Eggs! Who you tryin' to kid? You haven't been savin' any money. Been givin' it away as fast as ya make it! Look, Hap, I need ya here.

Davis: What could I do . . . now?

Gordon: Takin' care of these crates on the ground is just as important as flying 'em upstairs. I gotta have a man

I can trust on the ground. I wish you'd take that job, Hap.[102]

. . .

(*Captain Jim Gordon, momentarily distracted, is about to fly into a mountain peak*)

Woody Jason: Pull 'er up!

Capt. Jim Gordon (John Wayne) (*narrowly missing the mountain*): Didja know I used to drive a roller coaster?

Jason: Delivering nitro?

Gordon: Yesss.

Jason: Were you killed?

Gordon: Uh-huh.[102]

. . .

I guess a man just doesn't figure it that way. When he's fighting for his country, everything that will help his country is important. What happens to *him* just isn't.[104]

. . .

Theodore Roosevelt: How did you manage to get to the top of San Juan Hill ahead of the rest of us?

Daniel F. Somers (John Wayne): I had the longest legs, I guess.[106]

. . .

Apologies won't bring back my men.[107]

. . .

Lt. Cmdr. Wedge Donovan (John Wayne): What training do they need?

Admiral: Training to fight.

Donovan: Training to fight?! You might as well start training them to drink![107]

. . .

Commander: And that's an order!

Lt. Cmdr. Wedge Donovan (John Wayne) (*reluctantly*): That's one way to win an argument.[107]

. . .

Yeah, doin' great . . . Watchin' my men get knocked off like ducks in a birdbath. What's the sense of it? That's what I'd like to know.[107]

. . .

I want ya to act like a soldier! Remember you're in command of a company of men! You've got the responsibility of their lives in your hands.[110]

. . .

War hurts everybody.[110]

. . .

I only learned one thing from General Morgan, Sandy. That's when you're surrounded and haven't a chance, attack.[111]

. . .

A serviceman is supposed to have a funeral. That's a tribute to the way he spent his life. Escort, firing squad, wrapped in the flag he served under and died for. In war you gotta forget those things and get buried the best way you can. You all knew Squarehead Larsen and Slug Mahan. They were just a couple of bluejackets who did their job, and did it well. The Thirty-four boat couldn't've gotten along without 'em. Squarehead Larsen, he was the best cook in the Navy. He loved the old *Arizona*. Now they're both gone. Slug, he was always quotin' verse, bits of poetry. So here's one for him. It's about the only one I know. "Under the wide and starry sky, Dig the grave, and let me lie. Glad did I live and gladly die, And I laid me down with a will. This be the verse you grave for me: *Here he lies where he longed to be; Home is the sailor, home from the sea, And the hunter home from the hill.*"[112]

. . .

They aren't forgotten, because they haven't died. They're living. Right out there. Collingwood and the rest. They'll keep on living as long as the regiment lives. The pay is thirteen dollars a month, their diet beans and hay. Maybe horsemeat before this campaign is over. They'll fight over cards or rotgut whiskey, but share the last drop in their canteens. Faces may change, names, but they're there. They're the regiment, the regular Army. Now, and fifty years from now.[116]

...

The Army is always the same. The sun and the moon change. The Army knows no seasons.[120]

...

(*Captain Nathan Brittles, nearing retirement, sits by his late wife's grave*)
Well, Mary, only six more days to go and your ol' Nathan'll be out of the Army. Haven't decided what I'll do yet. Somehow I just can't picture myself back there on the banks of the Wabash rockin' in a front porch. . . . No, I been thinkin' I'd maybe push on west. New settlements. California. We had some sad news today, Mary. George Custer was killed. His whole command. Myles Keogh among 'em. You remember Myles. Happy-go-lucky Irishman—who used to waltz so well with you! Yeah, I know, I . . . I guess I was a little jealous. Never could waltz, myself. Well, take the troop out in the morning. Cheyennes around. Gonna pick up the patrols and guide 'em on back north. Prob'ly be my last mission, Mary. Hard to believe it. Hard to believe. . . . [120]

...

You will have the men build their squad fires higher. Make the fullest show of bedding down for the night. And then we're sneaking out. Heading for the river. Going back![120]

...

(*On mustering out*)
Old soldiers, Miss Dandridge. Someday you'll learn how they hate to give up. Captain of the troop one day, every man's face turned toward ya, lieutenants jump when I growl. Now, tomorrow I'll be glad if a blacksmith asks me to shoe a horse.[120]

...

Men, I won't be goin' out with ya. I won't be here when ya return. Wish I could. But I know yer performance under a new commander'll make me proud of ya. 'Cause I've always been proud of ya.[120]

. . .

Capt. Nathan Brittles (John Wayne): Sergeant Tyree!
Sgt. Tyree: Yes, sir!
Brittles: I'm ordering you to volunteer again.[120]

. . .

Yes, we are too old for war. But old men should stop wars.[120]

. . .

If you're worried about my prospects, sir, they're the same as any man's in these times. I just came from five years in the Army. You're a soldier, you know what that means.[121]

. . .

Out here you gotta remember the book and learn a thousand things that have never been printed, probably never will be. Ya gotta learn right, and ya gotta learn fast. And any man that doesn't want to cooperate, I'll make him wish he hadn't been born. Before I'm through with ya, you're gonna move like one man and think like one man. If ya don't, you'll be dead. Now, you guys have had a nice easy day. I hope you enjoyed it. Because it's the last one you're gonna get for a long time.[122]

. . .

I'm gonna tell you somethin', Conway. I'm gonna tell all of ya. I'm gonna make it nice and simple so ya all understand it. They handed me you guys as a present, a regular Easter basket. And they told me to get ya into some kind of shape so ya could handle a little piece of this war. And that's what I'm gonna do! And that means I'm gonna tell ya what to do, every day and every minute of every day. I'm gonna tell ya how to button your buttons. I'll even tell ya when to blow your noses. And if ya do something I don't like, I'm gonna jump! And when I land, it'll hurt. I'm gonna ride ya till ya can't stand up. And when ya do stand up, you're gonna be Marines.[122]

. . .

Oh, guys make mistakes, I guess, but every one we make, a whole stack of chips goes with it. We make a mistake and some guy don't walk away. Forevermore he don't walk away. I guess all we can do is just take it and hope we don't make the same mistake again.[122]

. . .

But he did enlist. And he's here. Here he'll stay and here he'll serve.[123]

. . .

If you fail, I'll have ya spread-eagled on a wagon wheel. If you desert, you'll be found, tracked down, and broken into bits.[123]

. . .

This is the captain talking. Well, we asked for it. Now we got it. We're right in the middle of the entire Japanese Imperial fleet. We've got to sit here like a duck in a shooting gallery until Pearl acknowledges our contact message. Searchlights are poppin' all over the place, and destroyers are crankin' up depth charges. If Pearl acknowledges in time, we have a chance. With these overlapping targets, I intend to fire all tubes, cause so much excitement that we can make a break for it. That is all. That's enough.[124]

. . .

Ens. Caldwell (*after the Chief and Junior are killed*): I couldn't help it about the Chief, sir.

Lt. Cmdr. Duke Gifford (John Wayne): Remembering how he took care of you?

Caldwell: Yes, sir.

Gifford: Well, before you, he took care of Larry. Before Larry, he took care of me. And before me, it was Pop. Before Pop . . . Chiefs have been taking care of this man's navy for a long time, Mr. Caldwell. Don't worry about him. He's got a lot of good sailors to take care of back there.[124]

· · ·

When the command meets a commander for the first time, it's like a wedding. Nobody knows how it's going to turn out. Whether it'll be a happy golden anniversary or a divorce. We'll see.[125]

· · ·

Ya beef at the decisions *I* make but you're too soft to make 'em yourself. You just can't bring yourself to point your finger at a guy and say, "Go get killed!" You gotta tear your guts out worryin' about his flight record. Or because some dame back in the States is givin' him the brush-off. Or whether he knows whether his baby's born yet or not. You got enough troubles of your own for one man. Stop trying to pack everybody else's around. Schedule that mission![126]

· · ·

When I was a Marine, the Navy kept putting me on boats and taking me places. My bunk was always too short. The Navy would take me to an island someplace, put me on a beach where a lot of angry people would start shooting at me. And when the shooting died down, the Navy would put me back on a boat, where the bunk was too short, and take me to another island where more people would shoot at me. Now, during this, I became very annoyed with the Navy. But I kept my temper. I did not strike even one sailor. However, there is a limit to my patience. And if I have any more trouble with the Navy, *you* are nominated.[127]

· · ·

(*To a snoring soldier*)
I'm gonna ask your wife if you keep *her* up all night. You're a lousy guy to sleep with.[129]

. . .

(*On parachuting*)
I haven't jumped out of a ship in sixteen years. I'm not gonna start tonight.[129]

. . .

(*On professional soldiers from West Point*)
Partly they learn, partly they die. But I gotta float my stick same as you. I never saw one of 'em I had to be ashamed of.[130]

. . .

We're all human. But unfortunately, at sea, there's no chance to enjoy our humanity.[132]

. . .

There's been some trouble. I had to kill a soldier. He's hidden in the kitchen.[133]

. . .

Well, Doctor, war isn't exactly a civilized business![142]

. . .

I figgered any fella that shouldered a gun was deserving of respect.[143]

. . .

We've got a man down here ambushed. And bushed! Like to die if he don't get some carin' for.[146]

. . .

Ya can't give the enemy a break. Send 'em to hell![148]

. . .

(*On the stormy eve of the D-Day invasion*)
Lt. Col. Benjamin Vandervoort (John Wayne): After briefing session today, all troops will participate in ground tactics and deployment.
Capt. Harding: In this weather, sir?

Vandervoort: Well, of course, Harding, if you can ensure that we'll land in France in sunshine and dry weather . . .

Harding: I didn't mean that, sir.

Vandervoort: What *did* you mean?!

Harding: I meant, it isn't the weather, sir. It's the waiting. These men are itching to go.

Vandervoort: I don't think I have to remind you that this war's been going on for almost five years. Over half of Europe has been overrun and occupied. We're comparative newcomers. England's gone through a blitz, with a knife at her throat since 1940! I'm quite sure that they, too, are impatient and itching to go. Do I make myself clear?

Harding: Yes, sir. Quite clear.

Vandervoort: Three million men penned up on this island— all over England, in staging areas like this. We're on the threshold of the most crucial day of our times. Three million men out there. Keyed up. Waiting for the big step-off. We aren't exactly alone.[148]

* * *

You're gonna be landing in the dark. And on the other side of that hedgerow, a fella may not be wearing the same uniform you are.[148]

* * *

It's a hell of a war.[148]

* * *

What is there to think about? The Army's better off with ya than without ya. That's the test.[149]

* * *

Michael Patrick "Guns" Donovan (John Wayne): Well, there's not much to tell. We got blown off our can, and it was a destroyer. Ended up here on the island. There was a big Jap base down there. So we hid out back here in the hills, down in those caves. Tossed a few monkey wrenches into their machinery, threw 'em a few spitballs.

Amelia Sarah Dedham: It's hard to believe that war has ever been within a thousand miles of a place as peaceful as this.

Donovan: Mm-hmm. Frangipani and flamethrowers don't seem to go together, but that's the way it was.[150]

* * *

I don't write ya up because your record already looks like a lotta pig tracks. One more scratch on it and your career in this man's navy is ended.[154]

* * *

Capt. Rockwell Torrey (John Wayne): Get a message off to Pearl. "Have taken two torpedoes." Fill in our position. "Extent of damage unknown. Will advise."

Commander Burke: And break radio silence, sir?

Torrey: Burke, don't you think the Japanese know by now where we *are*?[154]

* * *

Admiral Kimmel: If you didn't have enough fuel to complete your mission, why didn't you turn back for Pearl?

Capt. Rockwell Torrey (John Wayne): My mission was to intercept and engage an enemy of greatly superior strength, sir. I could only take that one way: that my group was expendable.

Kimmel: I doubt if a court of inquiry will accept that. Captain, you're about to be caught in the vacuum between a peacetime Navy and a wartime Navy. Six months from now they'll be making admirals out of captains who exhibit some guts, but right now they're only reacting to the Pearl Harbor disaster, and punishment is the order of the day. Of course, you don't have to abide by what a court of inquiry decides. You can ask for general court-martial, get yourself a couple of crack sea lawyers, and make a fight of it.

Torrey: I wouldn't care to do that, sir.

Kimmel: Why not?

Torrey: Second-generation Navy, Admiral.[154]

. . .

All battles are fought by scared men who'd rather be some-place else.[154]

. . .

If I were running the Pentagon, I'd have stood you up against the wall. Instead, they'll probably pin a medal on ya. Have ya ever heard of the word "discipline"? A staff officer actin' like a kid playing cowboys and Indians is an example that might cost us a few thousand lives. What are you trying to prove, Marcus?[156]

. . .

Give this insubordinate son of a bitch every truck and blan-ket in the Third Army. And I don't care who you have to steal 'em from![156]

. . .

Out there, due process is a bullet.[159]

. . .

It's pretty hard to talk to anyone about this country until they've come over here and seen it. The last village that I visited, they didn't kill the chief. They tied him to a tree and brought his teenage daughters out in front of him and disemboweled them. Then forty of them abused his wife. And then they took a steel rod, broke every bone in her body. Somewhere during the process, she died.[159]

. . .

First we get some sack time, then we start all over again.[159]

. . .

(*Holding up an M16 rifle*)

Funny thing. A fella takes one of these into battle, and by the grace of God he comes out in one piece, he carries a strange sense of guilt all the rest of his life.[159]

. . .

(*On parachute jumping*)

Oh, first one's easy. It's the second one that's hard to get 'em to make.[159]

• • •

The recon was a success. Prob'ly be no trouble. But the word is "alert." Get ready![159]

• • •

Little Vietnamese boy: What will happen to me now?

Col. Mike Kirby (John Wayne): You let me worry about that, Green Beret. You're what this is all about.[159]

• • •

Well, you'll have to bear with our worryin', Colonel. We stay alive by bein' scared to death.[160]

• • •

I volunteered into this outfit and I'll volunteer out of it.[162]

• • •

Well, he's got you outnumbered. Let's start from there.[162]

• • •

Short Grub: You ain't expecting trouble, are you, John Henry?

Col. John Henry Thomas (John Wayne): Trouble? Well, let's see. . . . We got Maximilian on one hand and Juárez on the other, and bandits in between. And on top of that, we're Americans in Mexico taking a cavvy of horses to a very unpopular government. Why should we expect trouble?[162]

• • •

HOW to JUDGE a MAN'S CHARACTER

Measuring the Mark of a Man, and Recognizing Your Own Failings

In nearly every role he plays, Duke Wayne can assess a man's worth—or his evil—the way a jeweler can appraise a diamond. You cannot con John Wayne. He can tell a man's innate value even when that man himself has self-doubts. Moreover, Wayne is pretty good at looking into his ethical mirror. And he doesn't always like his own reflection. . . .

· · ·

They ain't nobody got me buffaloed.[33]

· · ·

Some men are like books written in a strange language. And that makes it awfully hard to read them.[60]

· · ·

I used to be a good cowhand, but . . . things happen.[85]

· · ·

Folks, it's true, I don't know much about the law. Ain't had much book learnin'. But the good Lord gave me a nose for smellin' a horse thief a mile off. And what you need in these parts is a marshal that's better at smellin' than spellin'.[91]

. . .

Ever since I got able to remember, I've been sproutin' and growin' too fast outta my britches. I reckon I never growed into 'em, inside. Until today. Kinda like bein' born all over again, right side up.[97]

. . .

(*A man died because of his friends' dereliction of duty*)
I hope you two had a good time, 'cause Hap paid the check.[102]

. . .

Seems like everybody around here's made up their mind but me. It ain't my money and it ain't my oil lands. I know how you folks feel, and I'd like to please ya. But still and all I guess I gotta sleep on this proposition for a while.[106]

. . .

A regular lollapaloozer![106]

. . .

I'm here with my hat in my hand and no alibis. I was wrong. Rotten wrong in everything. But I had to learn it the tough way.[107]

. . .

Why, Tito, I learned how to make cards stand up and say uncle before *I* could.[109]

. . .

Quirt Evans (John Wayne): I thought you weren't allowed to work on Sunday.

Penelope Worth: Oh, Quirt, there's nothing we're not allowed to do. It's just that we don't believe in doing what we know is wrong.

Evans: Well, that makes it pretty much each fella's own guess.

Worth: But each fella knows, inside.

Evans: Well, there's a lot of gents I wouldn't want to give that much leeway to.[114]

• • •

Thomas Dunson (John Wayne) (*giving gun back to a boy looking for a job*): Are you gonna use it?

Boy: No, but don't ever try to take it away from me again!

Dunson (*turning to a ranch hand*): He'll do.[117]

• • •

(*To someone looking out for your best interests*)

Ya got a lot of bloodhound in ya, Charlie. But ya can call off the dogs, 'cause I'm about five years smarter than I was a half an hour ago. And if you ever catch me feelin' sorry for myself again, ya got my permission to bop me right in the nose.[122]

• • •

(*In a posthumous letter from Sergeant Stryker [John Wayne], read by Private First Class Thomas*)

You've got to take care of your mother, and love her, and make her happy. Never hurt her or anyone as I did. Always do what your heart tells you is right. Maybe someone will write you someday and tell you about me. I want you to be like me in some things but not like me in others, because when you grow older and get to know more about me, you'll see that I've been a failure in many ways. This isn't what I wanted. Things just turned out that way. If there was only more time, I'd . . . (*"Guess he never finished," adds Thomas*)[122]

• • •

Lt. Col. Kirby Yorke (John Wayne): Is it dark enough for you to get in there?

Trooper Travis Tyree: With two men I pick, sir.

Yorke: Two men *you* pick? I know that you are an excellent judge of horseflesh, Trooper Tyree. Proved that when

you stole my horse. But how are ya as a judge of men for
a dangerous mission?

Tyree: I consider myself a good judge of the men I trust, sir.

Yorke: That's a good answer. Call your volunteers.[123]

* * *

As a hobby, he bites silver dollars in half.[127]

* * *

I've been kicked out of the Big Ten, the Ivy League, and
the Southern Conference. They wouldn't even let me coach
at Alcatraz.[128]

* * *

(*About a college football team*)
Why, with the material you have at hand at St. Anthony's,
you couldn't whip Vassar at tiddlywinks![128]

* * *

Look, this is a musical-comedy college, and nobody could
save it but Rodgers and Hammerstein! I couldn't help if I
wanted to.[128]

* * *

Bein' purdy isn't much. I know a lot of purdy people I
wouldn't trust with a busted nickel-plated watch. But some
others? Sump'n comes out of the inside of 'em, and ya know
ya can trust 'em.[130]

* * *

A man has weakness or strength, Schmidt. Weakness you
can hide, like red lead over a sprung rivet. But it'll give under strain. Strength, ya cannot defeat, ever.[132]

* * *

A miracle?! Me?![133]

* * *

The rudder's sluggish. The turnbuckles won't turn. The
capstan's rusted. The decks are warped. She's stubby and
high in the water. God help us in a rough sea. But you know
sump'n, baby? I kinda like her.[133]

...

Listen, Min, I'm trying to say I've been a fool, first class, senior grade, gold-braided.[136]

...

When I do something, I go all the way. Living, gambling, flying, I tap myself out. Guess that's the way I want it to be. Maybe even it's the way I am.[136]

...

Things are flying around in my head like feathers in a bag.[137]

...

Maybe I'm recovering some lost virtue myself.[138]

...

I can't recite any Psalms for ya, but I know about people who believe in God. Our friend didn't. He put his faith in his father, a man, a human being. That's an easy faith to lose. I know about that, too.[138]

...

John T. Chance (John Wayne): It's nice to see a smart kid for a change.
Stumpy: Yeah, he ain't like the usual kid with a gun.
Dude: Wonder if he's as good as Wheeler said?
Chance: I'd say he is. I'd say he's so good, he doesn't feel he has to prove it.[141]

...

(*On Tennesseans*)
Some of 'em don't bathe as often as polite folks'd think is necessary, but every one of 'em smells sweet to me.[143]

...

You're not much for this forgive-and-forget business, are you, Jim?[143]

...

There's one thing for sure: He's a bear cat for nerve.[143]

...

Kinda foolish to trust a stranger with a hunk o' diamond like that.[144]

. . .

(*Captain Jake Cutter handcuffs fugitive Paul Regret to a saddle to prevent his escape*)

Paul Regret: Cap'n Jake, you know, it's getting very tiresome lugging this saddle around. I don't suppose you'd take my word of honor that I won't try to escape?

Capt. Jake Cutter (John Wayne) (*incredulously*): Mon-soor, you are a lulu![145]

. . .

That's something no one ever accused me of—being civilized.[145]

. . .

Time we both quit, Crow. You don't like losing to me, and I don't like winning from you.[145]

. . .

Yet another one of those fellas uses that "my friend" stuff real careless.[145]

. . .

Liberty Valance is the toughest man south of the Picketwire. Next to me. . . .[146]

. . .

A month ago they were sayin' I was crazy, insane! Now they're callin' me a hero. But hero or crazy, I'm the same man.[149]

. . .

Cuthbert H. Humphrey, governor of our territory, is a cull. Do you know what a cull is, ma'am? A cull is a specimen that is so worthless that you have to cut him out of the herd. Now, if all the people in the world were put in one herd, Cuthbert is the one I would throw my rope at. At whom. At whom I would throw my rope at. Natural-born cull![151]

. . .

Gov. Cuthbert H. Humphrey: G.W., *you* are a ruffian!

G. W. McLintock (John Wayne): Cuthbert, *you* are right.[151]

• • •

How long do ya think ya can keep runnin' away? How long ya gonna flop around in cheap joints, hawkin' your soul?[152]

• • •

A man's generally no better'n he has to be.[152]

• • •

I spent my life learning the things I know about men and ships and how to use 'em in action. I just don't fit behind a desk. I'm not cut out for it. I feel dry-docked.[154]

• • •

Taw Jackson (John Wayne): Did you know why Pierce wanted you to kill me?

Lomax: Sure, so he could legally steal your land once he found there was gold on it. You were a hardworking rancher defending your property, yet it's you who gets shot, framed, and sent to jail. I always thought that was kind of amusing.

Jackson: Well, it's nice to find a fellow with a keen sense of humor.[157]

• • •

Ask him. Does he ride with warriors, or women?[157]

• • •

You all right? No . . . you ain't.[158]

• • •

You can never tell what's in a Chinaman's mind. That's the way he bests ya at cards.[161]

• • •

Martha McCandles: You haven't changed, have you, Jacob McCandles?

Jacob McCandles (John Wayne): Not one bit.[165]

• • •

Pop Dawson: Say, you don't look too good. The sight of blood bother you?

Jacob McCandles (John Wayne): Only my own.[165]

* * *

Well, I can't say I always decide right.[166]

* * *

Mrs. Lowe: All you do is drift.

Lane (John Wayne): It's what I'm good at.[168]

* * *

Gold has a way of bringing out the larceny in all of us, Mrs. Lowe.[168]

* * *

Them lily-livered law-bookers ain't gonna risk their necks, or you wouldn't be here![172]

* * *

They ain't comin'! I'll bet my drunken cat on that. Well, I ain't waitin' for 'em.[172]

* * *

Seems to me there's been enough shootin' around here, ma'am. I'm of a different brand than them that did it.[172]

* * *

Ma'am, my hide is tougher'n boot leather. But no man alive likes to be called high-smellin' and low-down![172]

* * *

I was readin' about old Queen Vic. Well, maybe she outlived her time. Maybe she was a museum piece. But she never lost her dignity nor sold her guns. She hung on to her pride and went out in style. Now, that's the kind of an old gal I'd like to meet![173]

* * *

SHOOTIN' IRONS, SHOTGUNS, and SHELLS

All Manner of Weaponry— and How to Use It

A John Wayne film that doesn't have at least some gunfire is rare indeed. Wayne almost always has a Colt .45 strapped to his leg or a Remington repeater in a handy rifle rack. Yet only a few of his characters die by the bullet, even though most of them live by it. So when the Duke talks about weaponry and how to use it, people tend to listen.

. . .

(*The Ringo Kid stops a stagecoach heading into Indian territory by standing in the middle of the trail and twirling his Winchester rifle*)

Ringo (John Wayne): I didn't expect to see you ridin' shotgun on this run, Marshal.

Marshal Curly: Going to Lordsburg? I figured you'd be there by this time.

Ringo: Nope. Lame horse. Well, it looks like you've got another passenger.

Curly (*aiming his shotgun meaningfully at Ringo*): Yeah . . . I'll take the Winchester.

Ringo (*quietly*): You may need me and this Winchester, Curly. . . . [85]

. . .

Sandy Poli: That's Papa! He's shooting at us!

John Devlin (John Wayne): All I want to know is, do you take after Papa or Mama?

Poli: Papa always wants to shoot things out. He has no more sense than you have. I do hope he doesn't kill us. He'd never get over it.

Devlin: Well, I'd feel kind of regretful about it myself. [111]

. . .

Penelope Worth (*nodding at Quirt Evans's holstered side-arm*): Surely you can walk to the barn without *that*.

Quirt Evans (John Wayne): What?

Worth: The gun!

Evans: Oh, well, it, uh, *balances* me. One leg's longer than the other. You know, the *weight*.

Worth: Thee are a liar. [114]

. . .

Boy: How'd you know when he was gonna draw?

Thomas Dunson (John Wayne): By watchin' his eyes. Remember that. [117]

. . .

Lock and load! [122]

. . .

Paul Regret: How do you know you killed him?

Capt. Jake Cutter (John Wayne): Wasn't time not to. [145]

. . .

Gimme that peashooter. [145]

. . .

Hey, pilgrim, you forgot your popgun! [146]

. . .

There's a lot of things I'm not sayin' to ya, mister, while you've got a sawed-off shotgun in my middle. [151]

. . .

(*After shooting a pair of desperadoes*)

Lomax: Mine hit the ground first.

Taw Jackson (John Wayne): Mine was taller.[157]

• • •

That's no way to use a handgun. Ya gotta draw and fire, and ya better be quicker than somebody else that's doing the same thing. Like this![158]

• • •

Sheriff J. P. Harrah: One of 'em got away, Cole!

Cole Thornton (John Wayne): You oughta know. *You* missed him.[158]

• • •

Cole Thornton (John Wayne): Did you get him?

Mississippi: Who?

Thornton: The fella that ran outta the church!

Mississippi: Well, yes and no.

Thornton: Yes and no? Whaddaya mean? Did ya or didn't ya?

Mississippi: I hit the sign, and the sign hit him.

Thornton: That's great.

Mississippi: He was limping when he left!

Thornton (*increasingly frustrated*): He was limpin' when he *got* here![158]

• • •

(*An injured Cole Thornton shoots gunslinger McLeod with a hidden rifle*)

McLeod (*dying*): You didn't give me any chance at all, did you?

Cole Thornton (John Wayne): No, I didn't. You're too good to give a chance to.

McLeod: Yeah. I let a one-armed man take me.[158]

• • •

Lawyer Goudy: Now, is it not true that you sprang upon old man Wharton and his two sons with a deadly six-shot revolver in your hand?

Rooster Cogburn (John Wayne): I always try to be ready.

Goudy: Was this revolver loaded and cocked?

Cogburn: Well, a gun that's *un*loaded and cocked ain't good for nothin'.[161]

...

Well, a fella that carries a big-bore Sharps carbine might come in handy—if we get jumped by elephants, or buffalo, or sump'n.[161]

...

Rooster Cogburn (John Wayne): Why, by God, girl, that's a Colt's Dragoon! You're no bigger'n a corn nubbin. What're you doing with all this pistol?

Mattie Ross: It belonged to my father. He carried it bravely in the war. And I intend to kill Tom Chaney with it if the law fails to do so.

Cogburn: Well, this'll sure get the job done—if you can find a fence post to rest it on while you take aim.[161]

...

Rooster Cogburn (John Wayne): I'll shoot the last man through the door and we'll have 'em over a barrel.

Man: You'll shoot 'em without a call?!

Cogburn: Well, I'll get 'em to know our intentions is serious! Oh, well, I'll holler down after I shoot, see if any of 'em wanna be taken alive. But when they won't, we'll shoot 'em as they come out the door.[161]

...

Mattie Ross (*watching Rooster load his revolver*): Why do you keep that one chamber empty?

Rooster Cogburn (John Wayne): So I won't shoot my foot off.[161]

...

Beau was a young colt then. No horse could run him into the ground. When that posse thinned out, I turned ol' Beau around and, takin' them reins in my teeth, I charged them boys firin' two Navy sixes! They must've all been married men that loved their families, 'cause they scattered and run for home.[161]

• • •

I know him—well. I shot him in the lip last August over at Winding Stair Mountains. He was lucky that day, all right. My shootin' was off.[161]

• • •

(*Shooting tips*)
Windage and elevation, Mrs. Langdon. Windage and elevation.[162]

• • •

James Pepper: What are you going to do?
John Simpson Chisum (John Wayne): What I ought to have done twenty-five years ago. Pat, get the men out of South Camp. Trace, you round up everybody that can ride a horse or pull a trigger. Let's break out some Winchesters![163]

• • •

He stuck his butt up, that's what he did. Boy, when you're in that kind of a gunfight, keep your butt down. That's the thing to remember. There's always some bustard on the other side who's got enough sense of humor to shoot you there instead of the head, every time.[165]

• • •

(*McQ prepares to leave a gun shop with a MAC-10 submachine gun*)
Jack, gun-shop owner: You're not going to take it, are you?
Lon McQ (John Wayne): Just say it's a loan.
Jack: Lon, it's not licensed!
McQ: Jack, neither am I.[170]

• • •

Well, Judge, out there in the Territory, they don't know about all these newfangled laws. *We* know it, but they don't. They're still shootin' in the same direction—at me![172]

• • •

Eula Goodnight: There are nine men with him. How can you best them?

Rooster Cogburn: Well, ma'am, I got my Navy Colt sidearm and a Winchester rifle on my saddle and a packet full of cartridges.[172]

. . .

They chased me until I got tired of it. Then I just whirled my old horse, bore around, took them reins in my teeth, and rid right at them villains. And I was shootin' my saddle pistol in one hand and whirlin' my Winchester with the other. Never took aim! Just snap-shot—and got 'em all.[172]

. . .

J. B. Books (John Wayne): See that tree on the left, with the divided trunk? You take the right side. Now, aim well and put five slugs in it.

Boy: Why not six?

Books: Ya keep your hammer on an empty chamber, for safety.

Boy: And if you're going out to face somebody?

Books: Well, load six, if your insides tells ya to.[173]

. . .

There's more to bein' a man than handlin' a gun.[173]

. . .

It isn't always being fast or even accurate that counts. It's being willing. I found out early that most men, regardless of cause or need, aren't willing. They blink an eye or draw a breath before they pull the trigger. I won't.[173]

. . .

(*On mixing whiskey and weapons*)
Oh! I hope you're smart enough to know that that who-hit-John don't go with guns. . . .[173]

. . .

A man should know how to handle a gun, use it with discretion.[173]

. . .

MAKE MINE a DOUBLE

Taking a Snort Now and Then

John Wayne wasn't afraid of a little liquor every once in a while, whether in real life or on the screen. But in his films he is a responsible drinker (mostly!), rarely shooting anyone because he is on a bender or picking a fight because he is sloshed. Oh, he has his rascally moments in his cups, to be sure. And he isn't shy about saying so. . . .

...

Let's go to Hefty's and knock one off.[33]

...

You did a good job, Doc. Even if you was drunk![85]

...

(*To bartender*)
I want a glass of milk. Plain. No rum . . . and no comments. I like milk.[101]

...

Stay here. I'll git. I can always drink by myself.[105]

...

Boy, he hops to it like a drunkard at a Fourth of July barbecue.[118]

...

Set 'em up, bartender. Milk for the infant, and a cool, cool beer for me.[118]

* * *

Capt. Nathan Brittles (John Wayne): Ya got a breath on ya like a hot mince pie!

Sgt. Quincannon (*smelling of whiskey*): Ah, Captain darlin', as you well know I took the Pledge after Chapultepec.

Brittles: And Bull Run, and Gettysburg, and Shiloh. And St. Patrick's Day. And the Fourth of July!

Quincannon: Aw, ha ha, Captain darlin' . . .

Brittles: Beats me where you hide the stuff.[120]

* * *

The only tax you ever paid was a whiskey tax![120]

* * *

We'll get ya a little whiskey, men. It'll be all right![120]

* * *

Nobody starts out to get blind, staggerin', stinkin', fallin'-down drunk![122]

* * *

Elsa Keller: What else is there to do?

Capt. Karl Ehrlich (John Wayne): Have a drink, perhaps. Would that help?

Keller: It never hurts. . . .[132]

* * *

E pluribus unum. Have a drink.[136]

* * *

Damn the martinis. Full speed ahead.[136]

* * *

I used to make excuses when I drank in the afternoon too.[136]

* * *

Best desert remedy on the market. . . .[138]

* * *

Nothin' like soakin' your insides while ya can. . . .[138]

· · ·

All right, quit! Nobody's tryin' to stop ya. If ya wanna quit, quit! Go on back to the bottle. Get drunk. One thing, though. Somebody throws a dollar in a spittoon, don't expect *me* to do somethin' about it. Just get down on your knees and go after it.[141]

· · ·

All I want is a drink. . . .[142]

· · ·

(*Hands whiskey to crying woman*)
Here. Take this. It'll steady ya down.[142]

· · ·

Quite a speech. Guess I'm feelin' my liquor.[142]

· · ·

Let's wet our whistles. Words are dusty.[143]

· · ·

Crack out a couple of jugs and bring that gee-tar.[143]

· · ·

I figgered we'd crack a jug and tell each other our troubles.[143]

· · ·

I was wonderin', ya think there'd be a mouthful of that corn juice left? We could kinda cut the tar out of our throats?[143]

· · ·

I'll be below gettin' washed on the outside and wet down inside.[143]

· · ·

Well, you've got a lot of drinking to catch up on.[144]

· · ·

Aw, where's that whiskey?![144]

· · ·

What's your pleasure, folks? We've hit it big, and we're buying![144]

· · ·

It ain't mannerly out West to let a fella drink by himself.[146]

* * *

Pompey, go find Doc Willoughby. If he's sober, bring him back.[146]

* * *

Woman: You have been drinking a little, hm?
Sean Mercer (John Wayne): No, ma'am, I've been drinking a lot.[147]

* * *

I got a touch of a hangover, bureaucrat. Don't push me.[151]

* * *

Running Buffalo: Long time we don't get drunk together!
G. W. McLintock (John Wayne): And it's gonna be a lot longer time, because it's against the law and you're with the sheriff![151]

* * *

Shall we celebrate with a drink?[151]

* * *

You know, if we had any moral character, we wouldn't be standing here covered with mud, drinking, when we should be washing.[151]

* * *

I been doin' some thinkin' drinkin', Bunny.[151]

* * *

Katherine McLintock: I don't intend to stand here and hold a midnight conversation with an intoxicated man!
G. W. McLintock (John Wayne): And I'm *not* intoxicated. . . . Yet![151]

* * *

Don't make me feel like I'm drinking alone, ma'am. . . .[151]

* * *

Katherine McLintock: You smell of beer!

* * *

G. W. McLintock (John Wayne): Well, naturally! I'm drinking beer. . . .[151]

. . .

We both know what's eating you, Paul. You can't wash it out with booze.[154]

. . .

Gen. Mike Randolph (John Wayne): Did you find anything to drink around here?
(*Col. David "Mickey" Marcus hands him a canteen*)
Randolph: I don't mean water.
Col. David "Mickey" Marcus: *I* don't mean water![156]

. . .

Sheriff J. P. Harrah: Cole . . . Cole, they laughed at me. Right in front of McLeod, they just laughed at me.
Cole Thornton (John Wayne): They've *been* laughing at you. For a couple of months. You just haven't been sober enough to hear it.[158]

. . .

Mattie Ross: Well, I hope you don't think I'm going to keep you in whiskey!
Rooster Cogburn (John Wayne): I don't buy that. I confiscate it. And a touch of it wouldn't do you any harm against the night air!
Mattie: No, thank you.
Cogburn: Well, it's the real article! Genuine, double-rectified bust head. Aged in the keg.[161]

. . .

Mattie Ross: I'll tell the story if you stop drinking.
Rooster Cogburn (John Wayne): Let it go! That, baby sister, is no trade![161]

. . .

Col. James Langdon (*discussing the late Civil War*): Let's just say we haven't seen the end.

(*Langdon drinks from a bottle of whiskey and hands it to John Henry Thomas, who takes a gulp, then makes a face*)

Col. John Henry Thomas (John Wayne): You'll see it quick enough if you keep drinkin' *this* stuff.[162]

* * *

Coffee?! I think we can do better than that.[163]

* * *

(*At the end of the Civil War, Cord McNally looks up two Confederates he once fought against*)

Cord McNally (John Wayne): Glad you fellas weathered the storm.

Capt. Pierre Cordona: Well, it's a simple life, Colonel. No wine, no women, no song.

Sgt. Tuscarora Phillips: And no whiskey!

McNally: Well, I can remedy that—if you two don't mind drinkin' with a Bluebelly.

Phillips: Colonel, suh, I'd drink with the Devil himself!

Cordona: I feel just like he does!

McNally (*smiling, pointing to a saloon*): We're headed in the right direction![164]

* * *

None of that cow purch. Give us whiskey![164]

* * *

Shut up and pour.[166]

* * *

If that's that old Tennessee sour mash, put a little in there. Good for my rheumatism.[166]

* * *

I ain't had a drink since breakfast![172]

* * *

Who's payin' the rent around here?! Him or me? You can't lock up a man's whiskey![172]

* * *

Come on, sister! Don't tell me you stand in judgment of a man who pulls a cork every now and then?[172]

...

Why do people wish to be sober? Life ain't a easy game, sister. Don't hurt to make a fool o' yourself once in a while.[172]

...

J. B. Books (John Wayne): Good morning, sir.
Bartender: Good morning.
Books: This is my birthday. Gimme the best in the house.[173]

...

A HEALTHY MISTRUST
of AUTHORITY

Politics, Government, and
International Relations

Let's be honest: John Wayne is rarely gung-ho about government, lawyers, or any other group that tries to regulate the average citizen's behavior. He trusts human nature more than legislatures, his own gut more than judges and juries. And occasionally, he even has something to say about the world at large. . . .

. . .

Dink Hooley: Where's this cousin of yours at?

Dare Rudd (John Wayne): Wyoming.

Hooley: Where do you figure Wyoming's at?

Rudd: Right over yonder behind that hill—unless somebody's moved it.[80]

. . .

Tucson Smith: You know, there used to be a time when being an American meant something.

Stony Brooke (John Wayne): It still does. It stands for freedom and fair play.

Lullaby Joslin: But this madman's grabbing everything in sight. He's become a dictator.

Brooke: All the more reason why we gotta fight! The men who opened up this country didn't sit around crying for help. They *did* something![86]

* * *

They think more of money than they do of men.[90]

* * *

We've obeyed the law and they've broken it.[90]

* * *

That election was about as honest as a three-dollar bill.[95]

* * *

For those, I suppose your new city administration'll double my taxes. Taxes?! I haven't got a dime![109]

* * *

Speaking of politics, where we're going, there are only two parties: the quick and the dead.[111]

* * *

But it's a lot of hooey! Fixin' everybody up when they let out their first squawk. Givin' 'em pointers on good government between bottle feedings. And teachin' 'em in school to be good little ladies and gentlemen and not smack each other around.[113]

* * *

There are a lot of wonderful things written into our Constitution that were meant for honest, decent citizens. I resent the fact that it can be used and abused by the very people that want to destroy it.[127]

* * *

Look, baby. I don't know the *why*. I've heard all the jive. This one's a Commie because Momma won't tuck him in at night. That one because girls wouldn't welcome him with open arms. I don't know the *why*. The *what*, I do know. It's like when I was wearing a uniform. I shot at the guy on the other side of the perimeter because he was the enemy. Hey, we better get outta here or I'll start talkin' politics![127]

* * *

(*Looking at the lights of China from a prison cell*)
Hello, Amoy, you dog-eared old postcard.[133]

. . .

I hate the Reds because they closed a lot of Chinese ports where I have dames![133]

. . .

Patience was made in China.[133]

. . .

(*On Russians*)
I met lots of 'em in Germany. Got drunk with 'em. I sang their songs and they sang mine. It was a beautiful friendship that gradually ripened into complete apathy, baby.[137]

. . .

(*On slavery*)
But there are men in my country who would die to end that evil. It cannot long endure.[140]

. . .

Tennesseans ain't exactly against fighting. But they ain't much for listening to speeches.[143]

. . .

"Republic" . . . I like the sound of the word. It means people can live free, talk free, go or come, buy or sell, be drunk or sober, however they choose. Some words give ya a feeling. "Republic" is one of those words that makes me tight in the throat. Same tightness a man gets when his baby takes his first step, or his first baby shaves, and makes his first sound like a man. Some words can give ya a feeling that make your heart warm. "Republic" is one of those words.[143]

. . .

Political arguments don't flavor folks' supper.[143]

. . .

Well, I know those law books mean a lot to you. But not out here. Out here a man settles his own problems.[146]

. . .

I do not attempt to explore the depths of the Oriental mind.[150]

...

These settlers get burned out, there'll be a lot of hollerin' that this country is too wild to be a state. We'll go on bein' a territory some more, with a lot of political appointees runnin' it according to what they learned in some college where they think that cows are somethin' you milk and Indians are somethin' in front of a cigar store.[151]

...

There's no such thing as free land. You make these homesteads go, you'll have earned every acre of it. But ya just can't make 'em go on the Mesa Verde. God made that country for buffalo. Serves pretty well for cattle. But it hates the plow. And even the government should know that you can't farm six thousand feet above sea level.[151]

...

The government never gave anybody anything![151]

...

(*On European Jews and the formation of Israel*)
If anybody ever deserved a home on the basis of sheer gallantry, it's those poor devils from those camps.[156]

...

And the government has promised me a posse—which I figger'll be long on promise and short on posse.[172]

...

OLD COOTS

Longtime Friendship, Aches and Pains, and Facing the Big Adiós

Advancing age is a frequent topic in Wayne's later movies. The perspective it gives to his roles only increases the depth of his characters. Rarely lapsing into nostalgia, he frequently ruminates about his longtime saddle pals, complains most avidly about the lack of creature comforts due a man of a certain maturity, and considers when and where he will enter the box canyon of his life.

...

I'm glad you decided to drift along with me. It's kinda lonesome trailing alone.[54]

...

Why, you cantankerous old coyote![71]

...

Aw, I was only dryin' your beard, ya old Rocky Mountain canary![106]

...

I like grumpy old cusses. Hope to live long enough to be one.[108]

...

Nothing's going to happen to us. We won't turn up the well-known toes until Old Man Time catches up with us.[111]

...

Hello, you weather-beaten old hangman![114]

. . .

Well, we water our horses out of the same trough.[114]

. . .

Quirt Evans (John Wayne): He was a big fella. A cattleman.
   He swung a wide loop in his younger days, I think.
Penelope Worth: A wide loop?
Evans: He wasn't too careful whose calf he threw a rope at.[114]

. . .

Well, Pearly, ya old hay-shaker, ya got me.[118]

. . .

Ya got an old maid's failings: Ya worry![122]

. . .

I'm mellow in my old age, I guess.[122]

. . .

Well, I've knocked around these waters from Port Arthur to
Singapore in every kind of a ship, under a half a dozen flags.
Does that answer your question?[133]

. . .

Is that old goat still creakin' around? Why doesn't somebody bury him?![135]

. . .

My bones is cold tonight.[135]

. . .

We get to be bored as we get older.[145]

. . .

Oh, I'll bet that old boy was a man to stand aside from
when he was young and limber.[145]

. . .

When you're as old as I am, you'll thank me for this.[151]

. . .

The last time I saw you two, you were ten jumps ahead of a
posse raising dust from Mexico.[158]

. . .

He was carrying around a twenty-one-foot tapeworm along with his business responsibilities. That aged him.[161]

. . .

(*Wil Andersen is desperate for cowboys to drive his herd*)
Wil Andersen (John Wayne): Well, guess I'll go over to the Bigelow place and see what I can turn up. Maybe Henry . . .
Annie Andersen: Henry Bigelow is sixty years old, Wil!
Wil Andersen (*smiling*): So am I.[166]

. . .

Miserable old age. I hate it.[166]

. . .

I'm sorry. A man gets older, it's harder to say that. He tries to bull his way through.[168]

. . .

I got a saddle that's older than you, Mrs. Lowe. . . .[168]

. . .

Gone to seed, have I? Gone to seed . . . A man does his job, defends the code, what does he get out of it? Disgrace and abuse.[172]

. . .

Well, see who they have to come to when they got a real job to be done? The ol' Rat Killer. Well, I'll be in fine feather tomorrow.[172]

. . .

Well, my tail feathers may droop a little, and my wattles show, but I can still outcrow anything in the barnyard.[172]

. . .

You can tell your mother that a tuckered-out old man needs a room.[173]

. . .

THE ROAD to BOOT HILL

The Meaning of Life, and the Last Roundup

Not all John Wayne's characters live to the end of the movie. SPOILER ALERT: Sergeant John M. Stryker on Iwo Jima. J. B. Books on the dusty streets of Carson City. Wil Andersen on the trail to Belle Fourche. Wayne's characters are invariably tough hombres who know death might lie over the next fold of dung-colored hills or sneak up on him with each creak of the swinging saloon doors. But the shadow of certain doom produces in them no gripping fear, just acceptance, an existential understanding that everyone who lives must ultimately die. And in that understanding comes a sense of what we almost might call peace, even spiritual serenity.

...

Well, Zeke, old Windy's gone on another trail.[24]

...

Mrs. Worth: But what harm can there be in a little dough-nut? Unless one eats so many of them that they explode—which is likely to happen to you, young man!

Quirt Evans (John Wayne): Well, there's worse ways of checking out.[114]

...

Get a shovel and my Bible and I'll read over him.[117]

＊＊＊

We'll bury him . . . and I'll read over him in the morning.[117]

＊＊＊

There's quitters to be buried. I'll read over 'em in the morning.[117]

＊＊＊

(*At a frontier funeral*)
I also commend to your keeping, Sir, the soul of Rome Clay, late brigadier general, Confederate States Army. Known to his comrades here, Sir, as Trooper John Smith, United States Cavalry. A gallant soldier and a Christian gentleman.[120]

＊＊＊

Sgt. John Stryker (John Wayne): That little voice whisperin' in your ear again?

Frightened soldier: Uh-huh.

Stryker: Don't worry about it. I've known a million guys that've heard it. Most of 'em make it. A few don't. Percentage is on your side.

Soldier: Did you ever hear it?

Stryker: No.

Soldier: Don't you ever worry about it?

Stryker: What good would it do?

Soldier: You're indestructible.

Stryker: Well, stick close to me and maybe a little of it'll rub off on ya.[122]

＊＊＊

(*At the scene of a brutal Indian massacre*)

Lt. Col. Kirby Yorke (John Wayne): Corporal Bell . . . (*Places hand on corporal's shoulder*) Sorry, son.

Cpl. Bell: May I have permission to go forward, sir?

Yorke: Stay here.

Bell: But it's my wife! If it was yours, wouldn't you wanna go?!

Yorke: Yes, I would. But if I had a friend, he'd keep me here. Stay with me, boy. . . .[123]

· · ·

I guess it's up to me to say something. The most appropriate thing I can think of is the last part of the Burial at Sea, the Navy prayer book. Goes like this: We commend their souls to God and commit their bodies to the deep, in sure and certain hope of the resurrection into eternal life through Jesus Christ, at whose coming to judge the world, the sea shall give up her dead.[124]

· · ·

Everybody gets dead. It was his turn.[130]

· · ·

The Greeks believed that a man was immortal as long as his name was remembered on Earth.[132]

· · ·

Cathy Grainger: Why did you kill him?

Capt. Tom Wilder (John Wayne): Well, it seemed like a good idea.[133]

· · ·

(*In a rage, Brad Jorgensen tries to crush the skull of a dead Comanche warrior*)

Rev. Clayton: Jorgensen!

Ethan Edwards (John Wayne): Why don't you finish the job?

(*Edwards shoots out the eyes of the Comanche warrior*)

Clayton: What good did that do ya?

Edwards: By what *you* preach, none. But what that Comanche believes, ain't got no eyes, he can't enter the spirit land. Has to wander forever between the winds. You get it, Reverend.[135]

· · ·

Ethan Edwards (John Wayne): I'm gonna tell you somethin'. Didn't mean to speak of it, but I'm gonna tell ya now. Ya

remember that scalp strung on Scar's lance? Long and
wavy?

Martin Pawley: Yeah, I saw it. And don't try to tell me it was
Aunt Martha's or Lucy's.

Edwards: It was your mother's.[135]

. . .

Come on, he's paid his bills.[138]

. . .

He was a good guy almost all the way. If his pa hadn't tripped
him up, he'd've done all right. He spent all that junk on healin'
the sick and helpin' the lowly. Me pickin' on him?! For slippin'
at the finish? I slipped all the way.[138]

. . .

No complaints. No complaints.[138]

. . .

Burt: Oh, Señor Chance, what do you wish me to do with
these three dead men?

John T. Chance (John Wayne): Well, you're the undertaker,
Burt. Bury 'em. Another one down by the bridge. Send
in your bill and the county'll pay you.

Burt: No need for that. Each one of them had two new fifty-
dollar gold pieces in his pocket.

Chance (*thoughtfully*): Price is going up.[141]

. . .

Hannah Hunter: Medicine is the most noble and unselfish . . .

Col. John Marlowe (John Wayne): Sure, noble profession, noble oath. Lanterns held on high, so high they won't admit they're gropin' for . . .

Hunter: But you're . . . you're *unfair*!

Marlowe: Unfair?! There was a girl. Not much older than that
boy in there. I wasn't unfair then, understand, because
they used a lot of fancy words that an ordinary section
hand wouldn't understand. So I held her down while two
of 'em worked on her. I trusted doctors then. Believed in

'em. Because I was in love and I didn't wanna see her die. A tumor, they said it was. And it had to come out right away. So they stuck a leather strap in her mouth, so she could bite off her screams while they cut away to get in there. And what did they find?! Nothing! Oh, they were sorry. Sure, they'd made a mistake! They had something to talk about before their next little experiment. And what about me?! They left me beggin' her not to die. And I lost my wife! And I didn't kill either one of 'em. Must've been crazy, or too conventional.[142]

· · ·

I always figgered to die. The question is when.[145]

· · ·

Graile: You killed him?

Capt. Jake Cutter (John Wayne): Seemed like the thing to do at the moment.[145]

· · ·

Bud Elder: I'm going with you. I can draw pretty fast. We'll be famous, like the Dalton Brothers!

John Elder (John Wayne): Yeah, they're famous—but they're just a little bit dead. They were hung![155]

· · ·

(*Cole Thornton delivers to a father the body of his son, who has just killed himself to avoid a lingering death after being gutshot by Thornton*)

Kevin MacDonald: You said he was asleep. How do you know he was asleep?

Cole Thornton (John Wayne): He told me that. Told me his name. That's how I knew where to bring him. And he said you told him what happens to a man that's gutshot. How he hasn't got much of a chance. Did you tell him that?

MacDonald: Yeah, I told him that.

Thornton: Well then, you're partly to blame. You'll find two bullets in him. One of 'em's mine. He was hurtin' worse'n he could stand. Had a handgun that I didn't see. Any more *questions* you wanna ask?

MacDonald: No. I guess you're tellin' the truth. I guess if you weren't, you would never've brought him here. I'm much obliged to ya for that.

Thornton (*sighing*): It don't help much.

(*Thornton turns his horse and rides away*)[158]

• • •

Rooster Cogburn (John Wayne): Boots, I got Hayes and some youngster outside with Moon and Quincy. I want you to bury 'em for me. I'm in a hurry.

Capt. Boots Finch: They're dead?

Cogburn: Well, I wouldn't want you to bury 'em if they wasn't.[161]

• • •

I can't do a thing for ya, son. Your partner has killed ya and I've done for him. I'll see ya get buried.[161]

• • •

Damn that Texan! When ya need him, he's dead.[161]

• • •

That Texican. Saved my neck twice. Once after he was dead.[161]

• • •

Sometimes it's hard to understand the drift of things. This was a good boy. He'd have been a good man. He didn't get his chance. Death can come for ya any place, any time. It's not welcome, but if you've done all you can do, and it's yer best, in a way, I guess yer ready for it.[166]

• • •

Well, it's not how yer buried. It's how they remember ya.[166]

• • •

Cowboy: We've got a right to know what we're gettin' into.

Lane (John Wayne): A grave, more'n likely, if you come along with us.

Cowboy: Then why should we?

Lane: Beats the hell outta me.[168]

Lightfoot: J.D., gimme my five dollars. You get shot tonight, I disappear. Oh, I'll come back and bury you, mumble something Christian over your grave.

J. D. Cahill (John Wayne): Lightfoot, your kindness overwhelms me.[169]

• • •

Eula Goodnight: Marshal, I'd like to say a few words over the dead. Good or bad, they're God's own.

Rooster Cogburn (John Wayne): Well, they look like they're past carin', but go ahead.[172]

• • •

My being here, maybe that's news. But dying is my own business.[173]

• • •

A man's death is about the most private thing in his life. . . .[173]

• • •

It's usually some six-fingered bustard that couldn't hit a cow in the tit with a tin cup that does ya in.[173]

• • •

I'm a dying man, scared of the dark.[173]

• • •

A MISCELLANY
of JOHN WAYNE
QUOTES

On Religion, Leadership, Employment, the Utterly Unclassifiable, and More

These witty, often funny quotes are too random to deserve chapter headings in themselves, but you never know if you might find an occasion when one of these quotes—from the worlds of crime, critters, capitalism, and you-name-it— might prove useful.

LEADERSHIP
How to Take Charge

When we leave here, I'm in complete charge, and *I* give all orders.[67]

. . .

It's gotta be my way—on the side of law![67]

. . .

I know one rotten apple can spoil a barrel. Now just stay in line and quit shootin' off your mouth. When we make camp tonight, if you got anything to say, I'll listen to ya.[92]

. . .

This isn't my show. It's ours. I didn't ask to run it. But as long as I *am* running it, you're gonna take orders from me and like it.[92]

. . .

Listen, men! We've driven all day through a furnace. We've only just made camp. You're hot and tired and hungry. Go on back to your tents and let the women feed ya. Take a swim, cool off. We can get there![92]

. . .

There was an agreement made when you signed on. You agreed to finish this drive. I'm gonna hold you to it.[117]

. . .

Only the man who commands can be blamed. Rests on me. Mission failure![120]

. . .

Mr. Cohill, it is a bitter thing indeed to learn that an officer who has had nine years' experience in the cavalry—the officer to whom I am surrendering command of this troop in two more days—should have so little grasp of leadership as to allow himself to be chivvied into a go at fisticuffs while taps still sounds over a brave man's grave. God help this troop when I'm gone.[120]

. . .

If you're nervous, count your toes. I'll do the masterminding around here![122]

. . .

There is no room in my tent for those who fear—or question my orders.[134]

. . .

I'm givin' the orders. *I'm* giving the orders! Or we're splittin' up here and now.[135]

. . .

Paul, you're forcing me to throw my weight at you. Fish or cut bait. Get on your feet or take your troubles elsewhere. I've got a ship to run.[154]

. . .

Capt. Coleman: Oh, uh, I noticed a load of corrugated tin has miraculously appeared overnight.

Capt. MacDaniel: Sergeant Petersen provided it.

Coleman: Well, that's a good man you've got there.

Col. Mike Kirby (John Wayne): Sergeant Petersen say where he got it?

MacDaniel: He, uh, said the Good Fairy left it.

Kirby (*smiling*): I hope he said the Good Fairy left it, *sir*![159]

. . .

Dinnertime will come and go without notice on this trip. Get on your horse![161]

. . .

Sister, you pay heed to every word I say till this thing is over.[172]

. . .

ANIMALS
How to Consider Critters

(*Looking at his dying horse*)
Wish it was me that got sick instead of him. I could tell 'em where it hurts; he can't.[105]

. . .

Contrary animal, the deer. Gentle on the hoof, tough on the plate.[111]

. . .

I wouldn't give a plug nickel for a horse that wouldn't fight. They'll let you down when the goin' gets tough.[130]

. . .

I hoped for a horse, but there's nothing wrong with a good, strong mule.[143]

. . .

Another thing about Alaska: the polar bear! He can go for six months without any "attentions." But after six months, a polar bear gets a little nervous—and starts clawin' up his fellow animals to death! Now, it's the same way with a gold miner. . . .[144]

* * *

(*Capt. Jake Cutter prepares to take his prisoner, Paul Regret, on a trail ride to jail*)

Paul Regret: You say this trip'll take about five days?

Capt. Jake Cutter (John Wayne): Right. Step aboard.

Regret: What? On this mule?

Cutter: On the mule.

Regret: Ridin' him's gonna slow us down!

Cutter (*mounting his horse*): Oh, very sad. But on the other hand, if you were to take off into the tall and uncut, I could run ya down real easy.[145]

* * *

Paul Regret: I'm beginning to hate this mule already. He's got a mean look.

Capt. Jake Cutter (John Wayne): His name is Mabel. . . .[145]

* * *

Mon-soor, you haven't got the sense of a jackrabbit, lettin' hot horses drink! Keep 'em away from the water until they've cooled out! Or are horses sump'n else you don't know anything about?[145]

* * *

Sean Mercer (John Wayne): Pockets, what are you tryin' to do?

Pockets: I'm trying to milk this goat.

Mercer: That's the wrong kind of a goat; it's a ram![147]

* * *

Cats don't belong to nobody. He just rooms with me. Of course, I depend on him.[161]

* * *

Mattie Ross: Trust you to buy another tall horse.

Rooster Cogburn (John Wayne): Yeah. He's not as game as Beau, but Stonehill says he can jump a four-rail fence.

Mattie: You are too old and fat to be jumping horses.

Cogburn: Well, come see a fat old man some time!

(*Jumps fence and rides away*)[161]

· · ·

(*Discussing a horse with no saddle*)

Jacob McCandles (John Wayne): Throw a blanket on him.

James McCandles: I can ride without a blanket.

Jacob McCandles: I'm not worrying about your butt! It's *his* back![165]

· · ·

Ya know, trail drivin' is no Sunday-school picnic. Ya gotta figger yer dealin' with the dumbest, orneriest critter on God's green earth. A cow's nothing but a lot of trouble tied up in a leather bag. A horse ain't much better.[166]

· · ·

YOU GO YOUR WAY, I'LL GO MINE
How to Say Goodbye

Our trails fork here.[24]

· · ·

Don't let yer rails get rusty![35]

· · ·

Well, so long, Moses. And I hope you get out of the wilderness![63]

· · ·

Adiós, compañero.[118]

· · ·

Don't be a fool just because I was. Shove off![133]

· · ·

If this be forever, baby, then forever fare-the-well.[137]

. . .

Woman: Maybe I'll never see you again.

Col. Davy Crockett (John Wayne): If that's what's written, that's what's written. When it's time, it's time. Talkin' only makes it harder. . . .[143]

. . .

Well, ma'am, this is where our trails part.[172]

. . .

HOME
How to Snuggle In

Michaeleen: Aw, that's nothin' but a wee humble cottage. . . .

Sean Thornton (John Wayne): That little place across the brook. That *humble cottage*. Who owns it now?

Michaeleen: The widow Tillane. Not that she lives there.

Thornton: Think she'd sell it?

Michaeleen: I doubt it.

Thornton: Don't bet on it. Because I'm buying it!

Michaeleen: Now why would ya . . . why would a Yankee from Pittsburgh want to buy it?

Thornton: I'll tell ya why, Michaeleen Og Flynn. Young, small Michael Flynn, who used to wipe my runny nose when I was a kid. Because I'm Sean Thornton, and I was born in that little cottage over there. And I've come home, and home I'm gonna stay. Now does that answer your questions once and for all, you nosy little man?!

Michaeleen: Seaneen Thornton! And look at ya now! Saints preserve us! What do they feed you Irishmen there in Pittsburgh?

Thornton: Steel, Michael Og! Steel in pig-iron furnaces so hot a man forgets his fear of hell.[126]

. . .

Paul Regret: How're we gonna eat?

Capt. Jake Cutter (John Wayne): Ya ever been out in the fresh air? Side o' bacon, beans, coffeepot, and a fryin' pan. All the comforts of home.[145]

. . .

I guess I'll have to be a good host in my own home.[151]

. . .

THE WORKING LIFE
How to Handle a Job

Boss: You are fired!
Biff Smith (John Wayne): All right, boss. But I think you're lacking in imagination.[76]

. . .

(*In joyful disbelief*)
A hundred dollars a week?! You mean . . . a *week*?[78]

. . .

You see, I was born here and lived here all my life. And I like it. New York, well, it's too big. Too many people. Besides, I'd feel kinda foolish going all the way down there just to play hockey. Seems like a man oughta have a regular job. I wanna build something and see it grow. I'll show you what I mean. In here's my chicken house. I've got ten of the finest chickens in this country. Prizewinners. And I'm gonna watch 'em grow into the biggest flock in Maine. Take a look![78]

. . .

Fine. But after this, before you call me off a job, be sure you want me, 'cause I'm particular about how I waste my time.[103]

. . .

Anything that ties ya down is no good—like a steady job.[105]

. . .

Can't be fired; ain't been hired.[106]

. . .

Lady, I'd rather walk for somebody else than work for you.[108]

. . .

G. W. McLintock (John Wayne): I been punched many a time in my life, but never for hiring anybody.

Devlin Warren: Aw, I don't know what to say. I never begged before. It turned my stomach! I suppose I should've been grateful you gave me the job.

McLintock: Gave?! Boy, you got it all wrong. I don't give jobs; I hire men.

Drago (*to Warren*): You intend to give this man a full day's work, don't you, boy?

Warren: You mean, you're still hiring me, Mr. McLintock? Well, yes, sir! I mean, I'll certainly deliver a full day's work.

McLintock: For that, I'll pay you a fair day's wage. You won't *give* me anything and I won't *give* you anything. We both hold up our heads.[151]

. . .

Everybody works for somebody. Me, I work for everybody in these United States that steps into a butcher shop for a T-bone steak.[151]

. . .

I met him down near the border. Said he wanted me to work with him on a job. Range war. But he said it'd be easy. All we had to worry about was a drunken sheriff. You sure you don't want some coffee?[158]

. . .

(*When your employees come in late*)
Well, I want each one of you fellas to buy yourself a dollar Ingersoll watch. Ya can't break 'em with a hammer and won't lose more'n a minute a month.[166]

. . .

Cheer up! All we can lose is our jobs.[171]

· · ·

I am retired, relieved, and rejoiced![172]

· · ·

CRIME, COURTS, AND CORRUPTION
How to Find Justice—or Make Your Own

Ruth Cameron: They say you're going to hunt down Flack and Lopez.

Breck Coleman (John Wayne): That's what I aim to do.

Cameron: But you can't do this awful thing—take two lives.

Coleman: Frontier justice.[24]

· · ·

Pa Bascom: What did they do, Coleman?

Breck Coleman (John Wayne): Killed my best friend. I been on their trail ever since.

Bascom: That's a serious charge. If you're sure, we'll call a settlers' meeting in the morning to try 'em.

Coleman: You can call a settlers' meeting to bury 'em!

Bascom: What do you mean?

Coleman: I kill my own rats.[24]

· · ·

(*On intimidation by a rich man*)
Sounds like a polite form of cattle rustlin' to me.[71]

· · ·

Stony Brooke (John Wayne): Just a minute! What kind of a farce do you call this?

Mayor Gil Byron: Don't you approve of the way we conduct court?

Brooke: This isn't a court; it's a three-ring circus.

Judge Henry J. Hixon: Careful, young man. . . .

Brooke: Of what? You're sworn to uphold the laws of this

territory, and what do you do? (*Nods toward the mayor*)
Jump like a rabbit every time *he* cracks a whip.

Judge Hixon: One more word from you and I'll fine you for
contempt of this court!

Brooke: Words fail to express my contempt for this court.[83]

• • •

You turn me over to that sheriff, I'm a dead Comanche,
probably shot in the back trying to "escape." But if I resist
arrest . . . Well, there's my horse. I've got an even chance.
What would you do in my place?[83]

• • •

I'm dumb enough to think that smart marshals do their
shootin' first and their talkin' afterward. Folks, this country has more laws than there are ways to skin a skunk. Why,
back East they tell me there's even a law against spittin'!
But remember this: Before ya can try 'em for anything, you
gotta catch 'em. I can catch 'em![91]

• • •

Man gets shot that's got a gun, there's room for reasonable
doubt. Man gets shot that hasn't got a gun, what would *you*
call it?[141]

• • •

Cold-blooded murder. But I can live with it.[146]

• • •

Judge Parker . . . Old carpetbagger. But he knows his rats!
We had a good court going around here till them pettifog-
ging lawyers moved in![161]

• • •

Mattie Ross: I want Tom Chaney to hang for killing my
father. It's little to me how many dogs and senators he
killed in Texas.

Rooster Cogburn (John Wayne): You can tell him to his face,
you can spit in his eye, you can make him eat sand out of

the road, you can shoot him in the foot and I'll hold him for you—but first we gotta catch him.[161]

. . .

Mattie Ross: Never did get you for stealing that money?

Rooster Cogburn (John Wayne): Why, I didn't consider it stealin'!

Mattie: It didn't belong to you.

Cogburn: I needed a road stake. It was like that little high-interest bank in New Mexico. Needed a road stake, and there it was! I never robbed no citizen, taken a man's watch!

Mattie: It's all stealing.

Cogburn: That's the position them New Mexicans took! I had to flee for my life.[161]

. . .

(LaBoeuf walks up to Captain Boots Finch and Rooster Cogburn)

Capt. Boots Finch: So this is the man shot Ned Pepper's horse from under him.

Rooster Cogburn (John Wayne): Yeah! This is the famous horse killer from El Paso. He believes in puttin' everybody afoot. Says there'll be less mischief that way.

LaBoeuf: Fewer horses, fewer horse thieves.[161]

. . .

Lon McQ (John Wayne): Peters is a hood and everybody knew it!

Capt. Edward Kosterman: Yeah, and you weren't satisfied with throwing him up on the roof! You had to go up there and throw him back down! Six months in the hospital! Four lawyers screaming about his civil rights!

McQ: Well, it kept him off the street, didn't it?[170]

. . .

There ain't no justice in the West no more. Men with sand in their craws bein' pushed aside by duded-up Yankee lawyers who won spellin' bees back home.[172]

. . .

Eula Goodnight: You're too late.

Rooster Cogburn (John Wayne): Too late to stop 'em, but not too late to hang 'em.[172]

. . .

Judge: Rooster, any deputy who shoots and kills sixty-four suspects in eight years is breaking the law, not aiding and abetting it.

Rooster Cogburn (John Wayne): Now, let's get this straight, Judge. Only sixty of 'em died. None was shot but in the line of duty or in defense of my person or fleein' justice![172]

. . .

FILTHY LUCRE
Knowing the Value of Things, If Not the Price

Horseflesh comes kinda high out here.[58]

. . .

The day has passed when a guy can go out and make a fortune. A little fellow hasn't a chance.[76]

. . .

Ya know, I'm gonna like this dashing-tycoon business.[106]

. . .

(*Steve Williams [John Wayne] rejects an offer to return to college-football coaching*)

Oh, it's a fine game, football. Noble game. Originated in England in 1823 by an enterprising young man named William Webb Ellis—who studied for the ministry, by the way. Found his team behind in a soccer game. So he picked up the ball and ran through the amazed opponents for a thoroughly illegal touchdown. And that's how football was born—illegitimately. So it moved to America, where someone took advantage of a loophole in the rules and invented a formation called the Flying Wedge. So many young men were maimed and killed by this clever maneuver that President Roosevelt—Theodore Roosevelt—had to call the colleges together and ask 'em to make the game less brutal. He was, of course, defeated in the next election. In spite of this setback, football became an industry. The price of a good running back often surpassed the salary of a professor. And once some righteous committee unearthed this well-known fact, it was always the coach that took it on the chin. I just got tired of pickin' myself up.[128]

. . .

Well, as I understand it, a tycoon is a man who has far-flung financial operations. Now, during football season, I get out a little card, which gives my estimate of the numerical worth of the various college teams. If your estimate is better than mine, I pay as high as five to one. During baseball season, I do the same thing. Of course, I've given up basketball in order to maintain the high ethical standard of my firm. But you can still get action on prizefighting, hockey, and the eight ball in the side pocket. I'm a tycoon.[128]

. . .

No, I'm selling horses for thirty-five dollars in preference to twenty-five.[162]

. . .

A fool comes to town with a fistful of gold dust, and every jackass from fifty miles around lights out after him.[166]

. . .

Mob money—squeezed outta hookers and skimmed off of casinos.[171]

Judge: People with money to invest go where they're pro-
tected by the law, not shot by it.

Rooster Cogburn (John Wayne): Is that the kind of law my
deputy got yesterday?! I was proud to tell his wife I shot
his killers![172]

WHO ARE YOU?
How to Describe Yourself

Well, there's not much to tell. I'm just a cowboy, drifting
from place to place.[65]

My friends just call me Ringo. Nickname I had as a kid.
Right name's Henry.[85]

They call me Duke Fergus. Montana. And if you're ever
travelin' through and want to paddle your feet in fresh water,
look me up.[109]

Flaxen Tarry: Come on, King.

Duke Fergus (John Wayne): The name's Duke, lady.

Tarry: You've been promoted![109]

We're pals. You wouldn't expect a pal to call me mister,
would ya?[114]

Fellas my age generally call me G.W., or McLintock. Youngsters call me *Mister* McLintock.[151]

John Fain: Who are you?

Jacob McCandles (John Wayne): Jacob McCandles.

Fain: I thought you was dead.

McCandles: Not hardly.[165]

. . .

GRUB
How to Eat

Waiter: What's your pleasure?

Lynn Hollister (John Wayne): Throwing eggs in an electric fan, but that's out of season, so just give me a cup of coffee.[95]

. . .

(*On lamb chops*)
I don't like 'em. I like steak![105]

. . .

Funny thing about pancakes: I lose my appetite for 'em after the first coupla dozen.[114]

. . .

I could eat a yearling steer—if I could catch one.[114]

. . .

Rooster Cogburn (John Wayne): Gimme your cup.

Mattie Ross: I don't drink coffee, thank you.

Cogburn: Well, now, what *do* you drink?

Mattie: I'm partial to cold buttermilk.

Cogburn: Well, we ain't got none of that. We ain't got no lemonade, neither![161]

. . .

DUH!
How to Make Sense of the Senseless

They forgot this is the only car in the valley. I just followed the tracks.[62]

. . .

Hey, Lullaby, wake up! It's time to go to sleep![82]

. . .

I don't see how even a clumsy galoot could shoot himself in his own right hand.[101]

. . .

Michele de la Becque: Were you shot down?

Pat Talbot (John Wayne): My plane was. I couldn't figure a way to stay up without it, so I came down too.[104]

. . .

Lawyer Goudy: I believe you testified that you backed away from old man Wharton.

Rooster Cogburn (John Wayne): Yes, sir.

Goudy: Which direction were you going?

Cogburn: Backward! I always go backward when I'm backin' away.[161]

. . .

GOD, RELIGION, AND SPIRITUALITY
How to Handle the Holy

Quirt Evans (John Wayne) (*pointing at a wall plaque*): That on the wall. "Each human being has an integrity that can be hurt only by the act of that same human being and not by the act of another human being." Is that Quaker stuff?

Penelope Worth: Mm-hmm.

Evans: You mean nobody can hurt you but yourself?

Worth: That's a Friend's belief.

Evans: Well, supposin' someone whacks you over the head with a branding iron? Won't that hurt?

Worth: Physically, of course. But in reality it would injure only the person doing the act or force of violence. Only the doer can be hurt by a mean or evil act.

Evans: Are there very many of you Quakers?

Worth: Very few.

Evans: I sort of figured that.[114]

. . .

I didn't think religious people were so sudden and direct.[114]

• • •

Penelope Worth: Quirt, please stay away from Laredo Stevens.

Quirt Evans (John Wayne): He owes me money. And don't worry; I might come out on top.

Worth: That'd be even worse.

Evans: Worse! Then it'd be worse if *he* goes down than if *I* go down?

Worth: Of course. Don't you *see* that?

Evans: Oh, I know, I'd be a guy with a marred soul.

Worth: Don't make it sound so crude, Quirt. You see why: I couldn't love you.

Evans: All right, I won't look up Laredo. It's better this way. Every time he opens a door, every time he hears foot-steps comin' around a corner, Laredo'll start sweatin', thinkin' it's me. His food won't sit well the rest of his life.

(*Penelope stares bemusedly at Quirt, unsure whether he's serious*)

Evans: Well, all right. . . . But if I'm gonna be holy, I gotta get some fun out of it![114]

• • •

Thank you, God Almighty.[129]

• • •

I've seen these do-gooders before. Mostly doing good for themselves. Believing in God is different than drooling over rubies and emeralds.[138]

• • •

Sometimes I wonder which side God's on.[148]

• • •

God willin' and the river don't rise.[159]

• • •

James Pepper: You know, there's an old saying, Miss Sally. There's no law west of Dodge, and no God west of the Pecos. Right, Mr. Chisum?

John Simpson Chisum (John Wayne): Wrong, Mr. Pepper.
'Cause no matter where people go, sooner or later there's
the law. And sooner or later they find that God's already
been there.[163]

. . .

YOU TALK TOO MUCH
How to Get Someone to Shut Their Trap

Ah, save yer breath.[38]

. . .

Shut up and get busy.[63]

. . .

If you're trying to alibi the way you've been living, we'll run
outta gas.[102]

. . .

You're building me up for something, Skinny. Let's have
it![110]

. . .

Are ya ever gonna run down and let me talk?[114]

. . .

Soldier: I'm sorry, sir. . . .
Capt. Nathan Brittles (John Wayne): Oh, shut up![120]

. . .

Man: Are you telling me I can't talk?
Sgt. John Stryker (John Wayne): I'm telling you when ya
can't talk to *me*![122]

. . .

Ya know something, Joe? I got a bad ear. I can't hear a
thing yer sayin'.[130]

. . .

I'd be obliged if you'd come to the point, ma'am.[135]

. . .

Watch out, Pat, you'll blow up and bust![141]

. . .

Now *I'm* runnin' outta breath. You talk if you want to.[141]

• • •

Forget it. He's just spittin' out words to see where they splatter.[145]

• • •

You're whistling in the wind, Katie.[151]

• • •

Let's get to the rat killin'.[151]

• • •

You're going a little fast for me. You mind trottin' through that again?[162]

• • •

(*Cord McNally knocks out a bad guy to rescue his friend Shasta*)

Shasta: Well, you certainly took long enough! I was running out of things to say!

Cord McNally (John Wayne): That, I can't believe![164]

• • •

You're short on ears and long on mouth![165]

• • •

Big mouth don't make a big man.[166]

• • •

You have said enough, Judge. None of it to my credit or my likin'.[172]

• • •

Mr. Dobkins, you're goin' the long way around the barn.[173]

• • •

Marshal: To put it in a nutshell, you've plumb wore us out.

J. B. Books (John Wayne): Put it in a nutshell?! You couldn't put it in a barrel without a bottom! You're the longest-winded bastard I ever listened to.[173]

• • •

I'VE GOT A BAD FEELING ABOUT THIS
How to Deal with a Deteriorating Situation

Breck Coleman (John Wayne): Say, Zeke, who was that he-grizzly that just went by?

Zeke: Why, that's Red Flack. He's bullwhackin' for Wellmore. He's gonna whack Wellmore's train clear through to Oregon.

Windy Bill: You reckon you'll ever find out who downed old Ben?

Coleman (*looking in Flack's direction*): It's just possible that a certain low-down coyote left his sign there.[24]

* * *

Things are too peaceful.[38]

* * *

You know, we oughta give up this racket, though. Gonna lead us both to a rope necktie one of these days.[51]

* * *

(*Dare Rudd and Dink Hooley are thrown out of the casino*)

Dare Rudd (John Wayne): I guess that'll teach that fella not to pull any aces out of his sleeve.

Dink Hooley: Aw, why don't you quit playin' cards? You always lose your shirt or get one torn off your back.

Rudd: I whipped him, didn't I?

Hooley: Hah! That's what *you* think! It's a good thing I stepped in when I did or you might've got yourself a black eye.

Rudd: Yeah? I'm beginning to think Wyoming isn't such a friendly place.[80]

* * *

I'm a tough bird. An awful tough old bird. But I ain't goin' back in there![118]

* * *

(Captain Nathan Brittles and his cavalry patrol, en route to Sudrow's Wells, observe an entire Arapaho village on the move)

Capt. Nathan Brittles (John Wayne): I don't like it, Mr. Cohill. I don't like it at all.

Lt. Cohill: Arapaho, sir?

Brittles: We're turning east, gentlemen. Give 'em a wide berth. Approach Sudrow's Wells from Twin Forks.

Cohill: But we'll lose a half a day that way, sir!

Lt. Pennell: The ladies may miss the stage, sir.

Brittles: Would you rather have 'em miss their scalps, sir?[120]

. . .

Lady, we gotta get outta here![121]

. . .

There's a boy up on that hill didn't listen to me. He's dead![129]

. . .

I told you twice not to. But you do what you wanna do.[130]

. . .

Rev. Clayton: Ethan, I gotta ask you and Martin to take a ride with me down to the state capital.

Ethan Edwards (John Wayne): Is this an invite to a necktie party, Reverend?[135]

. . .

Holy mother of the pyramids![138]

. . .

Talking about whose ox gets gored, figure this: Fella gets in the habit o' goring oxes, whets his appetite. He may come up north next and gore yours. Men, we're in a little fix, sorta.[143]

. . .

(Taw Jackson is shaving, in his long johns, while wearing a holster and sidearm as Lomax enters)

Lomax: Do you always wear a gun over your underwear?

Taw Jackson (John Wayne): Just lately.[157]

. . .

(*Taw Jackson and Levi have successfully bargained with Chief Wild Horse in his encampment*)

Levi (*interpreting*): It is done. And he wants me to stay for dinner! But you're not welcome. Having a white man in his camp offends him.

Taw Jackson (John Wayne) (*angrily*): Well, you can tell him . . .

Levi: What?

Jackson (*looking at the armed Indians backing the chief*): Nothing.[157]

• • •

That shivaree you put on in there interrupted my supper and wore out our welcome. Now we'll have to find someplace else to eat.[158]

• • •

Cole Thornton (John Wayne): J.P., why don't you settle down?

Sheriff J. P. Harrah: I just can't help it, Cole. I've got the shakes so bad I . . .

Thornton: You've had 'em before.

Harrah: Yeah, but not with a hole in my leg, and a bunch of unfriendly people hanging around outside just waiting for somebody to pop through that . . .

Thornton: What do you wanna do?! Quit?[158]

• • •

(*Colonel John Henry Thomas and Colonel James Langdon ride out to parley with the villainous leader of a bandit army*)

Col. John Henry Thomas: Is the flap on your holster snapped or unsnapped, my Confederate friend?

Col. James Langdon: Snapped, my Yankee friend.

Thomas: Then I guess I'm his pigeon.[162]

• • •

Jacob McCandles (John Wayne): What do you do when cockroaches get in the woodwork, Michael?

James McCandles (*jumping in*): Smoke 'em out?

Jacob McCandles: That's right.

Michael McCandles: Why not wait until they make a move?

Jacob McCandles: Because waiting is good for them and bad for us. You get impatient, nervy, careless, and maybe dead. I've seen it.[165]

. . .

It may mean nuthin', but I'm gonna take a pass at our back-track.[168]

. . .

Come a-runnin'![168]

. . .

I got a hunch we're just a little way from a lot of trouble.[172]

. . .

UNCLASSIFIABLE
Short on Context, Long on Attitude

Hope I ain't crowdin' you folks none.[85]

. . .

I figure if you pen up a wolf long enough he's bound to howl.[95]

. . .

Cherry Malotte: Oh, how does Mr. Glennister look when he's acting brilliant?

Roy Glennister (John Wayne): Little bubbles come out of my mouth and I smoke.[100]

. . .

Hold the team, Smoky![106]

. . .

I'm still kicking, Mr. President![106]

. . .

(*On why he's so quiet*)
Maybe because my granny always says the second fiddler's got to wait his turn before he can sing out good and loud.[106]

. . .

Well, on second thought, I don't guess you make the rules. Keep talking, sailor.[107]

. . .

It's no skin off your moccasins if you let a little water over that ditch.[114]

. . .

Well, he can keep squattin' on his hunkers from now till Christmas, 'cause we ain't gonna *be* there.[118]

. . .

Chawin' tobacco's a bad habit. Been known to turn a man's stomach.[120]

. . .

You can bust your tuchus with ideas like that.[129]

. . .

I'm a jet man, not a gigolo![137]

. . .

(*Time to party*)
It means out of these deerskins and into our foofaraw![143]

. . .

(*When your dance partner falls down*)
Sorry, sir. She sorta came loose.[143]

. . .

Michelle Bonet: You're fooling me. . . .
Sam McCord (John Wayne): I was never more serious in my
    life.[144]

. . .

I better get steamed, cleaned, and shaved before I get on that boat.[144]

. . .

Looks like this little fracas is about over.[145]

. . .

Lem: Hey, Mr. Mac, what does "unprepossessing" mean?
G. W. McLintock (John Wayne): I was called that once, Lem.

Looked it up in the dictionary. It's best you don't know what it means.[151]

. . .

Now, Katherine, are you going to believe what you see, or what I tell you?[151]

. . .

Cole Thornton (John Wayne): Why do you wanna keep stickin' yer nose into this?

Mississippi: Maybe I could help. You saved my life two times.

Thornton: But I'm gonna be too busy to keep doing that![158]

. . .

Last time, you took the front door and I took the back. This time, we'll do 'er the other way around.[158]

. . .

(*Jacob McCandles sees a sheepherder about to be hanged by vigilantes and begins talking to himself*)

Jacob McCandles (John Wayne): No, sir. No, sir, I ain't. Haven't butted into anybody's business since I was eighteen years old, at which time it almost got me killed. Ain't gonna start that again.

(*His dog growls angrily in the direction of the vigilantes*)

McCandles: What's the matter? (*He looks toward the vigilantes, one of whom kicks a young boy*) Aw, what'd he have to go and do that for?[165]

. . .

As my Mexican friend said, To the pure life![173]

. . .

BONUS CHAPTER: DUKE ON TV

Speeches, Specials, and Celebrity Sit-Downs

John Wayne didn't appear on television very often. So when he did, it was a big deal. In his one-on-one interviews, he is charming, often self-deprecating, and surprisingly candid about his life and his movies. These interviews show the private, very human side of the mythic John Wayne persona. And you'll also find a couple of really fun quotes courtesy of British actor Michael Caine, admittedly secondhand but too good not to include here. Even though these quotes don't come from John Wayne's feature films, I felt certain the readers of this book would enjoy having them here— all sourced, so you can use them yourself with full confidence.

1970s PSA FOR THE AMERICAN CANCER SOCIETY

The American Cancer Society is asking you for help again. And pilgrim, if you don't give it to 'em, I'm gonna kick you in the butt!

· · ·

"LUCY AND JOHN WAYNE," *THE LUCY SHOW* (1966)
Written by Bob O'Brien

(*On actors*)
You know what I think ages 'em? Staying up all night watching their old movies on television.

. . .

THE DEAN MARTIN SHOW (1967)
Head writer: Harry Crane

(*On his hopes for his baby daughter*)
I'd just like to stick around long enough to see she gets started right. I'd like her to know some of the values that we knew as kids—some of those values that too many people these days are thinking are old-fashioned. Most of all, I want her to be grateful as I am every day of my life to live in these United States. I know it may sound a little corny, but the first thing my daughter's learning from me is the Lord's Prayer and some of the Psalms. And I really don't care if she ever memorizes the Gettysburg Address, just so long as she understands it. And since little girls are seldom called upon to defend their country, she may never have to raise her hand for the oath, but I certainly want her to respect all those who do. I guess that's about what I want for my daughter, Dean.

. . .

SWING OUT, SWEET LAND (TV SPECIAL, 1970)
Written by Paul W. Keyes

Countries are like people. Some take themselves so seriously that you won't get a laugh out of 'em in a hundred years. And others are more apt than not to stick their tongue in their cheek and tell funny stories about themselves. And America, thank God, is one of those yarn-spinning places.

. . .

Seventeen seventy-five. With freedom in their hearts, powder in their muskets, and the British in their sights, the men who came here looking for liberty made a down payment on it.

. . .

The Old West, the Wild West, is long gone. But that doesn't matter.

. . .

By the time the century ended, we had close to seventy-six million between our oceans. The new nation had become the dream of people all over the world, and millions came in leaps and bounds with little more than the clothes on their backs and hope in their hearts. And all they asked was a chance to put their two hands to work in our free marketplace. Europe's poorest became America's middle class. Men willing to work found no limit on their ambitions. And so in our first two centuries in this God-given land, men with a dream had converted untold acres of forests and lakes and rivers and plains, mountains and valleys into a land of opportunity.

. . .

I'm a lucky fella, for many reasons. Lucky that I was brought up to believe in a lot of things I've found worthwhile. I believe in common decency, without which no society or goodwill can exist. I believe in my country, my family, my fellow man, and my God. I believe in straight talk and freedom—with an accent on the *free,* which is still the best four-letter word I know. I believe in giving a fella a second, even a third chance. But keep yer eye on him. I believe the moon's a nice place to visit, but I wouldn't wanna live there because this country, on this planet, is man's last chance to make a go of it for humanity. And I believe there's time in my life and yours to get this country in such shape that God'd be proud of it. I believe your kids and mine are just you 'n' me gettin' a second crack at the world. And our job is to see that they don't make all the mistakes we did, and don't invent too many of their own. I believe ninety-nine percent of 'em are a credit to their folks, a pride to their country, and deserve a pat on their backs from all of us for being what they are, and not waving a white flag at life. I believe in hope for people of all ages. That equal opportunity is based on equal obligation. And speaking of opportunity, American opportunity has no limits, has been known to knock more than once. How about you very young people who see a tough life ahead? Well, when Lee surrendered to Grant at Appomattox, Booker T. Washington was a nine-year-old slave. Yet by the time he was twenty-eight he became president of Tuskegee Institute. And at eight months, Neil Armstrong took his first small baby steps toward mankind and fell flat on his face. At six years old, Mickey Mantle was settling for a base on balls. At seven, Wilt Chamberlain nailed a practice hoop over his garage—without a ladder. And at eight, Charles Lindbergh was flying a kite, wondering how it'd feel to be up that high. At nine, Burt Bacharach was thinking the piano lessons would never end. How many of ya are pushin' fifty and complaining that the country is going to hell? Crispus Attucks was in his forties when he died on State Street in Boston, fighting for the freedom that we share. And John F. Kennedy was forty-four when he asked not what his country could do for him, but what he could do for his country. And how many of ya over sixty-five are just settling down to rest after a busy life? Well, a fella by the name of Eisenhower—who had already lived one lifetime, as a soldier—was reelected to the presidency when he was sixty-seven years young. Well, by now, I've made my point—or I never will. Oh, there's one other thing. Every man and woman or child I've ever known, met, seen, or heard of wants one thing more than anything else in the world. That one thing is *tomorrow*. Tomorrow. That's the only thing any of us have going for us. And I believe this: If tomorrow all of us, every single one of us, gets out of bed and says, *This is my country, and I'm gonna do good for it,* we'll make the greatest step forward since the Pilgrim's foot found Plymouth Rock. Tomorrow, remember: *This is my country and I'm gonna do good for it!* Just might work. We'll never know unless we give it a fair try. Oh yeah, and there's one other thing. I'll say it tomorrow because I say it every day of my life: God bless America.

. . .

ACADEMY AWARD ACCEPTANCE SPEECH (1971)

But tonight I don't feel very clever or very witty. I feel very grateful, very humble, and all thanks to many, many people.

. . .

JOHN WAYNE INTERVIEW WITH PHIL DONAHUE (1976)

(*Nodding toward the live audience*)
I'm not quite sure about anything—particularly in front of a bunch of women!

. . .

(*Asked if he fought much as a kid*)
My name was Marion Michael Morrison. Do *you* think I ever fought?

. . .

(*On Californians' mellowness*)
The only thing that's quick-tempered in this state is the weather.

. . .

I understood liberal as . . . Maybe I read the wrong dictionary. But I thought that a liberal was a man who would listen to everybody's point of view, and then make up his mind. I made up my mind pretty fast, but . . . but I don't know any of these so-called liberals that listen to anything but their own mouth.

• • •

Violence . . . that's not it at all. Naturally, since I've been in Westerns, which are our folklore, in which men were fighting against the elements, very few of them had any trouble where they had to go lie down on a couch! They were too busy staying alive. And naturally you'd get the impression of a quick, cold, violent reaction. But in my pictures, it's been more illusion than violence.

• • •

I was very lucky in my career. I had a lot of very stable people in the business who were friends of mine. And every time that I got out of line, John Ford or Howard Hawks or Henry Hathaway or Harry Carey would belt me over the head. So it took me a long time to find out that I was a star.

• • •

I had a dog, an Airedale dog, when I was a little kid. I had an Airedale dog called Duke. And he'd follow me to school and stop at the fire station. The firemen knew the dog's name, so they called him Big Duke and me Little Duke. That's true!

• • •

(*On sex*)
It's not a spectator sport.

• • •

(*On why he won't pose naked*)
Too many calluses.

• • •

My favorite book? It's got H-O-L-Y on it.

...

I guess the first time that I was really recognized in show business was, I was going to the University of Southern California, and we just started having good ball clubs. Or being recognized by the East, Middle West, and South. And so the Business became very interested. They got us jobs during the summer. And I went on John Ford's set. And they'd had a habit of, they'd say to ya, "Oh, you play football. Well, how do you get down?" So you'd get down. They'd push and pull you. And this got a little boring. So when they'd ask me, I'd just brace myself on all four limbs—which is *not* the way, position, to be in if you're in a football game. And Ford had played a little ball, so he said, "Just stop me." And he kicked my feet out from under me and my face went down in that so-called mud, which was made of plaster on this phony mountain in the set. And I said, "Well, let's do her again." And he started around me, and I whirled and kicked him, hit him right on the chest, and down he went. There was a dead silence. And he started to laugh. *There* was one time when I was purdy near *not* in the motion picture business!

...

(*On the fight scene in* The Quiet Man)
That was an easy fight.

...

(*On Hollywood gossip*)
It seems like everybody has two businesses: theirs and mine.

...

I like to see a good-lookin' woman!

...

(*On old age*)
I don't chase girls quite as fast. . . .

...

I have seven children that I am very proud of. Four of 'em already grown up. And I know a lot of it's luck. And I know also a lot of it's that they felt love and security at home. That's all I can tell ya.

. . .

(*On his fondness for Hispanic women*)
Well, it seems when I'm not working, when I'm on vacation, I've always headed south. So I've seen more of 'em, had more contact with 'em, than I've had in the north.

. . .

I will try and never fail the wonderful country that I live in. And I will continue to respect men who I think are doing a good job for our country.

. . .

(*Asked what was the most dangerous stunt he ever did*)
Talk back to Marlene Dietrich.

. . .

JOHN WAYNE'S FINAL INTERVIEW, WITH BARBARA WALTERS (JANUARY 1979)

I know I'm a good actor. I've been at it for fifty years. I should have learned something!

. . .

I like to drink. And I like women. And I've probably been a lot softer than I should be on occasion with 'em. And a lot tougher on some men—mainly myself.

. . .

The American people have taken you to their hearts and they expect a certain thing out of you. Don't disappoint them. And I think it was the best advice I was ever given in my life.

. . .

I am me. . . . I am *me*.

. . .

ACTOR MICHAEL CAINE ON MEETING JOHN WAYNE, *THE GRAHAM NORTON SHOW* (2018)

Michael Caine remembered John Wayne fondly, and eagerly shared these two quotes from a conversation he had with the Duke in the 1960s.

Talk low, talk slow, and don't say too much.

⋯

Never wear suede shoes. You'll be in the gents' toilet taking a pee, and the guy next door is taking a pee, and he's gonna recognize you. And he's gonna turn and say, "My god!" And he's gonna piss all over your suede shoes.

⋯

APPENDIX A

Production Notes, Capsule Reviews, and Every Movie in Alphabetical Order

*Worth watching
+Essential

Note: Featured actors are those players listed in a film's opening screen credits. Names of actors, writers, and directors are given as in the film credits (with more common spellings in parentheses), unless otherwise noted, as in cases of lost films.

ADVENTURE'S END
Featured actors: John Wayne, Diana Gibson, Montagu Love, Moroni Olsen, Paul White, Maurice Black, George Cleveland, P. J. Kelly, Cameron Hall, James T. Mack, Britt Wood, William Sundholm, Ben Carter, Wally Howe, Jimmie Lucas, and Glenn Strange
Screenplay by Ben Grauman Kohn, Scott Darling, and Sidney Sutherland
Story by Ben Ames Williams
Directed by Arthur Lubin
Produced and distributed by Universal Pictures
Release date: December 5, 1937

This is a so-called lost or missing film in the John Wayne catalogue. See also *The Oregon Trail* (1936). Several films from the late 1920s are also lost, but Wayne didn't have a lead role in them as he did in this one. In the story, Duke Slade (John Wayne) leaves his New England home to become a pearl hunter in the South Seas. After violating a local taboo, Duke and his native buddy Kalo escape on a whaler bound for Massachusetts. Once at sea, Duke must face a hostile crew and a forced marriage to the captain's daughter. Sharks, mutineers, rambunctious whales, and fistfights follow—leaving John Wayne fans to lament that this is one of the few Duke films they can't see.

THE ALAMO+

Featured actors: John Wayne, Richard Widmark, Laurence Harvey, Frankie Avalon, Patrick Wayne, Linda Cristal, Joan O'Brien, Chill Wills, Joseph Calleia, Ken Curtis, Carlos Arruza, Jester Hairston, Veda Ann Borg, John Dierkes, Denver Pyle, Aissa Wayne, Hank Worden, Bill Henry (William Henry), Bill Daniel, Wesley Lau, Chuck Roberson, Guinn Williams (Guinn "Big Boy" Williams), Olive Carey, Ruben Padilla, and Richard Boone
Screenplay by James Edward Grant
Directed by John Wayne
Produced by Batjac Productions/The Alamo Company
Distributed by United Artists
Release date: October 24, 1960

The Alamo is possibly the quintessential account of that famous 1836 battle, if not in terms of historical accuracy, at least in the excitement and the personalities (Jim Bowie, Will Travis, Sam Houston, and Davy Crockett, the last portrayed by John Wayne). While all the stars (including Richard Widmark, Richard Boone, and Laurence Harvey) get their fair share of screen time, this is a John Wayne movie, make no mistake. And Duke is at the height of his powers as an actor and a screen presence. The fine quality of the production, dialogue, and acting makes you wonder why Wayne didn't direct his films more often. Some viewers might complain that at nearly three hours, the film seems bloated, but if so, put your viewing speed at 1.25 for the first half, then settle in at normal speed for the magnificent second half, with its glorious speeches, dramatic anticipation, and explosive battle scenes. Besides the big-name stars, the movie has outstanding secondary support from the likes of Chill Wills, Ken Curtis, Denver Pyle, and (uncredited) Joe and Tap Canutt, sons of Wayne's early-day costar and stuntman par excellence Yakima Canutt.

ALLEGHENY UPRISING

Featured actors: Claire Trevor, John Wayne, George Sanders, Brian Donlevy, Wilfrid Lawson, Robert Barrat, John F. Hamilton, Moroni Olsen, and Eddie Quillan
Screenplay by P. J. Wolfson
Based on a story by Neil H. Swanson
Directed by William A. Seiter
Produced and distributed by RKO Radio Pictures
Release date: October 24, 1939

Pennsylvania pioneers fight off Native Americans around the time of the French and Indian War while contending with smugglers and a corrupt British military. John Wayne as colonist Jim Smith organizes a militia to search out the Indians who massacred some of the region's settlers. The leader of the illegal traders who armed the Indians sets up Smith to take the fall for a murder. The drama hinges on whether

Smith's friends can collect the evidence needed to set him free. George Sanders as a stern but clueless British officer, Claire Trevor as John Wayne's love interest, and Brian Donlevy as the heavy add class to the proceedings, but even they can't overcome a lackluster script or Wayne's inhibited acting.

ANGEL AND THE BADMAN+

Featured actors: John Wayne, Gail Russell, Harry Carey, Bruce Cabot, Irene Rich, Lee Dixon, Stephen Grant, Tom Powers, Paul Hurst, Olin Howlin (Olin Howland), John Halloran, Joan Barton, Craig Woods, and Marshall Reed
Screenplay by James Edward Grant
Directed by James Edward Grant
Produced by John Wayne Productions/Patnel Productions
Distributed by Republic Pictures
Release date: February 15, 1947

In the West of yore, a wounded and nearly delirious gunslinger, Quirt Evans (John Wayne), seeks help from a Quaker rancher and his beautiful daughter (Gail Russell) to get him to the nearest telegraph office to file a mining claim. Nursed back to health by the generous Quakers, Evans must confront a team of baddies (led by Bruce Cabot) who want to jump his claim. At the same time, Evans must decide whether he can abandon his violent life in favor of the peace-loving woman who desires him. An excellent script and fine acting all around (with stellar support from Harry Carey, who has a small but pivotal role) earn this a star. It may also be the first film in which Wayne uses his iconic I've-had-enough-of-this, half-smoked-cigarette toss.

ANNIE LAURIE

Featured actors: Lillian Gish, Norman Kerry, Creighton Hale, and Joseph Striker
Screenplay and story by Josephine Lovett
Titles by Marian Ainslee and Ruth Cummings
Directed by John S. Robertson
Produced and distributed by Metro-Goldwyn-Mayer (MGM)
Release date: May 11, 1927

The MacDonalds and the Campbells duke it out in auld Scotland. When the body of a MacDonald is carried into the family castle, the head of the clan vows that a Campbell shall pay the price. The bad blood between them only grows more bitter when the MacDonalds exact their revenge and kidnap Enid, a Campbell daughter. If you think this sounds like a Scottish Highlands version of the Hatfields and the McCoys, you wouldn't be far off. A kilt-wearing John Wayne is supposedly in there, somewhere, as an extra, along with a few of his USC football buddies.

ARIZONA

Also titled MEN ARE LIKE THAT

Featured actors: Laura La Plante, John Wayne, June Clyde, Forrest
Stanley, and Nena Quartaro (Nina Quartero)
Dialogue and adaptation by Robert Riskin
Based on a play by Augustus Thomas
Directed by George B. Seitz
Produced and distributed by Columbia Pictures
Release date: August 16, 1931

John Wayne's first movie for Columbia is a meaningless piece of fluff that doesn't even have the benefit of being truly awful, just merely boring. Here he plays former football hero Bob Denton, a newly graduated West Pointer assigned to the Arizona army post presided over by the guardian who raised him—and who has just married the girl Wayne dumped on graduation. Denton, after finding that his old girlfriend has married his guardian, secretly marries her sister, a plot twist that leads to his possibly losing his commission. Not drama and not comedy, this trifle quickly wears itself thin in a cinematic no-man's-land in which Wayne shows neither the promise nor the charm of his leading-man debut the previous year in *The Big Trail*.

BABY FACE

Featured actors: Barbara Stanwyck, George Brent, Donald Cook,
Alphonse Ethier, Henry Kolker, Margaret Lindsay, Arthur Hohl, John
Wayne, Robert Barrat, Douglas Dumbrille (Douglass Dumbrille), and
Theresa Harris
Screenplay by Gene Markey and Kathryn Scola
Story by Mark Canfield (Darryl F. Zanuck)
Directed by Alfred E. Green
Produced and distributed by Warner Bros.
Release date: June 23, 1933

Barbara Stanwyck is smooth, sexy, and in charge in this pre-code drama about a woman working her way through the glass ceiling. Lily Powers (Stanwyck) is a tavern-keeper's daughter with no future among the steel mills of Erie, Pennsylvania. When her wicked father dies in an explosion, she makes her way to New York City, determined to get ahead—even if she has to use her physical charms to get there. Wayne is a sad-sack wannabe lover who gets tossed aside in favor of his boss. You'd be advised to toss aside this movie—except for Stanwyck's impeccable performance. Billed eighth in this soapy thriller, John Wayne enters the film at twenty-one minutes from the start and is completely overwhelmed by Stanwyck.

BACK TO BATAAN

Featured actors: John Wayne, Anthony Quinn, Beulah Bondi, Fely
Franquelli, Richard Loo, Philip Ahn, J. Alex Havier (Alex Havier),

"Ducky" Louie, Lawrence Tierney, Leonard Strong, Paul Fix, Abner
Biberman, and Vladimir Sokoloff
Screenplay by Ben Barzman and Richard H. Landau
Original story by Aeneas MacKenzie and William Gordon
Directed by Edward Dmytryk
Produced and distributed by RKO Radio Pictures
Release date: June 25, 1945

Coming at the tail end of World War II, *Back to Bataan* is a thriller de-
signed to raise the patriotic spirits of its American audience. Via flash-
backs, we learn that Colonel Joe Madden (John Wayne) has organized a
group of Filipino scouts on Corregidor to defend against the Japanese in-
vaders of the Philippines. Accidentally discovering a POW camp holding
Americans and Filipino patriots, Madden leads his ragtag troops to the
rescue against impossible odds. A young Anthony Quinn, as the son of a
fabled Filipino hero, adds some fun to the proceedings. Long on action,
short on witty dialogue, the film is an enjoyable bit of low-key American
war propaganda.

THE BARBARIAN AND THE GEISHA
Featured actors: John Wayne, Eiko Ando, Sam Jaffe, and So
Yamamura (Sō Yamamura)
Screenplay by Charles Grayson
Story by Ellis St. Joseph
Directed by John Huston
Produced and distributed by Twentieth Century–Fox
Release date: September 30, 1958

In 1856, at a time when Japan has closed its doors to foreigners, diplo-
mat Townsend Harris (John Wayne) is sent to serve as America's con-
sul general and help open trade with the West. Arriving in the port city
of Shimoda, Harris and his interpreter (Sam Jaffe) are shunned by the
populace and the local leaders. Soon Harris begins to make some small
progress. But when passing American sailors jump off a cholera ship and
bring devastation to Shimoda, Harris's task begins to look hopeless. The
slow pace of the film is unexpected from someone like director John Huston (who later disavowed the final cut). And Wayne seems uncomfortable
with the forced nature of the script's formal nineteenth-century manner
of speech. The filmed-in-Japan locations make this watchable.

BARDELYS THE MAGNIFICENT
Featured actors: John Gilbert, Eleanor Boardman, Roy D'Arcy, Lionel
Belmore, Emily Fitzroy, George K. Arthur, Arthur Lubin, Theodor von
Eltz (Theodore von Eltz), Karl Dane, Fred Malatesta, and
John T. Murray
Titles by Marian Ainslee
Based on a novel by Rafael Sabatini

Adaptation by Dorothy Farnum
Directed by King Vidor
Produced and distributed by Metro-Goldwyn-Mayer (MGM)
Release date: September 30, 1926

In the John Wayne canon, *Bardelys the Magnificent* is notable strictly for being the actor's second appearance on film. Marquis Christian de Bardelys (John Gilbert), a favorite of Louis XIII, attempts to woo the beautiful and wealthy Roxalanne at the king's behest to bring her family's fortune under the king's control. But dashing ladies' man Bardelys gets more than he bargained for when he is accused of treason by Roxalanne, who mistakenly thinks Bardelys has wronged her. John Wayne has a fleeting moment in the film as a guard. Other uncredited bit players include Joan Crawford and Lou Costello, so Wayne is in good company among the extras.

BIG JAKE+
Featured actors: John Wayne, Richard Boone, Patrick Wayne, Christopher Mitchum, Bruce Cabot, Bobby Vinton, Glenn Corbett, John Doucette, Jim Davis, John Agar, Harry Carey, Jr., Gregg Palmer, Roy Jenson, Virginia Capers, William Walker (Bill Walker), John McLiam, Bernard Fox, Don Epperson, Jim Burk, Dean Smith, Ethan Wayne, Hank Worden, Tom Hennesy, Chuck Roberson, Robert Warner, Jeff Wingfield, Jerry Gatlin, Everett Creach, and Maureen O'Hara
Screenplay by Harry Julian Fink and R. M. Fink
Directed by George Sherman and John Wayne (uncredited)
Produced by Batjac Productions
Distributed by National General Pictures
Release date: May 26, 1971

There are only a handful of tough hombres who can stand up to John Wayne, face-to-face, on the big screen. Victor McLaglen is one, for sure. Lee Marvin is another. That's about it . . . until you get to Richard Boone. And make no mistake: Boone is big and bad and menacing in *Big Jake*. But John Wayne, despite nearing the end of his career, is up to the task. The year is 1909, and Wayne plays rancher Jacob "Big Jake" McCandles, whose grandson has been kidnapped by a fearsome gang of desperadoes. The kidnapping element recalls *The Searchers*, and this film is as violent (especially the first scene—whoa!) and in-your-face as that classic. Wayne was so concerned about *Big Jake*'s violence that he inserted several comical scenes to counterbalance the harsher ones. The comedy, though, just gets in the way of what is a damn good actioner, with Wayne in top form. Assisting Duke in roles large and small are Maureen O'Hara, Patrick Wayne, Bruce Cabot, Hank Worden, gravelly-voiced Jim Davis, Harry Carey, Jr., Chris "Robert's son" Mitchum, John Doucette, pop singer Bobby Vinton, and John Agar.

BIG JIM McLAIN
Featured actors: John Wayne, Nancy Olson, James Arness, Alan Napier, Veda Ann Borg, Hans Conried, Hal Baylor, Gayne Whitman, Gordon Jones, Robert Keys, John Hubbard, Madame Soo Yong (Soo Yong), Honolulu Chief of Police Dan Liu, and Red McQueen (Vernon "Red" McQueen)
Screenplay by James Edward Grant, Richard English, and Eric Taylor
Directed by Edward Ludwig
Produced by Wayne-Fellows Productions
Distributed by Warner Bros.
Release date: August 30, 1952

John Wayne is a Commie hunter for the House Un-American Activities Committee during the Red Scare of the early 1950s. Plotted as a police procedural, the story line follows investigators Jim McLain (John Wayne) and Mal Baxter (James Arness) in Hawaii as they attempt to track down a Communist cell on Oahu. Pure propaganda, poorly acted, and a blot on Wayne's "mature" oeuvre. On the other hand, the film, a box-office success, is interesting for its peek into postwar Honolulu, replete with slack-key guitars, too-small Hawaiian shirts, ukuleles, hula girls, outrigger canoes, and other aspects of a lifestyle long since vanished. Hans Conried provides some comic relief, for what it's worth, and Veda Ann Borg, as Madge, the man-eating lush, is funny as hell. Side note: Shortly after filming *Big Jim McLain*, John Wayne supposedly declined the lead role in the planned TV series *Gunsmoke*, and instead recommended his acting pal James Arness to star. Wayne even introduced the first episode. *Gunsmoke* (1955–75) went on to become one of broadcasting's longest-running programs.

THE BIG STAMPEDE
Featured actors: John Wayne, Duke the Horse, Noah Beery, Paul Hurst, Mae Madison, Sherwood Bailey, Luis Alberni, and Berton Churchill
Screenplay and dialogue by Kurt Kempler
Story by Marion Jackson
Directed by Tenny Wright
Produced by Leon Schlesinger Studios/Warner Bros. (as A Four Star Western)
Distributed by Warner Bros. (as Vitagraph Pictures, Inc.)
Release date: October 8, 1932

John Wayne is Deputy Sheriff John Steele, sent by the governor to find out who's causing mischief among the cattle ranches on the New Mexico plains. Working undercover in the guise of a drunken layabout, Steele targets a group of high-profile ranchers who moonlight as rustlers, sowing fear among the pioneers and thus stunting the growth of New Mexico toward statehood. Wayne's horse, named Duke, hogs some of the limelight thanks to its almost human reactions to some of the goings-on. Not a bad oater, though Wayne has yet to find his comfort zone—especially when it comes to his (lack of) dialogue.

THE BIG TRAIL+

Featured actors: John Wayne, Marguerite Churchill, El Brendel, Tully Marshall, Tyrone Power (Tyrone Power, Sr.), David Rollins, Frederick Burton, Ian Keith, Charles Stevens, and Louise Carver
Story by Hal G. Evarts
Directed by Raoul Walsh
Produced and distributed by Fox Film Corporation
Release date: October 24, 1930

This picture makes clear why John Wayne became a movie star. In his first feature film as a principal actor, a handsome, young (twenty-three years old) Wayne plays Breck Coleman, a frontiersman who signs on to guide a wagon train. His real goal, though, is to find the killer of an old friend. *The Big Trail* is a Big Production, with hundreds of extras, thousands of horses and cattle, and sprawling Western countryside. The cinematography is stylish, visually delightful. So realistic are the action scenes, you well may wonder if this movie was the cause of the "No animals were harmed . . ." movement in later years. And you may well say to yourself, "This was made in 1930?! Incredible!" The movie is worth watching for those values alone, but even more so to see Duke's first important film role.

THE BLACK WATCH

Featured actors: Victor McLaglen, Myrna Loy, David Torrence, David Rollins, Cyril Chadwick, Lumsden Hare, Roy D'Arcy, David Percy, Mitchell Lewis, Claud King (Claude King), and Walter Long
Dialogue by James Kevin McGuinness
Scenario by John Stone
Story by Talbot Mundy
Directed by John Ford
Produced and distributed by Fox Film Corporation
Release date: May 8, 1929

Scotland's fearsome fighting unit, the Black Watch, is shipping out to France at the start of World War I, but Captain Donald King (Victor McLaglen) has inexplicably dropped off the roster. The men think it's a case of cowardice, but King has been assigned in confidence to travel to the Khyber Pass to prevent religious fanatics from wreaking havoc on British-controlled India. Lots of fun, and McLaglen is terrific as the unwilling secret agent. John Wayne has an inconsequential spot as a fellow soldier, but one can only wonder what it was like for McLaglen and Wayne to be on the same set under the same director, John Ford, who would put them together again, gloriously, some twenty-three years later in *The Quiet Man*, among other memorable films.

BLOOD ALLEY*
Featured actors: John Wayne, Lauren Bacall, Paul Fix, Joy Kim,
Berry Kroger (Berry Kroeger), Mike Mazurki, and Anita Ekberg
Screenplay by A. S. Fleischman
Based on a novel by A. S. Fleischman
Directed by William A. Wellman
Produced by Batjac Productions
Distributed by Warner Bros.
Release date: October 1, 1955

In postwar China, Wayne plays Tom Wilder, a second-rate freighter captain locked up in prison by the newly installed Red Chinese government. With some unexpected assistance (in the form of a Russian uniform and a loaded pistol smuggled into his cell), the nearly stir-crazy captain makes his escape. The trouble is, his help comes from the residents of a village who desperately want to escape the Red Chinese. In exchange for breaking him out of incarceration, they want Captain Wilder to lead them to freedom—to Hong Kong, by ship, at night, in the fog, without charts. *Blood Alley* is a rollicking adventure story, made even better by the able presence of Lauren Bacall.

BLUE STEEL
Featured actors: John Wayne, Eleanor Hunt, George Hayes (George
"Gabby" Hayes), Edward Peil (Edward Peil, Sr.), Yakima Canutt, Lafe
McKee, George Cleveland, and Earl Dwire
Screenplay and story by Robert Bradbury (Robert N. Bradbury)
Directed by Robert Bradbury (Robert N. Bradbury)
Produced and distributed by Monogram Pictures (as Lone Star
Productions)
Release date: May 10, 1934

The people of Yucca City don't know how good they have it, literally. Gold lies just below the muddy surface of the town, and the bad guys want to get their hands on it. All they have to do is drive the good citizens out so they can take over and collect the riches. John Wayne as tramp cowboy John Carruthers finds himself in the thick of things when the sheriff (George Hayes) catches him stealing from a local innkeeper. Supposedly. The bad guys, led by the Polka Dot Bandit (Yakima Canutt), keep the supply trains from reaching the remote settlement in an attempt to force the citizens to abandon Yucca City. But Carruthers, now revealed to be an undercover U.S. marshal, offers to break through the siege and bring in the goods.

BORN RECKLESS
Featured actors: Edmund Lowe, Catherine Dale Owen,
Marguerite Churchill, Lee Tracy, Warren Hymer, William
Harrigan, Frank Albertson, Ilka Chase, Ferike Boros, Paul Porcasi,

*Joe Brown, Ben Bard, Pat Somerset, Eddie Gribbon, Mike Donlin,
and Paul Page*
Screenplay and dialogue by Dudley Nichols
Based on a novel by Donald Henderson Clarke
Directed by John Ford
Produced by John Ford Productions and Fox Film Corporation
Distributed by Fox Film Corporation
Release date: May 11, 1930

John Ford creates a worthwhile peek into the criminal life of lower-middle-class Manhattan in the years following the Great War. After being convicted of robbery, mobster Louis Beretti (Edmund Lowe) is "sentenced" to volunteer for World War I, and returns Stateside with military honors. He soon enters the nightclub scene, teetering on the edge of criminality. When he finds himself the rescuer of a missing child, Beretti must decide if playing the hero is worth paying the ultimate price. The film is notable for uncredited bit players who include Ward Bond, future cowboy star Bill Elliott, Jack Pennick, Randolph Scott, and John Wayne, who also served as a prop man.

BORN TO THE WEST
Also titled HELL TOWN
*Featured actors: John Wayne, Marsha Hunt, John Mack Brown
(Johnny Mack Brown), John Patterson, Monte Blue, and Lucien
Littlefield*
Screenplay by Stuart Anthony and Robert Yost
Based on a novel by Zane Grey
Directed by Charles Barton
Produced and distributed by Paramount Pictures
Release date: December 10, 1937

What happens when no-account, unemployed gambler Dare Rudd (John Wayne) is offered a job by his successful cousin in untamed Wyoming? That's the premise of this sagebrush saga in which Duke plays against type. Dare and his saddle pal Dinkey Hooley are a pair of tramp cowhands getting mixed up with the wrong crowd. Dare says no to his cousin's job offer, but has second thoughts when the attractive Judy Worstall (Marsha Hunt) enters the picture. Can Dare go legit, or will his wild, gambling inclinations get in the way of success—and wooing the beautiful gal he loves? All in all, *Born to the West* is an average film in just about any way you can describe.

BRANNIGAN
*Featured actors: John Wayne, Richard Attenborough, Judy Geeson,
Mel Ferrer, John Vernon, Daniel Pilon, Ralph Meeker, John Stride,
James Booth, Arthur Batanides, Barry Dennen, Lesley Anne Down
(Lesley-Anne Down), Del Henney, Brian Glover, Stewart Bevan,*

Janette Legge, Pauline Delany (Pauline Delaney), Anthony Booth,
Tony Robinson, Don Henderson, Kathryn Leigh Scott, and Enid
Jaynes
Screenplay by Christopher Trumbo, Michael Butler, William P.
McGivern, and William Norton (William W. Norton)
Based on a story by Christopher Trumbo and Michael Butler
Directed by Douglas Hickox
Produced by Wellborn Ltd.
Distributed by United Artists
Release date: March 13, 1975

John Wayne is modern-day Chicago police detective Jim Brannigan, assigned to retrieve a fugitive in London. Think *McQ* set in Piccadilly Circus instead of Seattle. Little action, less wit, and no great lines. Don't
hope for more than one stupid semi-comedic bar fight and one halfway-
decent car chase. The scene in which an assassin mistakes a diminu-
tive 100-pound young blond woman for the six-foot-four, 250-pound
Wayne strains credulity to the point of speechlessness. And the seventies
soundtrack, like something *Superfly* left on the cutting-room floor, does
no honor to the Duke.

BROWN OF HARVARD

Featured actors: Jack Pickford, Mary Brian, Mary Alden, Francis X.
Bushman, Jr., and William Haines
Screenplay by A. P. Younger (Andrew Percival Younger)
Titles by Joe Farnham
Based on a play by Rida Johnson Young
Adaptation by Donald Ogden Stewart
Directed by Jack Conway
Produced and distributed by Metro-Goldwyn-Mayer (MGM)
Release date: April 19, 1926

Tom Brown (William Haines) enters Harvard to find fun, frolic, and
fame on the football field. He's a Lothario, a womanizer, and is happy to
leave a string of broken hearts in his path. He even (literally) cuts notches
in his belt for every new girl who falls in love with him. But when Brown
sets his sights on Mary, the daughter of a Harvard professor, shy, retiring
Bob MacAndrews (Francis X. Bushman, Jr.) decides enough is enough.
The crunch comes during a game against Yale when Tom must decide
what is more important—his own reputation or the good of the team.
Bushman asked for a stand-in during a scene in which he is tackled while
making a touchdown; John Wayne, a USC football player and part-time
prop man at the time, was brought in to do the job. Don't expect any
dashing close-ups of the eighteen-year-old Wayne in this blink-and-
you'll-miss-it appearance, notable only because it marks the future star's
first screen foray. Note: IMDb and Fred Landesman in *The John Wayne*
Filmography spell Bushman's character as McAndrew and McAndrews,

respectively, but in my video copy, the title cards (which appear to be original) use MacAndrews.

CAHILL, UNITED STATES MARSHAL
Featured actors: John Wayne, Gary Grimes, Neville Brand, Clay O'Brien, Marie Windsor, Morgan Paull, Dan Vadis, Royal Dano, Scott Walker, Denver Pyle, Jackie Coogan, Rayford Barnes, Dan Kemp, Harry Carey, Jr., Walter Barnes, Paul Fix, Pepper Martin, Vance Davis, Ken Wolger (Kenneth Wolger), Hank Worden, James Nusser, Murray MacLeod, Hunter von Leer, Ralph Volkie, Chuck Roberson, and George Kennedy
Screenplay by Harry Julian Fink and Rita M. Fink
Story by Barney Slater
Directed by Andrew V. McLaglen
Produced by Batjac Productions
Distributed by Warner Bros.
Release date: June 14, 1973

John Wayne plays the title role, a Texas lawman whose wanderings in search of bad guys has left his motherless sons without parental love and guidance. In a Freudian effort to seek their father's attention, the boys get mixed up with a crew of outlaws. Despite the mounting evidence against them, Wayne is blinded to their culpability by a father's love. The action and plot are solid, but Wayne here is clearly past his prime. He sounds froggy and looks tired—plus he's a little long in the tooth to be the father of a teen and a tween. The film is a pleasant distraction but adds nothing to Wayne's monumental legacy. Elmer Bernstein scored the soundtrack, so at least there's that in the movie's favor. Among the fine supporting actors: George Kennedy, Neville Brand, Hank Worden, Harry Carey, Jr., Jackie "Uncle Fester" Coogan, Denver Pyle, Royal Dano, and Paul Fix.

CALIFORNIA STRAIGHT AHEAD!
Featured actors: John Wayne, Louise Latimer, Robert McWade, Theodore von Eltz, Tully Marshall, Emerson Treacy, Harry Allen, LeRoy Mason, Grace Goodall, Olaf Hytten, and Monty Vandergrift
Screenplay by Scott Darling
Original story by Herman Boxer
Directed by Arthur Lubin
Produced and distributed by Universal Pictures
Release date: April 16, 1937

Nobody will ever mistake this for a typical John Wayne movie. In his third outing with Universal, Wayne plays Chicagoland bus driver (!!) Biff Smith. At the urging of his girlfriend, Smith leaves his dead-end (but enjoyable) job and joins his buddy in a freight-hauling business. Together they take on the crooked trucking industry. When disaster strikes while

Biff is in jail (!!), he vows to seek revenge. At this stage in John Wayne's career, Universal surely knew what Wayne was good at—ropin' and ridin' and romancin'—so why the boys in the head office decided to put him in this gritty urban drama is a mystery. Early Bogart, Cagney, Raft, sure. But Duke?! It's not a bad movie, just . . . disconcerting.

CANCEL MY RESERVATION

Featured actors: Bob Hope, Eva Marie Saint, Ralph Bellamy, Forrest Tucker, Anne Archer, Keenan Wynn, Henry Darrow, and Chief Dan George
Screenplay by Arthur Marx and Robert Fisher (Bob Fisher)
Based on a novel by Louis L'Amour
Directed by Paul Bogart
Produced by Naho Enterprises
Distributed by Warner Bros.
Release date: September 21, 1972

TV talk-show host Dan Bartlett (Bob Hope) arrives in Arizona for some R & R after his doctor says he needs a mental-health break from the hectic pace of New York City. A dead body in his house doesn't help calm his nerves, especially when the corpse goes missing only to reappear in his car, where the local sheriff finds it. The result of all this? A highly unfunny Bob Hope comedy. Unfortunately, with the talent at hand, it could have been hilarious, considering the costars include Keenan Wynn, Ralph Bellamy, Anne Archer, Forrest Tucker, Doodles Weaver, Pat Morita, Chief Dan George, and Eva Marie Saint. Blame scripter Bob Fisher (if you must blame anyone), who was primarily a writer for TV sitcoms, which this film resembles. John Wayne, as himself, has a cameo in a dream sequence in which Hope is about to get lynched. "I'd like to help ya," says Wayne, "but it's not my picture." That line is the funniest thing in the entire film, which tells you how dreadful it is.

CAST A GIANT SHADOW*

Featured actors: Kirk Douglas, Senta Berger, James Donald, Stathis Giallelis, Luther Adler, Topol, Ruth White, Gordon Jackson, Michael Hordern, Allan Cuthbertson, Jeremy Kemp, Michael Shillo, Sean Barrett, Rina Ganor, Roland Bartrop, Robert Gardett, Michael Balston, Claude Aliotti, Samra Dedes, Michael Shagrir, Hillel Rave, Frank Lattimore (Frank Latimore), Ken Buckle, Rodd Dana (Rod Dana), Arthur Hansel, Robert Ross, Don Sturkie (Dan Sturkie), Shlomo Hermon, Angie Dickinson, Frank Sinatra, Yul Brynner, and John Wayne
Screenplay by Melville Shavelson
Based on a book by Ted Berkman
Directed by Melville Shavelson

Produced by Batjac Productions, Bryna Productions, Llenroc
Productions, and the Mirisch Corporation
Distributed by United Artists
Release date: March 30, 1966

This film would have made an interesting double feature paired with *Exodus,* since they're both about the violent founding of the nation of Israel in 1948. Kirk Douglas and John Wayne once again share the screen as in 1965's *In Harm's Way.* This time, though, Douglas is the star and Wayne is a featured player. Douglas is a U.S. Army colonel who volunteers to advise the nascent Israeli army as the new nation prepares to announce its independence, despite threats from the surrounding Arab nations to push the Jews into the sea. The movie is packed with action, and well worth watching. Douglas is excellent, as he is in almost everything he does. But Duke Wayne is reduced to a minor role, though he's every inch John Wayne in his powerful moments before the camera. He plays a U.S. general who finds Douglas to be nothing but a pain in the rear. With costars Topol (in his first English-language film role), Senta Berger, and Angie Dickinson, plus "special appearances by" Frank Sinatra and Yul Brynner.

CENTRAL AIRPORT
Featured actors: Richard Barthelmess, Sally Eilers, Tom Brown,
Grant Mitchell, James Murray, Claire McDowell, Willard Robertson,
Arthur Vinton, and Charles Sellon
Screenplay by Rian James and James Seymour
Based on a story by Jack Moffitt
Directed by William A. Wellman
Produced by First National Pictures
Distributed by Warner Bros.
Release date: March 29, 1933

In this aviation drama, famed pilot Jim Blaine (Richard Barthelmess) is blamed for an air crash that wasn't his fault. His reputation in tatters, he's lucky to get a job in an aerial circus. While performing with the flying troupe, Jim falls in love with parachutist and fellow performer Jill Collins but is reluctant to marry her because a pilot's life is too precarious. Jim's brother Neil, also a pilot, steps into the breach, woos Jill, and marries her, despite Jim's continuing love for her. During a stormy flight, Neil's passenger plane goes down in the ocean, and Jim takes a seaplane to the rescue. John Wayne gets no credit (literally and figuratively) as a copilot in the plane wreck who gives his life for one of the downed passengers.

CHEER UP AND SMILE
Featured actors: Dixie Lee, Arthur Lake, Olga Baclanova,
"Whispering" Jack Smith, Johnny Arthur, Charles Judels, John
Darrow, Sumner Getchell, Franklin Pangborn, and Buddy Messinger

Dialogue and adaptation by Howard J. Green
Based on a story by Richard Edward Connell
Directed by Sidney Lanfield
Produced and distributed by Fox Film Corporation
Release date: June 22, 1930

A "lost" film, although IMDb says there is a copy at the UCLA Film and Television Archives. Arthur Lake, best known for his continuing role of Dagwood Bumstead in the *Blondie* series of movies, is Eddie Fripp, a pencil-neck geek who gets invited to join a college fraternity. Suspended over a hazing incident, Eddie leaves college and his girlfriend behind for the bright lights of New York. In an unbelievable chain of events, Eddie finds himself in a broadcast studio where he must sub for the radio station's singing star. Despite his reedy tenor, Eddie becomes a sensation. John Wayne has a bit part as "Roy."

CHISUM
Featured actors: John Wayne, Forrest Tucker, Christopher George, Ben Johnson, Glenn Corbett, Bruce Cabot, Andrew Prine, Patric Knowles, Richard Jaeckel, Lynda Day (Lynda Day George), John Agar, Lloyd Battista, Robert Donner, Ray Teal, Edward Faulkner, Ron Soble, John Mitchum, Glenn Langan, Alan Baxter, Alberto Morin, William Bryant, Pedro Armendariz, Jr. (Pedro Armendáriz, Jr.), Christopher Mitchum, John Pickard, Abraham Sofaer, Gregg Palmer, Hank Worden, Pedro Gonzalez Gonzalez, Jim Burk, Eddy Donno, Bob Morgan, Geoffrey Deuel, and Pamela McMyler
Screenplay by Andrew J. Fenady
Directed by Andrew V. McLaglen
Produced by Batjac Productions
Distributed by Warner Bros.
Release date: June 17, 1970

John Chisum (John Wayne) runs a big spread in New Mexico while fighting off a rival landowner and grappling with the thought of Billy the Kid trying to woo his niece. Too much of the action is in the hands of Duke's costars; Wayne himself doesn't have nearly as much screen time as a fan would like. The drama is weak, the action feeble. But it's an inoffensive vehicle, with gorgeous cinematography, that doesn't do any harm to the man's legacy. The failed potential is what hurts most, especially considering the side cast: Forrest Tucker, Hank Worden, Ben Johnson, Bruce Cabot, and Richard Jaeckel.

CIRCUS WORLD
Featured actors: John Wayne, Claudia Cardinale, Rita Hayworth, Lloyd Nolan, Richard Conte, John Smith, Katharyna, Katherine Kath, Wanda Rotha, Maggie MacGrath (Maggie Rennie), Miles Malleson, Jose Maria Cafarell (José Maria Cafarell), Kay Walsh,

Francois Calepides, Robert Cunningham, and Hans Dante (Hans Dantes)
Screenplay by Ben Hecht, Julian Halevy (Julian Zimet), and James Edward Grant
Story by by Philip Yordan (front for Bernard Gordon) and Nicholas Ray
Directed by Henry Hathaway
Produced by Samuel Bronston Productions
Distributed by Paramount Pictures
Release date: June 25, 1964

From the opening credits, you get the feeling this film might be worth watching: Rita Hayworth, Richard Conte, Lloyd Nolan, and a young Claudia Cardinale in her prime. (Surprisingly, considering Wayne's previous pictures, the rest of the supporting cast is made up of nobodies.) Circus promoter Matt Masters (John Wayne) has raised Toni Alfredo (Cardinale) for fourteen years, ever since the night her father, the circus's star aerialist, died in a fall from the trapeze. Toni's mother, Lili Alfredo (Rita Hayworth), abandoned her child and fled to Europe following her husband's death. Fast-forward: Masters decides to take his big top on the road to Europe for a grand tour. But will the now-despised Lili reenter the picture to reunite with her daughter—and Masters, the man she once loved? The action shots are often very good, but the painted backdrops are sometimes so phony as to be insulting. The superb stuntwork throughout compensates somewhat for the sappy plot, but there's little here to make up for Wayne's desultory acting. His age is clearly showing, his acting is too broad at times, and his voice is so scratchy that it sounds like it hurts him to speak.

COLLEGE COACH
Featured actors: Dick Powell, Ann Dvorak, Pat O'Brien, Arthur Byron, Lyle Talbot, Hugh Herbert, Arthur Hohl, Charles C. Wilson, Guinn Williams (Guinn "Big Boy" Williams), Nat Pendleton, Phillip Reed, Donald Meek, Berton Churchill, Harry Beresford, Herman Bing, Joe Sauers (Joe Sawyer), and Philip Faversham
Screenplay and story by Niven Busch and Manuel Seff
Directed by William A. Wellman
Produced and distributed by Warner Bros.
Release date: November 10, 1933

Calvert University is on the brink of bankruptcy. The board of trustees decides the only thing to do is to hire a big-name football coach who can bring the team a winning season—and ticket sales. Pat O'Brien is excellent as the self-important, not entirely trustworthy Coach Gore, who manages to assemble a winning team. Among the ringers Gore has plucked from other colleges is Phil Sargent (Dick Powell), a studious chemistry major who becomes a cornerstone of Calvert's backfield.

When Phil exits the roster to devote more time to his studies, the future of the team, and the college, is in doubt. John Wayne has a walk-on role as a student saying hi to Phil.

THE COMANCHEROS*
Featured actors: John Wayne, Stuart Whitman, Ina Balin, Nehemiah Persoff, Lee Marvin, Michael Ansara, Pat Wayne (Patrick Wayne), Bruce Cabot, Joan O'Brien, Jack Elam, Edgar Buchanan, Henry Daniell, and Richard Devon
Screenplay by James Edward Grant and Clair Huffaker
Based on a novel by Paul I. Wellman
Directed by Michael Curtiz
Produced and distributed by Twentieth Century–Fox
Release date: October 30, 1961

John Wayne, wearing one of his iconic pink shirts, plays Jake Cutter, a captain in the Texas Rangers who has been dispatched to arrest Paul Regret (Stuart Whitman) for a murder committed in a duel in Louisiana. The love-hate relationship between the two men ultimately grows into a solid bond as they seek out the Comancheros, a gang of desperadoes who sell guns to the Indians and rile them up. Lee Marvin, in an all-too-short role, is one of the few actors who can go head-to-head with Duke and make you think he might come out on top. As usual, Duke's revolving troupe of supporting players here includes some of the best in the business: Bruce Cabot, Edgar Buchanan, Nehemiah Persoff, Jack Elam, Michael Ansara, and a hilarious turn by Guinn "Big Boy" Williams as a not-quite-repentant gunrunner.

CONFLICT
Featured actors: John Wayne, Jean Rogers, Tommy Bupp, Frank Sheridan, Ward Bond, Eddie Borden, Harry Woods, Bryant Washburn, Lloyd Ingraham, Frank Hagney, Margaret Mann, and Bruce Mitchell
Screenplay by Charles Logue and Walter Weems
Based on a novel by Jack London
Directed by David Howard
Produced and distributed by Universal Pictures
Release date: November 28, 1936

Pat Glendon (John Wayne) is a two-bit palooka betting rummies that they can't hit him on the chin, until he comes face-to-face with "the world's champion knockout artist," Gus Carrigan (played by the eternally awesome Ward Bond). Next thing you know, Glendon is revealed to be a con man in with the Carrigan scam. Will he find his true north and return to honest ways, or delve deeper into the grifter lifestyle with Carrigan and his cronies? Although this is set in the West of yore, the tough-guy Universal approach to filmmaking makes this more like a Warner

Bros. gangster flick than the good old Lone Star Westerns where Wayne earned his spurs.

THE CONQUEROR
Featured actors: John Wayne, Susan Hayward, Pedro Armendariz (Pedro Armendáriz), Agnes Moorehead, Thomas Gomez, John Hoyt, William Conrad, Ted de Corsia, Leslie Bradley, Lee Van Cleef, Peter Mamakos, Leo Gordon, and Richard Loo
Screenplay by Oscar Millard
Directed by Dick Powell
Produced and distributed by RKO Radio Pictures
Release date: February 21, 1956

Okay, whose big fat idea was this, anyway?! The answer, apparently, was Howard Hughes, the head of RKO when the film was greenlit. Seriously, John Wayne as a Mongol warlord?! She-so-white Susan Hayward as a Tartar princess? A film about Asians with hardly an Asian to be seen. The dialogue is embarrassing beyond comprehension. (Mother: "Kumlik's daughter? Spawn of evil! Let your slaves have their sport with her. I will not have her within our tents." Wayne: "I say who stays in our tents. This woman is for my pleasure.") Don't be surprised if your ears start to bleed. And after all that, you still want to know the plot?! Fine. Temujin (Wayne) and his horde attack the caravan of Targutai and steal Targutai's fiancée, Bortai (Hayward). Targutai soon seeks his revenge while Temujin is busy trying to sweep Bortai off her feet with his bravery and falconry skill. (Had enough yet or shall I keep going? Trust me, that was plenty.) One must wonder whether Duke was intoxicated when he signed the contract after reading the script—*if* he even read the script in advance. *The Conqueror* is often described as Wayne's worst role ever—which is saying a lot, considering his uncredited bit part as a corpse in 1931's *The Deceiver*. The production costars Agnes Moorehead, Lee Van Cleef, and William Conrad, expert actors all, whose skills were sundered in this egregious stinkeroo and who were probably kicking themselves for years afterward.

THE COWBOYS+
Featured actors: John Wayne, Roscoe Lee Browne, Bruce Dern, Colleen Dewhurst, Slim Pickens, Lonny Chapman, Charles Tyner, Sarah Cunningham, Allyn Ann McLerie, Matt Clark, Maggie Costain, Alfred Barker, Jr., Nicolas Beauvy, Sean Kelly, Steve Benedict, A Martinez, Robert Carradine, Clay O'Brien, Norman Howell, Jr. (Norman Howell), Sam O'Brien, Stephen R. Hudis (Stephen Hudis), and Mike Pyeatt
Screenplay by Irving Ravetch, Harriet Frank, Jr., and William Dale Jennings
Based on a novel by William Dale Jennings

Directed by Mark Rydell
Produced by Warner Bros./Sanford Productions
Distributed by Warner Bros.
Release date: January 13, 1972

The Cowboys is a wholly satisfying movie—in production values, in plot, in acting, in pacing, and in John Wayne's spectacular performance, at once bold and nuanced. Rancher Wil Andersen (John Wayne) is left high and dry by his ranch hands, who have run off to try their luck at a nearby gold strike. Andersen desperately needs to get his cattle to market to pay his bills, so when a group of local schoolboys volunteers to play buckaroo and ride herd on the drive, Andersen reluctantly agrees. The perils they encounter are profound, and Wayne's determined efforts to move them forward are inspiring. At the finale, the boys' "plan" is incredibly satisfying on both a strategic and visceral level. The soundtrack by composer John Williams (*Star Wars, Harry Potter, Indiana Jones,* et al.) adds a tremendous zest to the goings-on. Interestingly, *The Cowboys* doesn't have a deep bench of acting talent, as do many of Wayne's post–World War II films, but all the players are capable, including a superlative Roscoe Lee Browne, a super-creepy Bruce Dern, Colleen Dewhurst, Slim Pickens, young Robert Carradine as one of the cowboys, and stuntman Tap Canutt (Yakima's son) as one of the rustlers.

DAKOTA*
Featured actors: John Wayne, Vera Hruba Ralston (Vera Ralston),
Walter Brennan, Ward Bond, Mike Mazurki, Ona Munson, Olive
Blakeney, Hugo Haas, Nicodemus Stewart (Nick Stewart), Paul Fix,
Grant Withers, Robert Livingston, Olin Howlin (Olin Howland),
Pierre Watkin, Robert H. Barrat (Robert Barrat), Jonathan Hale,
Bobby Blake (Robert Blake), Paul Hurst, Eddy Waller (Ed Waller),
Sarah Padden, Jack LaRue, George Cleveland, Selmer Jackson, Claire
DuBrey, and Roy Barcroft
Screenplay by Lawrence Hazard
Original story by Carl Foreman
Adaptation by Howard Estabrook
Directed by Joseph Kane
Produced and distributed by Republic Pictures
Release date: November 2, 1945

Get ready! Among the cast of this Western are Ward Bond, Mike Mazurki, and the inimitable Walter Brennan (the last of whom is by himself worth the price of admission). There's even a young Robert "Bobby" Blake, fresh off the set of an *Our Gang* short. And Yakima Canutt shows up in the credits as second-unit director, likely overseeing stunts and fight scenes. It's 1870s Chicago, and John Devlin (Wayne) is a playboy who has just married Sandra Poli (Vera Ralston) against her rich father's wishes. Off they go to Dakota Territory to find peace and to seek their fortune. Soon enough Wayne is going mano a mano with Bond's evil land speculator and his thugs. But when a natural disaster threatens the farmers of North Dakota, the odds get even longer for John Devlin.

DARK COMMAND

Featured actors: Claire Trevor, John Wayne, Walter Pidgeon, Roy Rogers, George Hayes (George "Gabby" Hayes), Porter Hall, Marjorie Main, Raymond Walburn, Joseph Sawyer (Joe Sawyer), Helen MacKellar, J. Farrell MacDonald, and Trevor Bardette
Screenplay by Grover Jones, Lionel Houser, and F. Hugh Herbert
Based on a novel by W. R. Burnett
Adaptation by Jan Fortune
Directed by Raoul Walsh
Produced and distributed by Republic Pictures
Release date: April 4, 1940

Bob Seton (John Wayne) is a brawler who specializes in knocking teeth loose so Doc Grunch (George "Gabby" Hayes), his dentist partner, can treat 'em and charge 'em. But the lighthearted start becomes more serious as we find ourselves in pre–Civil War "Bloody Kansas." Claire Trevor, excellent as ever, plays the love interest. Old-timers will enjoy recognizing Roy Rogers as the boy ingénue. The role of Seton comes at a transitional time in Wayne's career—from matinee cowboy star to actual actor. Bonus: Near the finale, Wayne shows up—as he did a year earlier in *Stagecoach*—in the twin-row-button Western bib shirt that would become a trademark of his, and he rocks it. But ultimately, despite some good lines and performances, the film becomes a soap opera rather than the adventure we might have hoped for.

THE DAWN RIDER

Featured actors: John Wayne, Marion Burns, Denny Meadows (Dennis Moore), Reed Howes, Joe DeGrasse (Joseph DeGrasse), Yakima Canutt, Earl Dwire, and Nelson McDowell
Screenplay by Robert N. Bradbury and Wellyn Totman (uncredited)
Story by Lloyd Nosler
Directed by R. N. Bradbury (Robert N. Bradbury)
Produced and distributed by Monogram Pictures (as Lone Star Productions)
Release date: June 20, 1935

John Mason (John Wayne) arrives in town to visit his father at the express office, only to be challenged to a (rousing) fistfight outside the local saloon. His sparring partner, Ben, as it turns out, works for John's dad, and the two young men soon become buddies. John and Ben enter the express office in the middle of a robbery, during which John's father is shot and killed. Vowing to find his father's killers, John is distracted when he falls in love with the beautiful Alice, who is also the object of Ben's attentions. Convinced that John has stolen Alice's favors, Ben removes the bullets from John's gun just as John prepares for a shoot-out with his father's murderer. Typical bullet-and-bronco Saturday-matinee fodder.

THE DECEIVER
Featured actors: Lloyd Hughes, Dorothy Sebastian, Ian Keith, Natalie Moorhead, Richard Tucker, George Byron, Greta Granstedt, Murray Kinnell, DeWitt Jennings, Al Ernest Garcia, Harvey Clark, Sidney Bracey, Frank Holliday, Colin Campbell, and Nick Copeland
Writers: Jack Cunningham, Charles Logue, and Jo Swerling
Based on a story by Abem Finkel and Bella Muni
Directed by Louis King
Produced and distributed by Columbia Pictures
Release date: November 22, 1931

Handsome rogue and Shakespearean actor Reginald Thorpe (Ian Keith) lures married high-society women into his romantic clutches, then blackmails them to guarantee his silence and preserve their reputations. He's ready to leave for the West Coast with his latest paramour, but must wait for a $10,000 payoff from one of the women he has ruined. If anyone ever deserved a knife in the back, it's Thorpe. To save actor Keith the indignity of lying across the floor as a dead man, John Wayne was assigned to stand in as the corpse. His budding career at Columbia was not looking promising.

DESERT COMMAND
See THE THREE MUSKETEERS

THE DESERT TRAIL
Featured actors: John Wayne, Mary Kornman, Paul Fix, Eddy Chandler, Carmen LaRoux (Carmen Laroux), Lafe McKee, Al Ferguson, and Henry Hall
Screenplay and story by Lindsley Parsons
Directed by Cullen Lewis (Lewis D. Collins)
Produced and distributed by Monogram Pictures (as Lone Star Productions)
Release date: April 22, 1935

John Scott (John Wayne) and his poker-playing buddy Kansas Charlie (Eddy Chandler) are on the road to Rattlesnake Gulch to take part in the rodeo. After getting shortchanged by the rodeo bosses, the boys take what's rightfully owed them, at gunpoint. Things deteriorate from there, and they're forced to assume false identities to protect themselves. Thanks to screenwriter Lindsley Parsons, there's a little more snappy dialogue than in the average Lone Star Wayne flick, but who can wrap their mind around Wayne being a bad guy engaging in a shoot-out with a legit posse? Weak narrative architecture hampers the full enjoyment of a movie that feels, at times, like it could go somewhere, but doesn't.

DONOVAN'S REEF*

Featured actors: John Wayne, Lee Marvin, Elizabeth Allen, Jack Warden, Cesar Romero, Dick Foran, Dorothy Lamour, Marcel Dalio, Mike Mazurki, Jacqueline Malouf, Cherylene Lee, Tim Stafford (Jeffrey Byron), Edgar Buchanan, and Jon Fong
Screenplay by Frank Nugent (Frank S. Nugent) and James Edward Grant
Story by Edmund Beloin and James A. Michener (uncredited)
Directed by John Ford
Produced by John Ford Productions
Distributed by Paramount Pictures
Release date: June 12, 1963

Saloon-keeper Michael Patrick "Guns" Donovan (John Wayne) and Thomas Aloysius "Boats" Gilhooley (Lee Marvin) are friendly rivals on the fictional Polynesian island of Haleakaloha who have had an annual birthday brawl for twenty-two years. A stuffy daughter from Boston comes out to the islands to ensure that her runaway father (Jack Warden), John Wayne's friend, doesn't inherit the family shipping business. It's a joy to watch Lee Marvin chew the scenery, but another semi-comical bar fight (with Mike Mazurki!) does nothing to enhance the action. With such a cast, including Dorothy Lamour and Cesar Romero, it's a shame the film never lives up to its potential. Even so, it's good fun, thus earns a watchability star. *Donovan's Reef* marks the last film on which Wayne and director John Ford worked together.

THE DRAW-BACK

Featured actors: Johnny Arthur, Kathryn McGuire, and Wallace Lupino
Directed by Norman Taurog
Produced by Tuxedo Comedies (Goodwill Production)
Distributed by Educational Film Exchanges
Release date: April 10, 1927

In this unfunny short, country bumpkin Horace Hayseed (Johnny Arthur) goes to college, where everyone makes fun of him—until he inadvertently becomes a football hero. The short film is little more than a series of weak gags by Arthur, who is an acquired taste at best. John Wayne (no screen credit) plays an opposing team member. His big scene occurs during a one-on-one standoff with Horace at the goal line.

THE DROP KICK

Starring Richard Barthelmess, Alberta Vaughn, Hedda Hopper, Barbara Kent, Eugene Strong, Dorothy Revier, James Bradbury

(James Bradbury, Jr.), Brooks Benedict, and George Pierce (George C. Pearce)
Scenario by Winifred Dunn
Based on a story by Katharine Brush
Directed by Millard Webb
Produced and distributed by First National Pictures
Release date: September 25, 1927

Jack Hamill (Richard Barthelmess) is the greatest dropkicker that Shoreham College has ever seen, so of course, all the girls are simply crazy about him. Meantime, Coach Hathaway has been embezzling money from the athletic department to underwrite his sexy bride's carefree spending habits. Will Jack fall into the clutches of the vampish wife, or stick to the straight and narrow and pursue Cecily, the good girl? John Wayne is recognizable about fifty-seven minutes into the movie as a fan at the football game, and also as a walk-on as one of the football players.

EL DORADO*

Featured actors: John Wayne, Robert Mitchum, James Caan, Charlene Holt, Paul Fix, Arthur Hunnicutt, Michele Carey, R. G. Armstrong, Edward Asner, Christopher George, Marina Ghane, John Gabriel, Robert Rothwell, Robert Donner, Adam Roarke, Victoria George, Jim Davis, Anne Newman (Anne Newman Bacal), Diane Strom, and Olaf Wieghorst
Screenplay by Leigh Brackett
Based on a novel by Harry Brown
Directed by Howard Hawks
Produced and distributed by Paramount Pictures
Release date: June 9, 1967

Wealthy Texas landowner Bart Jason (Ed Asner) hires a passel of gunslingers to get rid of a neighboring rancher so he can steal the man's water rights. Cole Thornton (John Wayne), a notorious pistolero, turns down a spot with Jason's thugs because it would mean going up against his old compañero, J. P. Harrah (Robert Mitchum), sheriff of El Dorado. Instead, Thornton and Harrah team up against the bad guys. But the sheriff is battling the bottle, and may not be fit enough to do the job. Because of the drunken-lawman plotline, many people, including the screenwriter, Leigh Brackett, say *El Dorado* is just a reworked version of *Rio Bravo* (which Brackett also wrote, so she should know). That theory isn't a stretch, either, especially if you consider Mitchum in the Dean Martin role, Arthur Hunnicutt in the Walter Brennan role, and James Caan in the Ricky Nelson role, all holed up in the sheriff's office waiting for the marshal to arrive in four or five days. But the film is good enough to stand on its own. *El Dorado* is a first-rate production (costumes by Edith Head, music scored and conducted by Nelson Riddle, etc.), and Wayne, once more clad in a dark-pink shirt, is his old self again following a few lackadaisical performances in recent pictures. The cast also includes Charlene Holt, the ever-present Paul Fix, Christopher George, Michele Carey, Jim Davis, Johnny Crawford of TV's *The Rifleman,* and in a small, uncredited role as Elmer the bartender, John Mitchum, brother of Robert. (Funny goof: Robert calls the bartender "Johnny" instead of "Elmer" near the film's end.)

THE FIGHTING KENTUCKIAN

Featured actors: John Wayne, Vera Ralston, Philip Dorn, Oliver Hardy, Marie Windsor, John Howard, Hugo Haas, Grant Withers, Odette Myrtil, Paul Fix, Mae Marsh, Jack Pennick, Mickey Simpson, Fred Graham, Mabelle Koenig, Shy Waggner, and Crystal White
Written and directed by George Waggner
Produced by Republic Pictures/John Wayne Productions
Distributed by Republic Pictures
Release date: September 15, 1949

Oliver Hardy?! That casting alone would seem to make this a must-see Wayne flick. Wayne looks dashing in his coonskin cap and buckskins, and Hardy does offer some comic relief, but even twenty minutes into the film it's not clear what the plot is. All in all, it's a bit of a mess. In short, the remnants of Napoleon's defeated French army have settled in Alabama, of all places, but they are being unwittingly taken advantage of by a local businessman. Wayne and his band of brothers are Kentucky militia in the early 1800s, but they seem to be marching for no purpose. Wayne leaves his regiment to take up with a French girl in Mobile, then fights to let her people keep their land. A so-so effort all around.

THE FIGHTING SEABEES*

Featured actors: John Wayne, Susan Hayward, Dennis O'Keefe, William Frawley, Leonid Kinskey, J. M. Kerrigan, Grant Withers, Paul Fix, Ben Welden, William Forrest, Addison Richards, Jay Norris, and Duncan Renaldo
Screenplay by Borden Chase and Aeneas MacKenzie
Original story by Borden Chase
Directed by Edward Ludwig
Produced and distributed by Republic Pictures
Release date: March 5, 1944

By the time this film was released, America had been in the war for nearly three years. Americans were tired of the news from the battlefronts— and of rationing, and blackouts, and their husbands and sons being overseas for months and years, perhaps never to return. What the country needed was some good old propaganda, which it got in spades with this rah-rah movie. Wayne plays Wedge Donovan, a tough-as-nails construction boss who persuades the U.S. Navy to let him create a construction brigade ("CB"—get it?) to build airfields, bridges, roads, and anything else the military needs in war zones. An unexpected highlight is a scene in which Wayne is jitterbugging—and man, that cat could swing! Despite the patriotic hucksterism, *The Fighting Seabees* has some good moments. Not a great film, but a darn good one.

FLAME OF BARBARY COAST
Featured actors: John Wayne, Ann Dvorak, Joseph Schildkraut,
William Frawley, Virginia Grey, Russell Hicks, Jack Norton, Paul Fix,
Manart Kippen, Eve Lynne, Marc Lawrence, Butterfly McQueen, Rex
Lease, Hank Bell, and Al Murphy
Screenplay by Borden Chase
Story by Prescott Chaplin
Directed by Joseph Kane
Produced and distributed by Republic Pictures
Release date: May 28, 1945

Duke Fergus (John Wayne) is a Montana horse rancher who comes to 1906 San Francisco to collect a debt from Tito Morrell, one of the city's biggest gamblers. To do so, he must face off against Morrell at one of the most notorious gambling dens on the Barbary Coast, El Dorado. After collecting, Duke goes on a tear through the city's other gambling houses with saloon singer Flaxen Tarry (Ann Dvorak) on his arm. Soon enough, the earth moves—but not because of romance (cue dramatic soundtrack). *Flame* is a good period piece of its kind. A tip of the hat to veteran character actors William Frawley and Butterfly McQueen for their portrayals.

FLYING LEATHERNECKS*
Featured actors: John Wayne, Robert Ryan, Don Taylor, Janis Carter,
Jay C. Flippen, William Harrigan, James Bell, Barry Kelley, Maurice
Jara, Adam Williams, James Dobson, Carleton Young, Steve Flagg
(Michael St. Angel), Brett King, and Gordon Gebert
Screenplay by James Edward Grant
Story by Kenneth Gamet
Directed by Nicholas Ray
Produced and distributed by RKO Radio Pictures
Release date: July 18, 1951

Shortly after the 1942 battle of Guadalcanal, Major Daniel Xavier Kirby (John Wayne) is assigned to lead Marine Fighter Squadron VMF 247, the Flying Leathernecks. The pilots are less than pleased that their old leader, Captain Carl "Griff" Griffin (Robert Ryan), wasn't appointed to lead, so Wayne has to be tougher than ever with his new crew. Major Kirby hopes to prove to the Marines that low-level flying, in concert with infantry strategy, can change the course of the war, but the age-old ways of the military prove to be a nearly insurmountable obstacle. Meantime, men are dying. . . . Wayne is at his peak, and costar Robert Ryan proves himself to be one of the few Hollywood actors who can hold his own alongside the charismatic Duke. Costarring is the always spot-on Jay C.

Flippen. Because the actors are better than the script, mark this film as a middling-to-good offering among Duke's World War II movies.

FLYING TIGERS*
Featured actors: John Wayne, John Carroll, Anna Lee, Paul Kelly, Gordon Jones, Mae Clarke, Addison Richards, Edmund MacDonald, Bill Shirley, Tom Neal, Malcolm "Bud" McTaggart, David Bruce, Chester Gan, James Dodd, Gregg Barton, and John James
Screenplay by Kenneth Gamet and Barry Trivers
Original story by Kenneth Gamet
Directed by David Miller
Produced and distributed by Republic Pictures
Release date: October 8, 1942

John Wayne plays Squadron Leader Jim Gordon of the First American Volunteer Group of pilots, the Flying Tigers, charged with keeping the air over Southwest China out of Japanese hands during World War II and at the same time doing their best to bring in desperately needed supplies. Trying to woo a pretty nurse (a subplot that goes nowhere) while inwardly torn up over the frequent loss of his young pilots, Gordon is a sensitive tough guy who can't be licked. The aerial scenes are thrilling. The supporting cast is terrific, especially John Carroll as lovable rogue and fellow pilot Woody Jason; he steals the show out from under Wayne.

FORT APACHE+
Featured actors: John Wayne, Henry Fonda, Shirley Temple, Pedro Armendariz (Pedro Armendáriz), Ward Bond, George O'Brien, Victor McLaglen, Anna Lee, Irene Rich, Dick Foran, Guy Kibbee, Grant Withers, Jack Pennick, Ray Hyke, Movita, Miguel Inclan (Miguel Inclán), Mary Gordon, Philip Keiffer (Philip Kieffer), Mae Marsh, Hank Worden, and John Agar
Screenplay by Frank S. Nugent
Based on a story by James Warner Bellah
Directed by John Ford
Produced by Argosy Pictures
Distributed by RKO Radio Pictures
Release date: March 18, 1948

This was the first film in the fabled Cavalry Trilogy (along with *She Wore a Yellow Ribbon* and *Rio Grande*), directed by John Ford and starring John Wayne. The place and time are an Army outpost in the 1880s Southwest during an Apache uprising. Overly officious Lieutenant Colonel Owen Thursday (Henry Fonda), accompanied by his attractive daughter (Shirley Temple), is sent to the fort to take command. Still smarting from his demotion from general, Thursday is bent on making a name for himself as an Indian fighter, even at the expense of his own men's lives. Kirby York (Wayne) is the experienced captain who tries to instill a sense of reality in the newly arrived commander. A superb Henry Fonda by rights should have received top billing, since the story revolves around his character and he has far more lines than Wayne. But Wayne's star was in the ascendant in Hollywood in the late forties. As good as the leads is the supporting cast: John Agar (in his film debut), Victor McLaglen, Ward Bond, Hank Worden, Grant Withers, and an all-grown-up Shirley Temple. *Fort Apache* is a must-watch film for any fan of John Wayne.

THE FORWARD PASS
Featured actors: Douglas Fairbanks, Jr., Loretta Young, Guinn Williams (Guinn "Big Boy" Williams), Marion Byron, Phyllis Crane, Bert Rome, Lane Chandler, Allan Lane, and Floyd Shackelford
Dialogue, titles, and scenario by Howard Emmett Rogers
Story by Harvey Gates
Directed by Eddie Cline (Edward Clive, per Vitaphone, 2003; Edward F. Kline, per the Internet Movie Database)
Produced and distributed by First National Pictures
Release date: November 10, 1929

Tired of getting hammered on the field, college quarterback Marty Reid (Douglas Fairbanks, Jr.) threatens to quit the game. The other teams are targeting him, it seems, and his own teammates are unable to protect him. Some of his fellow players accuse Reid of cowardice. Enter beautiful coed Patricia Carlyle (Loretta Young), who does her best to change his mind as he reconsiders his decision. But does she truly care about Reid, or is she playing an angle? Considered a lost film. John Wayne is an extra. College football dramas were a popular genre in the late 1920s.

FOUR SONS
Featured actors: Margaret Mann, James Hall, Charles Morton, Francis X. Bushman, Jr., George Meeker, June Collyer, Earle Foxe, Albert Gran, Frank Reicher, Archduke Leopold of Austria, Ferdinand Schumann-Heink, and Jack Pennick
Titles by H. H. Caldwell and Katharine Hilliker (as production editors)
Based on a story by Miss I. A. R. Wylie (I. A. R. Wylie)
Adaptation by Philip Klein
Directed by John Ford
Produced and distributed by Fox Film Corporation
Release date: February 13, 1928

Frau Bernle (Margaret Mann) is prepared to rest on her maternal laurels after raising four strapping sons in her picture-perfect Bavarian village of Burgendorf—until the specter of the Great War upends her world. She gives her life's savings to one of them so he can move to America, where he has a friend who will help settle him in. As for the other lads, one will remain at home to tend the cows, but the other two chaps must face the madness of the Russian front. It's a film both charming and disturbing, from master director John Ford. But if you can find John Wayne (uncredited, as a soldier), you'd probably do well at Where's Waldo? Some sources doubt whether Wayne was in the final cut.

GIRLS DEMAND EXCITEMENT

Featured actors: John Wayne, Virginia Cherrill, Marguerite Churchill, Edward Nugent (Edward J. Nugent), Helen Jerome Eddy, Terrance Ray, Martha Sleeper, and William Janney
Screenplay by by Harlan Thompson
Directed by Seymour Felix
Produced and distributed by Fox Film Corporation
Release date: February 8, 1931

Should females be allowed to attend classes at Bradbury College, an all-male institution? Peter Brooks (John Wayne) is a collegiate he-man woman hater entrapped by the feminine wiles of Joan Madison (Virginia Cherrill), an upper-crust man-eater. Thanks to his pull with his fellow (male) students, Brooks threatens to veto women on campus. Can a basketball game between the sexes make a difference? This film may or may not be lost, but it's nearly impossible to find online for streaming, rental, or purchase.

THE GREAT K & A TRAIN ROBBERY

Featured actors: Tom Mix, Tony the Wonder Horse, Dorothy Dwan, William Walling (Will Walling), Harry Grippe (Harry Gripp), Carl Miller, Edward Piel (Edward Piel, Sr.), and Curtis McHenry (Curtis "Snowball" McHenry)
Titles by Malcolm Stuart Boylan
Scenario by John Stone
Story by Paul Leicester Ford
Directed by Lewis Seiler
Produced by Lewis Seiler Productions
Distributed by Fox Film Corporation
Release date: October 17, 1926

A gang of bandits is getting tipped off whenever Eugene Cullen's railroad trains are carrying valuables. Cowboy-detective Tom Gordon (Tom Mix) goes undercover to learn the identity of the inside source. Because of his secret identity, Gordon is mistaken for one of the bandits, even though he is on the verge of capturing the gang. In the end, Tony the Wonder Horse and an unlikely ally, a hobo, give Gordon all the assistance he needs to catch the bad guys and clear his name. John Wayne (uncredited) is one of the railroad guards. At least, it sort of looks like John Wayne. . . .

THE GREATEST STORY EVER TOLD

Featured actors: Max von Sydow, Michael Anderson, Jr., Carroll Baker, Ina Balin, Pat Boone, Victor Buono, Richard Conte, Joanna

Dunham, Jose Ferrer (José Ferrer), Van Heflin, Charlton Heston,
Martin Landau, Angela Lansbury, Janet Margolin, David McCallum,
Roddy McDowall, Dorothy McGuire, Sal Mineo, Nehemiah Persoff,
Donald Pleasance, Sidney Poitier, Claude Rains, Gary Raymond,
Telly Savalas, Joseph Schildkraut, Paul Stewart, John Wayne, Shelly
Winters, Ed Wynn, John Abbott, Rodolfo Acosta, Michael Ansara,
Robert Blake, Burt Brinckerhoff, Robert Busch, John Considine,
Philip Coolidge, John Crawford, Frank de Kova (Frank DeKova),
Cyril Delevanti, Jamie Farr, David Hedison, Russell Johnson,
Mark Lenard, Robert Loggia, John Lupton, Peter Mann, Tom
Reese, Marian Seldes, David Sheiner, Frank Silvera, Joseph Sirola,
Abraham Sofaer, Harold J. Stone, Chet Stratton, Michael Tolan, and
Ron Whelan
Screenplay by James Lee Barrett and George Stevens
Based on the Old and New Testaments, a book by Fulton Oursler, and
writings by Henry Denker
Directed by George Stevens
Produced by George Stevens Productions
Distributed by United Artists
Release date: February 15, 1965

The star-filled extravaganza tells the Passion of the Christ in highly dramatic scenes. The movie is so stylized that it often comes across as a series of tableaux vivants rather than a typical movie with subplots and character development. Making the trial and Crucifixion of Christ into a boring lecture is a pretty good trick. Blame producer-director George Stevens. The film was largely panned by critics in its day. John Wayne, as the Roman centurion next to Jesus' cross, has a single line: "Truly, this man was the Son of God." The line, coming from a man of Wayne's cinematic background, is said to have caused audience laughter as much as anything.

THE GREEN BERETS*

Featured actors: John Wayne, David Janssen, Jim Hutton, Aldo Ray,
Raymond St. Jacques, Bruce Cabot, Jack Soo, George Takei, Patrick
Wayne, Luke Askew, Irene Tsu, Edward Faulkner, Jason Evers, Mike
Henry, Craig Jue, Chuck Roberson, Eddy Donno, Rudy Robbins, and
Richard "Cactus" Pryor
Screenplay by James Lee Barrett
Based on a novel by Robin Moore
Directed by John Wayne and Ray Kellogg
Produced by Batjac Productions
Distributed by Warner Bros./Seven Arts
Release date: June 17, 1968

As director of a film produced by his own production company about the Vietnam War, John Wayne had more freedom with *The Green*

Berets to express his personal political opinions than in any previous film he made. And the conservative Wayne made full use of the opportunity. The film was critically savaged, though it did well at the box office. As Colonel Mike Kirby of U.S. Army Special Forces, better known as the Green Berets because of their distinctive headgear, Wayne leads his valiant soldiers on a desperate foray behind enemy lines to capture a Vietcong general. At the same time, Colonel Kirby "proves" to an antiwar journalist (David Janssen) that the American mission is a righteous one and that the American fighting man is the best on earth. The pro-America point of view isn't as arch as it might have been, thankfully, but the propaganda element undercuts the film's good points (including several well-crafted battle sequences). Coming along for the ride are Jim Hutton, Aldo Ray (who should have been in every war movie ever made), Bruce Cabot, George "Mr. Sulu" Takei, Jack Soo, Patrick Wayne, and Vera Miles.

HANGMAN'S HOUSE
Featured actors: Victor McLaglen, June Collyer, Larry Kent, Earle Foxe, and Hobart Bosworth
Titles by Malcolm Stuart Boylan
Scenario by Marion Orth
Based a story by Donn Byrne (Brian Oswald Donn-Byrne)
Adaptation by Philip Klein
Directed by John Ford (uncredited)
Produced and distributed by Fox Film Corporation
Release date: May 13, 1928

Denis "Citizen" Hogan (Victor McLaglen), a commander in the French Foreign Legion, requests leave to return to his Irish homeland, where he plans to kill a man who informed on him years earlier. The fact that the informer has inveigled himself into a wealthy family and plans to wed their daughter, who doesn't love him, makes Hogan's mission all the sweeter. John Wayne is unrecognizable as the Condemned Man in a flashback scene some six minutes into the film, but careful viewers will make him out as a horse-race spectator starting at about thirty-eight minutes, wearing a jaunty cap, cheering exultantly, and nearly upsetting a wagon by his size.

HATARI!
Featured actors: John Wayne, Hardy Kruger (Hardy Krüger), Elsa Martinelli, Red Buttons, Gerard Blain (Gérard Blain), Bruce Cabot, Michele Girardon (Michèle Girardon), Valentin de Vargas, and Eduard Franz
Screenplay by Leigh Brackett
Based on a story by Harry Kurnitz
Directed by Howard Hawks

Produced by Malabar Productions
Distributed by Paramount Studios
Release date: May 24, 1962

A group of hard-bitten Africa hands capture big game for the world's zoos until one of their comrades is gored while chasing down a rhino. When he returns to their compound to await their friend's recovery, head man Sean Mercer (John Wayne) finds a young woman in his bed. She turns out to be Anna Maria "Dallas" D'Allesandro (Elsa Martinelli), the photographer Mercer hired sight unseen, thinking "Dallas" was a man. Inevitably, romance blossoms. Despite the glorious wildlife and magnificent scenery, the action is slow and the plot is thin. Nonetheless, with a score by Henry Mancini and costumes by the renowned Edith Head, *Hatari!* is a class-A production from start to finish. It's just not very . . . interesting. Co–principal actors: Red Buttons, Bruce Cabot, and the inspiring veldt of Tanzania.

HAUNTED GOLD

Featured actors: John Wayne, Duke the Horse, Sheila Terry, Harry Woods, Erville Alderson, Otto Hoffman, Martha Mattox, and Blue Washington
Screenplay and dialogue by Adele Buffington
Directed by Mack V. Wright
Produced by Leon Schlesinger Studios/Warner Bros. (as A Four Star Western)
Distributed by Warner Bros. (as Vitagraph Inc.)
Release date: December 17, 1932

A Western horror show? John Mason (John Wayne) receives an anonymous note instructing him to go to Gold City to "protect his interest" in an abandoned gold mine cofounded by his late father. While cooped up in a spooky mansion in the desolate town, he meets the daughter of his father's former partner, who unbeknownst to everyone was swindled out of his share by a suspicious caballero who just happens to be in Gold City at the same time as Mason. If this description sounds boring, it doesn't hold a candle to the movie itself, which gives fresh meaning to the word "unexciting." Add to that a Stepin Fetchit–style Black man who acts and is treated like an idiot as they call him "Smoky" and "Darky," actors who seem to forget their lines, and a plot not quite sophisticated enough for an *Our Gang* comedy, and you have the makings of . . . well, a horror show.

HELL TOWN
See BORN TO THE WEST

HELLFIGHTERS

Featured actors: John Wayne, Katharine Ross, Jim Hutton, Jay C. Flippen, Bruce Cabot, Edward Faulkner, Barbara Stuart, Edmund Hashim, Valentin De Vargas, Frances Fong, Alberto Morin, Alan

Caillou, Laraine Stephens, John Alderson, Lal Chand Mehra, Rudy
Diaz, Chris Chandler, William Hardy, Howard Finch, Cactus Pryor
(Richard "Cactus" Pryor), Big John Hamilton, Elizabeth Germaine,
and Vera Miles
Screenplay by Clair Huffaker
Directed by Andrew V. McLaglen
Produced and distributed by Universal Pictures
Release date: December 14, 1968

The art of putting out an oil-well blaze is practiced by few men, one of
whom was the well-known "Red" Adair, who served as a technical advi-
sor on this picture along with several other oil-fire experts from the Red
Adair Wild Well Control Company. If nothing else, *Hellfighters* has fact-
checking on its side. John Wayne stars as Chance Buckman, based to
some extent on the exploits of Adair himself. For years, Buckman has fo-
cused on his career to the detriment of his family obligations. Following
a freak accident, Buckman begins to reassess his priorities in life. That
fresh perspective comes in handy when his feisty daughter (Katharine
Ross) begins to show an interest in Buckman's work and in his cocky un-
derling (Jim Hutton), neither of which makes the old man happy. A comical bar fight midway through the plot serves no purpose except to show
that Duke can still throw a punch. Overall, despite lots of action, explo-
sions, and flames, the plot wears thin quickly. Also on the bill are Vera
Miles, Bruce Cabot, and Jay C. Flippen.

THE HIGH AND THE MIGHTY*

Featured actors: John Wayne, Claire Trevor, Laraine Day, Robert Stack,
Jan Sterling, Phil Harris, Robert Newton, David Brian, Paul Kelly,
Sidney Blackmer, Julie Bishop, Gonzalez Gonzalez (Pedro Gonzalez
Gonzalez), John Howard, Wally Brown, William Campbell, Ann Doran,
John Qualen, Paul Fix, George Chandler, Joy Kim, Michael Wellman,
Douglas Fowley, Regis Toomey, Carl Switzer (Carl "Alfalfa" Switzer),
Robert Keys, William Dewolf Hopper (William Hopper), William
Schallert, Julie Mitchum, Doe Avedon, Karen Sharpe, and John Smith
Screenplay by Ernest K. Gann
Based on a novel by Ernest K. Gann
Directed by William A. Wellman
Produced by Wayne-Fellows Productions
Distributed by Warner Bros.
Release date: July 3, 1954

Commercial airline pilot Dan Roman (John Wayne) hesitantly returns
to the cockpit after suffering a devastating crash that killed his wife
and only child. Suffering from intense guilt because he alone survived,
Roman signs on as copilot for a Hawaii-California transpacific flight.
Engine trouble threatens to turn the aircraft into a *Lifeboat* situation,
with each passenger's life story flashing across the screen as impending

doom . . . er, impends. The ensemble nature of the cast and script means that Wayne is off-screen for much of the film, but don't let that stop you from watching this gripping adventure. The film could have served as the model for such 1970s big-production, multi-star disaster flicks as *Airport, The Towering Inferno,* and *The Poseidon Adventure.* Music is by Dimitri Tiomkin—very high class! The costars are simply pitch-perfect, especially Robert Stack, Claire Trevor, John Qualen, Phil Harris, Robert Newton, Pedro Gonzalez Gonzalez, Carl "Alfalfa" Switzer, George Chandler, Robert Easton, William Schallert, and, of course, Paul "the Fixture" Fix, who appeared in so many Wayne movies.

HIS PRIVATE SECRETARY

Featured actors: Evalyn Knapp, John Wayne, Reginald Barlow, Alec B. Francis, Arthur Hoyt, Natalie Kingston, Patrick Cunning, Al St. John, Hugh Kidder, and Mickey Rentschler
Story by Lew Collins (Lewis D. Collins)
Adaptation and continuity by John Francis Natteford (Jack Natteford)
Directed by Philip H. Whitman (Phil Whitman)
Produced by Screencraft Productions/Showmen's Pictures
Distributed by Marcy Pictures Corporation
Release date: June 10, 1933

Billed second to Evalyn Knapp, John Wayne sheds his cowpuncher duds for the tuxedoed trappings of a modern-day playboy, Dick Wallace. Wallace's millionaire father soon has enough of Dick's lack of motivation and puts him to work as a debt collector, which leads to his falling in love with a minister's granddaughter, Marion Hall. When they marry, Dick's father threatens to disown the couple, certain that Marion, whom he has never met, must be a gold digger. Marion attempts to visit the father in his office to plead her case, but is mistaken for a secretarial applicant and hired to be the old man's assistant. Meantime, Dick is falling back into his old ways, drinking and dancing late into the nights—without his wife. Being cast as a roguish Lothario was not Wayne's only career misstep (his previous and next films are also contemporary urban flicks), but he soon got back into his Western roles where he was a more natural fit.

A HOME-MADE MAN

Featured actors: Lloyd Hamilton, Lucille Hutton, and Kewpie Morgan
Scenario by Norman Taurog
Directed by Norman Taurog
Produced by Lloyd Hamilton Corporation
Distributed by Educational Film Exchanges
Release date: July 17, 1928

Lloyd Hamilton was among the most respected silent comedy stars of the teens and twenties, earning plaudits from contemporaries like

Charlie Chaplin and Buster Keaton. Unfortunately, because he died young, at age forty-three, and few of his films still exist, modern audiences are generally unaware of this comic actor. In this comedy short, the star works at a soda fountain in a gym, where, of course, he makes a mess of things. Laughter ensues, and Hamilton is reassigned to the gymnasium, where more funny disasters follow. John Wayne, in a brief bit, portrays the uncredited Man on Stool in the soda fountain scene.

HONDO+

Featured actors: John Wayne, Geraldine Page, Ward Bond, Michael Pate, James Arness, Rodolfo Acosta, Leo Gordon, Tom Irish, Lee Aaker, Paul Fix, and Rayford Barnes
Screenplay by James Edward Grant
Based on a story by Louis L'Amour
Directed by John Farrow
Produced by Wayne-Fellows Productions
Distributed by Warner Bros.
Release date: November 27, 1953

In 1870 New Mexico, Apache warrior-chief Vittorio and his band go on the warpath to rid the American Southwest of the white man. Cavalry scout Hondo Lane (John Wayne) is on his way to the fort to report the news of the bellicose Indians when he loses his horse. He makes his way on foot to a remote ranch where a widow (Geraldine Page) and her young son have been living in peace with the Apaches for years. But as the U.S. Army and the Apaches go to war, the fate of the local ranchers is in grave doubt. John Wayne's initial screen appearance here is every bit as dramatic as in *Stagecoach*—maybe even more so. With his buckskin shirt, colorful neckerchief, battered and tasseled hat, and grim expression, Duke embodies the abiding legend of John Wayne in those opening scenes. Costars and supporters include Geraldine Page in her first feature film, a bearded Ward Bond, James Arness (in his third Waynester in little more than a year), heavy Leo Gordon, and the omnipresent Paul Fix.

THE HORSE SOLDIERS*

Featured actors: John Wayne, William Holden, Constance Towers, Judson Pratt, Hoot Gibson, Ken Curtis, Willis Bouchey, Bing Russell, O. Z. Whitehead, Hank Worden, Chuck Hayward, Denver Pyle, Strother Martin, Basil Ruysdael, Carleton Young, William Leslie, William Henry, Walter Reed, Anna Lee, William Forrest, Ron Hagerthy, Russell Simpson, and Althea Gibson
Screenplay by John Lee Mahin and Martin Rackin
Based on a novel by Harold Sinclair
Directed by John Ford
Produced by the Mirisch Company/Mahin-Rackin Productions

Distributed by United Artists
Release date: June 12, 1959

The year is 1863, the height of the Civil War. The Union's siege of Vicksburg is at a standstill, so General Ulysses S. Grant sends Colonel John Marlowe (John Wayne) and his short brigade on a vital assignment—to destroy the rebels' main supply depot at Newton Station. The chances of success are slim, but the mission's importance to the Union cause spurs the men to face the enormous challenge ahead. Enter Major Henry Kendall (second-billed William Holden), regimental surgeon, whose concern for the health and safety of the troopers runs counter to Marlowe's leave-the-wounded-behind determination. With its superb direction by John Ford, consistently strong acting by the entire cast, and tale of grand adventure, *The Horse Soldiers,* while not a perfect film, is a laudable addition to Duke's cinematic canon. Wayne's penchant for wearing dark-pink or red decorative clothing (in this case, his neckerchief and union suit) is especially apparent here. Popping up now and then are early-day Western star Hoot Gibson, Ken "Festus" Curtis, Hank Worden, Western perennial Denver Pyle, and Strother Martin.

HOW THE WEST WAS WON*

Featured actors: Carroll Baker, Lee J. Cobb, Henry Fonda, Carolyn Jones, Karl Malden, Gregory Peck, George Peppard, Robert Preston, Debbie Reynolds, James Stewart, Eli Wallach, John Wayne, Richard Widmark, Brigid Bazlen, Walter Brennan, David Brian, Andy Devine, Raymond Massey, Agnes Moorehead, Henry Morgan (Harry Morgan), Thelma Ritter, Mickey Shaughnessy, Russ Tamblyn, and Spencer Tracy as the narrator
Screenplay by James R. Webb
Based on the Life *magazine series "How the West Was Won"*
Directed by John Ford ("The Civil War"), George Marshall ("The Railroad"), and Henry Hathaway ("The Rivers," "The Plains," and "The Outlaws")
Produced and distributed by Metro-Goldwyn-Mayer (MGM)/ Cinerama Productions
Release date: November 7, 1962

Much like *The Longest Day,* this film is a sprawling epic filled with every star in the cinematic heavens. Some might say it's bloated (at two hours forty-two minutes, it *is* overlong). Some might call it pompous (with an overarching narration by no less than Spencer Tracy, plus a musical "Overture," "Entr'acte," and "Exit"). But no matter how you look at it, *How the West Was Won* is a must-see for any cinephile, not just fans of Duke. Wayne's screen time is limited to a cameo appearance, though he's still worth watching. Wayne plays General William Tecumseh Sherman in the Civil War section (directed by John Ford) of this family saga, convincing General Ulysses S. Grant not to resign his commission in the wake of negative news reports about his leadership abilities. Elsewhere, it's lots of fun picking out character actors you love in roles small and smaller: Andy Devine, Harry Morgan, Willis Bouchey, Ken Curtis, Jay C. Flippen, Raymond Massey, Walter Brennan, and a young Harry Dean Stanton, among many others.

THE HURRICANE EXPRESS
Featured actors: Tully Marshall, Conway Tearle, John Wayne, Shirley Gray (Shirley Grey), Edmund Breese, Lloyd Whitlock, Al Bridge, Mathew Betz (Matthew Betz), Joseph Girard (Joseph W. Girard), James Burtis, Ernie S. Adams (Ernie Adams), Charles King, Al Ferguson, and Glenn Strange
Screenplay by George Morgan and J. P. McGowan
Story by Colbert Clark, Barney Sarecky (Barney A. Sarecky), and Wyndham Gittens
Directed by Armand Schaefer and J. P. McGowan
Produced and distributed by Mascot Pictures
Release date: August 9, 1932

Someone with a grudge against the railroad, a mysterious person known only as the Wrecker (after his penchant for wrecking locomotives), must be caught! Able to conceal his identity, the Wrecker creates havoc with little challenge, seemingly at will. Enter Larry Baker (John Wayne), an airplane pilot whose engineer father was killed by the Wrecker. Baker is just the man to catch the crook. This weekly serial (later edited into a standalone movie) is so boring that one wonders what made children come back to the theater week after week, other than in hope of seeing the series' final installment, proof that this travesty was finished.

I COVER THE WAR!
Featured actors: John Wayne, Gwen Gaze, Don Barkely (Don Barclay), Charles Brokaw, James Bush, Pat Somerset, Richard Tucker, Major Sam Harris (Sam Harris), Olaf Hytten, Arthur Aylsworth (Arthur Aylesworth), and Franklyn Parker (Franklin Parker)
Screenplay by George Waggner
Original story idea by Bernard McConville
Directed by Arthur Lubin
Produced and distributed by Universal Pictures
Release date: June 29, 1937

John Wayne plays Bob Adams, a newsreel cameraman covering an Arab rebellion in fictional Samari. His goal: to capture rebel chieftain El Kadar on film. Unfortunately, he first has to deal with bloodthirsty insurrectionists, the colonial English army in charge of Samari, the attractive daughter of an army officer, and his sibling, Don, who has quit college to become a newsman like his big brother. When Don is tricked into aiding gunrunners, he is suspected of being one himself. But Bob has little time to help his younger brother, because after getting his pictures, he must escape from the clutches of the Arab chieftain and save the English army from certain disaster.

I MARRIED A WOMAN

Featured actors: George Gobel, Diana Dors, Adolphe Menjou, Jessie Royce Landis, Nita Talbot, William Redfield, Steve Dunne (Stephen Dunne), John McGiver, and Steve Pendleton
Screenplay by Goodman Ace
Directed by Hal Kanter
Produced by Gomalco Productions
Distributed by RKO Radio Pictures
Release date: May 23, 1958

Ad exec Marshall Briggs (George Gobel) may lose a big brewery account unless he comes up with a new promotion to follow on the heels of his successful Miss Luxenberg Beer campaign. His demanding but gorgeous wife (Diana Dors) is ready to announce she's pregnant, but then hides the news because she thinks Briggs might be running around on her. John Wayne, as himself, has only a walk-on (near the start and at the end) in this loser of a comedy. At least Duke's latter scene gets one of the movie's few smiles, though it's nothing memorable.

IDOL OF THE CROWDS

Featured actors: John Wayne, Sheila Bromley, Billy Burrud (Bill Burrud), Russell Hopton, Huntley Gordon, Charles Brokaw, Hal Neiman, Virginia Brissac, Frank Otto, Jane Johns, Clem Bevans, and George Lloyd
Screenplay and original story by George Waggner
Directed by Arthur Lubin
Produced and distributed by Universal Pictures
Release date: September 30, 1937

Johnny Hanson (John Wayne) is a semiretired amateur hockey player who wants nothing more than to raise chickens on his Maine farm. But then a pro team from New York comes a-calling. The big-city icemen, it turns out, need someone who can add pizzazz to the moribund squad. Country-bumpkin Hanson soon falls sway to the allures of the metropolis as he carries his team to victory after victory. The situation gets tense, though, when gamblers threaten to harm Hanson's younger brother unless the hockey star shaves some points in the big game. Cosmopolitan evils, gangsters, grifters, and two-timers do everything in their power to undermine Hanson's innate goodness. This is a John Wayne movie?!

IN HARM'S WAY

Featured actors: John Wayne, Kirk Douglas, Patricia Neal, Tom Tryon, Paula Prentiss, Brandon De Wilde, Jill Haworth, Dana

Andrews, Stanley Holloway, Burgess Meredith, Franchot Tone,
Patrick O'Neal, Carroll O'Connor, Slim Pickens, James Mitchum,
George Kennedy, Bruce Cabot, Barbara Bouchet, Tod Andrews, Larry
Hagman, Stewart Moss, Richard LePore, Chet Stratton, Soo Young
(Soo Yong), Dort Clark, Phil Mattingly, and Henry Fonda
Screenplay by Wendell Mayes
Based on a novel by James Bassett
Directed by Otto Preminger
Produced by Sigma Productions/Otto Preminger Films
Distributed by Paramount Pictures
Release date: March 31, 1965

This is the story of Pearl Harbor, a tale that has been told a thousand times. Navy captain Rockwell "Rock" Torrey (John Wayne) keeps his ship safe during the bombing of Pearl Harbor, but a subsequent accident stalls his career soon after. Kirk Douglas is competent as Wayne's scenery-chewing number two but really doesn't have enough to do in this actioner. No one will criticize a viewer for fast-forwarding through the slow-moving romantic bits, considering that Patricia Neal is unconvincing as the love interest. As was usual in most of Duke's later films, the secondary actors are first-rate, in particular Burgess Meredith, Dana Andrews, Paula Prentiss, Stanley Holloway, an aging Franchot Tone, Carroll "Archie Bunker" O'Connor, Slim Pickens, George Kennedy, mainstay Bruce Cabot, a pre–*I Dream of Jeannie* Larry Hagman, an uncredited Hugh O'Brian, and a special walk-on by Henry Fonda. And if you hear someone who sounds just like Robert Mitchum, it's his son James in a bit part.

IN OLD CALIFORNIA
Featured actors: John Wayne, Binnie Barnes, Albert Dekker, Helen
Parrish, Patsy Kelly, Edgar Kennedy, Dick Purcell, Harry Shannon,
Charles Halton, Emmett Lynn, Bob McKenzie (Robert McKenzie),
Milt Kibbee (Milton Kibbee), Paul Sutton, and Anne O'Neal
Screenplay by Gertrude Purcell and Frances Hyland
Original story by J. Robert Bren and Gladys Atwater
Directed by William McGann (William C. McGann)
Produced and distributed by Republic Pictures
Release date: May 31, 1942

Tom Craig (John Wayne), a druggist from Boston, arrives in Gold Rush–era California to set up shop in Sacramento. The Dawson Gang runs Sacramento, taking over farms and ranches with abandon. The fightin' pharmacist Craig rouses the citizenry to stand up to the bad guys. But when the battles are over, will he choose to marry the saloon singer with a heart of gold or the pretty Spanish señorita with pink ribbons for brains? Well, it goes downhill from there. This Republic Picture harks back to Wayne's 1930s oaters—and not in a good way. Any movie that starts with John Wayne entering as a fancy dude—let alone a milk-drinking pill peddler—doesn't have much of a chance to begin with.

IN OLD OKLAHOMA*
Also titled WAR OF THE WILDCATS
Featured actors: John Wayne, Martha Scott, Albert Dekker, George "Gabby" Hayes, Marjorie Rambeau, Dale Evans, Grant Withers, Sidney Blackmer, Paul Fix, Cecil Cunningham, Irving Bacon, Byron Foulger, Anne O'Neal, and Richard Graham
Screenplay by Ethel Hill and Eleanore Griffin
Original story by Thomson Burtis
Directed by Albert S. Rogell
Produced and distributed by Republic Pictures
Release date: December 5, 1943

John Wayne is back again as a leading man after a couple of unpromising tertiary roles. This time, it's 1906, and territorial Oklahoma is experiencing an oil boom. Daniel Somers (Wayne) is a footloose cowboy who points his Stetson at feisty schoolteacher Catherine Elizabeth Allen (Martha Scott). Problem is, the purdy schoolmarm has also attracted the attentions of ruthless oilman Jim Gardner (Albert Dekker). Wayne ends up working for Gardner, but with qualms. When Gardner makes a play to cheat the local Indians out of their oil rights, Wayne puts his foot down—and the fun begins. Character actor George "Gabby" Hayes teams with Wayne once again and is at his Gabbiest.

ISLAND IN THE SKY*
Featured actors: John Wayne, Lloyd Nolan, Walter Abel, James Arness, Andy Devine, Allyn Joslyn, James Lydon (Jimmy Lydon), Harry Carey, Jr., Hal Baylor, Sean McClory, Wally Cassell, Gordon Jones, Frank Fenton, Robert Keys, Sumner Getchell, Regis Toomey, Paul Fix, Jim Dugan, George Chandler, Louis Heydt (Louis Jean Heydt), Bob Steele, Darryl Hickman, Touch Connors (Mike Connors), Carl Switzer (Carl "Alfalfa" Switzer), Cass Gidley, Guy Anderson (Herbert Anderson), and Tony De Mario (Anthony De Mario)
Screenplay by Ernest K. Gann
Based on a novel by Ernest K. Gann
Directed by William A. Wellman
Produced by Wayne-Fellows Productions
Distributed by Warner Bros.
Release date: September 5, 1953

Captain Dooley (John Wayne) and the crew of a C-47 Skytrain transport plane crash-land in remote northeastern Canada in foul weather. There's little for them to do but wait for a rescue that may never come. The suspense is palpable, but would the producers really let John

Wayne die in the frozen wilderness? Well, maybe. As is so often the case in Duke's films of the 1940s and '50s, the supporting cast is stellar: Lloyd Nolan, James Arness, Harry Carey, Jr., Paul Fix, Louis Heydt, and Andy Devine. It even has Carl "Alfalfa" Switzer, from the old *Our Gang* series in the almost-not-there role of Lloyd Nolan's copilot. *Island in the Sky* is worth watching, but not quite up to the standards of "best of."

JET PILOT
Featured actors: John Wayne, Janet Leigh, Jay C. Flippen, Paul Fix, Richard Rober, Roland Winters, Hans Conried, and Ivan Triesault
Screenplay by Jules Furthman
Directed by Josef von Sternberg
Produced and distributed by RKO Radio Pictures
Release date: September 23, 1957

The story revolves around Colonel Jim Shannon (John Wayne), Air Force pilot and Alaska base commander. When his second-in-command forces down a Russian pilot over U.S. territory, they're all surprised to find it's a stunning and shapely woman. Once the men have slowed their heavy breathing for a minute, Anna Marladovna (Janet Leigh) announces she wants to defect. Wayne's dubious superiors command Wayne to seduce her so he can get into her head (and perhaps her pants) to learn if she's a spy. The sexual banter between Wayne and Leigh is fun, frequently hokey, and at times so outdated ("You sure are the Peruvian doughnuts!") that viewers today may not have a clue what they're talking about. *Jet Pilot* is an anti-Communist romance with a fair dose of drama, but not a film to be taken seriously. Supporting actors worth singling out: Jay C. Flippen, the always delightful Hans Conried, and Paul Fix.

KING OF THE PECOS
Featured actors: John Wayne, Muriel Evans, Cy Kendall, Jack Clifford (Jack Rube Clifford), Arthur Aylsworth (Arthur Aylesworth), Herbert Heywood, Frank Glendon (J. Frank Glendon), Edward Hearn, John Beck, Mary MacLaren, Bradley Metcalfe, and Yakima Canutt
Screenplay by Bernard McConville, Dorrell McGowan, and Stuart McGowan (Stuart E. McGowan)
Original story by Bernard McConville
Directed by Joseph Kane
Produced and distributed by Republic Pictures
Release date: March 9, 1936

John Clayborn's parents are gunned down by the land-grabbing son of a bitch Alexander "Salamander" Stiles, whose goal is to grab up the water rights to the Texas Pecos country and thereby control all the smaller ranchers. Fast-forward twenty years, and here comes the older John Clayborn (John Wayne), now calling himself John Clay. Clay is a full-fledged lawyer determined to fight for the ranchers and deal a blow against the evil land baron Stiles. The beginnings of a more mature John Wayne are starting to be apparent—a sense of becoming "John Wayne," though by no means yet the actor we will recognize in another five or ten years.

LADY AND GENT

Featured actors: George Bancroft, Wynne Gibson, Charles Starrett, James Gleason, John Wayne, Morgan Wallace, Billy Butts, and Joyce Compton
Written by Grover Jones and William Slavens McNutt
Directed by Stephen Roberts
Produced and distributed by Paramount Pictures
Release date: July 15, 1932

Buzz Kinney (John Wayne, in an uncharacteristic role) is an up-and-coming boxer who derails the career of veteran fighter Slag Bailey (George Bancroft) when he unexpectedly KO's the champ. Bailey and his saloon-keeper mistress end up raising the orphaned son of Bailey's late manager while Bailey ekes out a living in a steel mill, with occasional boxing bouts to earn some spare change. Late in the film, Bailey runs into Buzz Kinney again. Kinney is now on the skids in Palookaville, a punch-drunk pug and a personification of the perils of the prize ring. I'd recommend this film only for the most hardened Wayne enthusiasts, because Duke is largely absent, and what little dialogue he has is inconsequential. The movie itself, though, and leading man George Bancroft in particular, have a Depression-era appeal.

LADY FOR A NIGHT

Featured actors: Joan Blondell, John Wayne, Philip Merivale, Blanche Yurka, Ray Middleton, Edith Barrett, Leonid Kinskey, Hattie Noel, Montagu Love, Carmel Myers, Dorothy Burgess, Guy Usher, Ivan Miller, Patricia Knox, Lew Payton, Marilyn Hare, and the Hall Johnson Choir
Screenplay by Isabel Dawn and Boyce DeGaw
Based on a story by Garrett Fort
Directed by Leigh Jason
Produced and distributed by Republic Pictures
Release date: January 5, 1942

Jenny Blake (Joan Blondell) runs the *Memphis Belle* riverboat gambling den in cahoots with Jackson Morgan (John Wayne, playing against type as a playboy and conniver). When she is publicly humiliated by Memphis high society, she aims to get her revenge by marrying dipsomaniacal aristo Alan Alderson (Ray Middleton) to live in his mansion and flaunt his vaunted surname. Wayne doesn't take the move lying down, though, because he believes Jenny and he are meant to get hitched and be content to live on "the other side of town." Like some Wayne flicks of this period (especially *Seven Sinners* and *The Shepherd of the Hills*), it's a fun movie, but Wayne is secondary to his costars and the plot.

LADY FROM LOUISIANA
Featured actors: John Wayne, Ona Munson, Ray Middleton, Henry Stephenson, Helen Westley, Jack Pennick, Dorothy Dandridge, Shimen Ruskin, Jacqueline Dalya, Paul Scardon, Major James H. McNamara, James C. Morton, and Maurice Costello
Screenplay by Vera Caspary, Michael Hogan, and Guy Endore
Original story by Edward James and Francis Faragoh (Francis Edward Faragoh)
Directed by Bernard Vorhaus
Produced and distributed by Republic Pictures
Release date: April 22, 1941

New England attorney John Reynolds (John Wayne) is summoned by the honest folks of New Orleans to investigate a corrupt lottery operator. En route to N'Awlins by steamboat, Reynolds, representing the Anti-Lottery League, is captivated by Julie Mirbeau (Ona Munson), a lovely Southern belle—who just happens to be the daughter of the crook in question. Mere chance? At first entranced by the joys of the uninhibited city and the vivaciousness of his beautiful new girlfriend, Wayne soon senses that the concerns of the citizenry are correct. He renews his efforts to expose the criminal enterprise, but can he do that while still in love with Mlle. Mirbeau? *Quel dilemme!* While not a loser, *Lady from Louisiana* is inferior to other Wayne films of this era.

A LADY TAKES A CHANCE*
Featured actors: Jean Arthur, John Wayne, Charles Winninger, Phil Silvers, Mary Field, and Don Costello
Screenplay by Robert Ardrey
Original story by Jo Swerling
Directed by William A. Seiter
Produced by Frank Ross Productions
Distributed by RKO Radio Productions
Release date: August 19, 1943

Molly J. Truesdale (Jean Arthur) escapes her male admirers in New York City by taking a bus tour of "the West" in this romantic comedy. Molly meets broncobuster Duke Hudkins (John Wayne) at a rodeo and becomes deeply involved with his wacky group of misfits. Here Wayne is a fully formed handsome leading man, not just a cardboard cowboy. A comical bar fight ensues—a plot device that would become a recurring element in Wayne's later films, as you will note. Jean Arthur is charming and witty, and has some of the movie's best lines. Phil Silvers provides some laughs as the fast-talking tour guide.

THE LAWLESS FRONTIER

Featured actors: John Wayne, Sheila Terry, Jack Rockwell, George Hayes (George "Gabby" Hayes), Buffalo Bill, Jr. (Jay Wilsey), Yakima Canutt, Bud Wood (Gordon De Main), and Earl Dwire
Screenplay and story by R. N. Bradbury (Robert N. Bradbury)
Directed by R. N. Bradbury (Robert N. Bradbury)
Produced and distributed by Monogram Pictures (as Lone Star Productions)
Release date: November 22, 1934

John Tobin (John Wayne) arrives too late to save his rancher father from being murdered in his bed by notorious sidewinder and hoss thief Pandro Zanti ("half white and half Apache Indian," according to the wanted posters), but vows to search the wide world over, or at least the back lot of Monogram's Lone Star Productions, to find the killer. Wayne finally nabs the bad'un, only to be arrested for a crime he didn't commit while that hornswoggler Pandro makes trails. A good actioner, but unfortunately Wayne rarely rises above being a mere cowboy cutout in a white Stetson.

THE LAWLESS NINETIES

Featured actors: John Wayne, Ann Rutherford, Harry Woods, George Hayes (George "Gabby" Hayes), Al Bridge, Snowflake (Fred "Snowflake" Toones), Etta McDaniel, Tom Brower, Lane Chandler, Cliff Lyons, Jack Rockwell, Al Taylor, Charles King, George Cheseboro, Tracy Layne, Chuck Baldra, Sam Flint, and Tom London
Screenplay by Joseph Poland (Joseph F. Poland)
Original story by Joseph Poland (Joseph F. Poland) and Scott Pembroke
Directed by Joseph Kane
Produced and distributed by Republic Pictures
Release date: February 15, 1936

Another Republic Pictures production, a nice switch from the earlier Lone Star movies. Set in 1890 Wyoming, as the territory seeks statehood, a bloodthirsty opposition gang terrorizes the homesteaders who are in favor of joining the Union. John Tipton (John Wayne) is sent by the federal government to his native Wyoming to ensure that the statehood vote is carried out despite the bad guys' efforts to prevent it. Gunfights and horseback chases abound, but there's no logical explanation for the anti-statehood motivations. All in all, a so-so horse opera.

LAWLESS RANGE

Featured actors: John Wayne, Sheila Mannors (Sheila Bromley), Frank McGlynn, Jr., Jack Curtis, Wally Howe, Julia Griffith, Yakima Canutt, and Earl Dwire
Screenplay and story by Lindsley Parsons

Directed by R. N. Bradbury (Robert N. Bradbury)
Produced and distributed by Republic Pictures
Release date: November 4, 1935

John Middleton (John Wayne) is out to win the Cheyenne Rodeo but must give up that dream to aid his father's best friend, who's in deep trouble from evildoers trying to drive the ranchers out of Poqueno Valley. With help from the marshal of Elk City, Middleton masquerades as an outlaw to infiltrate the gang that is terrorizing the valley's settlers. As part of his strategy (apparently), Middleton rides across the prairie with a guitar, lip-synching his heart out. When Middleton discovers that the bad guys have put up a blockade aimed at stopping supplies to the ranchers in the valley, well, hell, he goes to work! And we go to sleep.

LEGEND OF THE LOST*
Featured actors: John Wayne, Sophia Loren, Rossano Brazzi, Kurt Kasznar, Sonia Moser, Angela Portaluri, and Ibrahim El Hadish
Screenplay by Robert Presnell, Jr., and Ben Hecht
Directed by Henry Hathaway
Produced by Batjac Productions/Dear Film Productions
Distributed by United Artists
Release date: December 17, 1957

John Wayne is Joe January, scoundrel, layabout, and expert guide to the Sahara. January agrees to lead a mysterious Frenchman, Paul Bonnard (Rossano Brazzi), on a ten-week quest deep into the desert in search of lost treasure. Accompanying the duo is Dita (Sophia Loren), a notorious thief, prostitute, and independent-minded cynic who has nothing to lose by the adventure ahead. Loren is at her most captivating, Brazzi lends an appealing earnestness to the plot, and Duke is at his Dukiest—brawny, contrarian, and with a mind and mouth all his own. The vast desert setting (filmed in Libya) is a visual spectacle of a backdrop.

THE LIFE OF JIMMY DOLAN
Featured actors: Douglas Fairbanks, Jr., Loretta Young, Aline MacMahon, Guy Kibbee, Lyle Talbot, Fifi Dorsay (Fifi D'Orsay), Harold Huber, Shirley Grey, George Meeker, John Wayne, and Arthur Hohl
Screenplay by David Boehm and Erwin Gelsey
Based on a play by Bertram Millhauser (Bertram Milhauser) and Beulah Marie Dix
Directed by Archie Mayo
Produced and distributed by Warner Bros.
Release date: June 13, 1933

Billed tenth, John Wayne is an afterthought in this boxing movie. Douglas Fairbanks, Jr., leads the cast as up-and-coming pugilist Jimmy Dolan, who presents himself to the public as a Boy Scout in boxing trunks but who is a heavy boozer and skirt chaser. At a wild drinking party, Dolan may or may not have drunkenly killed a reporter who threatened him. The boxer's pal and girlfriend drive the still-unconscious Dolan back to his training camp, where they steal his wallet and wristwatch. The couple then die in a fiery car crash as they attempt to skip town. Because Dolan's telltale belongings are found in the burned-out remains, the authorities assume Dolan died in the accident. That sets Dolan free to shed his cynical past and discover the better angels of American culture as he adopts a new identity—and a more accepting and generous nature. Sounds like Preston Sturges or Frank Capra should have helmed, although Archie Mayo does a workmanlike job in the director's chair. Wayne doesn't even enter the film until about 1:02:00 from the start, at which point we see him as a junior boxer, nervous about his big match. This doesn't really qualify as a "John Wayne" movie, and it's surprising that he took such a minor role at this stage in his career, making *The Life of Jimmy Dolan* one of the biggest wastes of movie talent in the year 1933.

THE LONE STAR RANGER

Featured actors: George O'Brien, Sue Carol, Walter McGrail, Warren Hymer, Russell Simpson, and Roy Stewart
Dialogue and scenario by John Hunter Booth and Seton I. Miller
Based on a novel by Zane Grey
Directed by A. F. Erickson
Produced and distributed by Fox Film Corporation
Release date: January 5, 1930

Buck Duane (George O'Brien), falsely accused of murder, flees town to join the Texas Rangers. If he can prove his honesty and dedication to law and order, he may be able to clear his name. Duane is ordered to track down a gang of cattle thieves and stop their rampaging. But Duane faces a dilemma: He discovers that the rustlers are being led by none other than the father of the girl he loves. His quandary? Since he's already accused of a crime, why should he sacrifice his newfound love for the sake of a justice system that has forsaken him? John Wayne is a stunt double, extra, and prop man in this B Western.

THE LONELY TRAIL

Featured actors: John Wayne, Ann Rutherford, Cy Kendall, Bob Kortman, Snowflake (Fred "Snowflake" Toones), Sam Flint, Denny Meadows (Dennis Moore), Jim Toney, Etta McDaniels (Etta McDaniel), Yakima Canutt, Lloyd Ingraham, James Marcus (James A. Marcus), Bob Burns, Rodney Hildebrand, Eugene Jackson, and Floyd Shackelford
Screenplay by Bernard McConville and Jack Natteford
Original story by Bernard McConville

Directed by Joseph Kane
Produced and distributed by Republic Pictures
Release date: May 25, 1936

John Wayne is John Ashley, an ex–Union soldier who returns to his home in Texas after the war only to find his hometown in distress. Carpetbaggers from up North are threatening to confiscate his family's farm for a pittance in back taxes. But it's not just Ashley's farm that's in danger; the entire town is being bled dry by the evil Yankee superintendent Benedict Holden and his troops. Ashley and his buddy, Jed Calicutt (Jim Toney), go undercover in hope of aiding their fellow Southerners and giving Holden a taste of his own medicine. When Ashley and Calicutt are captured, they face almost certain doom. Ho hum.

THE LONG VOYAGE HOME*

Featured actors: John Wayne, Barry Fitzgerald, Thomas Mitchell, Ian Hunter, John Qualen, Ward Bond, Wilfred Lawson (Wilfrid Lawson), Mildred Natwick, Arthur Shields, Joseph Sawyer (Joe Sawyer), J. M. Kerrigan, Rafaela Ottiano, and Carmen Morales
Based on four sea plays by Eugene O'Neill
Adaptation by Dudley Nichols
Directed by John Ford
Produced by Argosy Corporation/Walter Wanger Productions
Distributed by Masterpiece Productions
Release date: October 8, 1940

The opening credits are enough to excite a film buff, considering that John Wayne's costars include the always delightful Thomas Mitchell; the Auld Sod incarnate his blessed self, Barry Fitzgerald; the man with the memorable mug, Joe Sawyer; John Qualen; and Wayne's frequent acting pal, Western icon Ward Bond. The icing on the screen-credit cake is the director, John Ford. The trouble, from a fan's point of view, is that *The Long Voyage Home* is an ensemble performance, not a Duke Wayne star turn. One might reasonably ask why Wayne was given star billing, considering that he has far fewer lines and less screen time than Mitchell or Fitzgerald. Nonetheless, the film is interesting in its own right. The tale is of the merchant ship *Glencairn* on a dangerous mission in the early days of World War II. The plot delves into the lives of the international crew, a bunch of rootless men adrift, literally and figuratively, on an ocean of ennui, doubt, and fear.

THE LONGEST DAY*

Note: All credits appear at the end of the film.
Featured actors: Eddie Albert, Paul Anka, Arletty, Jean-Louis Barrault, Richard Beymer, Hans Christian Blech, Bourvil, Richard Burton, Wolfgang Büttner, Red Buttons, Pauline Carton, Sean Connery, Ray Danton, Irina Demich (Irina Demick), Fred Dur,

Fabian, Mel Ferrer, Henry Fonda, Steve Forrest, Gert Fröbe, Leo Genn, John Gregson, Paul Hartmann, Peter Helm, Werner Hinz, Donald Houston, Jeff Hunter (Jeffrey Hunter), Karl John, Curt Jürgens (Curd Jürgens), Alexander Knox, Peter Lawford, Fernand Ledoux, Christian Marquand, Dewey Martin, Roddy McDowall, Michael Medwin, Sal Mineo, Robert Mitchum, Kenneth More, Richard Münch, Edmond O'Brien, Leslie Phillips, Wolfgang Preiss, Ron Randell, Madeleine Renaud, Georges Riviere (Georges Rivière), Norman Rossington, Robert Ryan, Tommy Sands, George Segal, Jean Servais, Rod Steiger, Richard Todd, Tom Tryon, Peter van Eyck, Robert Wagner, Richard Wattis, Stuart Whitman, Georges Wilson, and John Wayne
Screenplay by Cornelius Ryan, with additional episodes by Romain Gary, James Jones, David Pursall, and Jack Seddon
Based on a book by Cornelius Ryan
Directed by Ken Annakin (British exterior episodes), Andrew Marton (American exterior episodes), and Bernhard Wicki (Bernard Wicki) (German episodes)
Produced by Darryl F. Zanuck Productions/Twentieth Century–Fox
Distributed by Twentieth Century–Fox
Release date: October 3, 1962

Arguably, *The Longest Day* is the ultimate film about D-Day, the 1944 Allied invasion of German-held France and the turning point of World War II. Go ahead and mention *Saving Private Ryan*, but *The Longest Day* is a broad overview of the events as they unfolded, from the viewpoint of the American paratroopers, the British sailors, the German officers, the French Resistance, and almost anyone else who was involved. No film about these events has managed to capture the breadth of the story and characters who made it happen as has *The Longest Day*. This is not strictly a John Wayne movie, though; the film features almost every significant actor in the early 1960s. Wayne's screen time is necessarily limited, considering the large and impressive cast. But he has a major role, especially in the first sixty minutes of this nearly three-hour flick. Wayne plays paratrooper Colonel Benjamin "Van" Vandervoort, who must prepare his men to parachute behind the Nazi lines. Wayne is a treat, no doubt, but the main reason to watch *The Longest Day* is that it is a sprawling epic, acted to perfection by a brilliant cast.

THE LUCKY TEXAN
Featured actors: John Wayne, Barbara Sheldon, Lloyd Whitlock, George Hayes (George "Gabby" Hayes), Yakima Canutt, Ed Parker (Eddie Parker), Gordon Demaine (Gordon De Main), and Earl `Dwire
Screenplay and story by Robert N. Bradbury

Directed by Robert N. Bradbury
Produced and distributed by Monogram Pictures (as Lone Star
Productions)
Release date: January 21, 1934

Jerry Mason (John Wayne) and old-timer Jake Benson (George Hayes) discover gold, Mason discovers Benson's beautiful granddaughter, the bad guys discover the goldfield, and we discover we'll never get back that 54:25 we invested in watching this cow-pie drivel. It's not all bad, though: An early film appearance by Hayes adds some sparkle to the proceedings, and Earl Dwire and Yakima Canutt are fun to watch as the bad guys going after Jake and Jerry's fortune.

McLINTOCK!+

Featured actors: John Wayne, Maureen O'Hara, Patrick Wayne,
Stefanie Powers, Jack Kruschen, Chill Wills, Yvonne De Carlo, Jerry
Van Dyke, Edgar Buchanan, Bruce Cabot, Perry Lopez, Strother
Martin, Gordon Jones, Robert Lowery, Hank Worden, Michael Pate,
Edward Faulkner, Mari Blanchard, Leo Gordon, Chuck Roberson,
Bob Steele, Aissa Wayne, and "Big" John Hamilton
Screenplay by James Edward Grant
Directed by Andrew V. McLaglen
Produced by Batjac Productions
Distributed by United Artists
Release date: November 13, 1963

The setting is the Western territories in the late 1800s. Wayne is George Washington "G.W." McLintock, a widely respected cattle baron who must deal with the social upheaval all around him. Settlers are coming in droves to farm the land where cattle have long grazed. The promise of statehood is threatened by petty disagreements among the residents. And to top it off, G.W.'s estranged (and demanding) wife, Kitty (Maureen O'Hara), has returned to the ranch after tasting the good life back East and in Europe. Cranky but good-humored, tough as rawhide but capable of love, McLintock is a put-upon man who finds himself in the role of lawgiver, embattled husband, and hardworking businessman, when all he wants to do is ride the range and drink whiskey. The script by James Edward Grant is full of delicious quotes from Wayne and his fellow cast members. As with so many of Wayne's midcareer and mature pictures, he is supported by a team of first-rate backup players, including regulars like Hank Worden, Bruce Cabot, Strother Martin, Edgar Buchanan, Patrick Wayne, and Chill Wills, plus Jerry Van Dyke, Stefanie Powers, and Yvonne "Lily Munster" De Carlo.

McQ

Featured actors: John Wayne, Eddie Albert, Diana Muldaur, Colleen
Dewhurst, Clu Gulager, David Huddleston, Jim Watkins (Julian

Christopher), Al Lettieri, Julie Adams, Roger E. Mosley, William
Bryant, Joe Tornatore, Richard Kelton, Dick Friel, Richard Eastham,
and Fred Waugh
Screenplay by Lawrence Roman
Directed by John Sturges
Produced by Batjac Productions and Levy-Gardner
Distributed by Warner Bros.
Release date: January 15, 1974

Seattle cop Lon McQ (John Wayne) tries to bring down the hoods who killed his buddy. But there's more: McQ is determined to smash a corrupt police department that is dealing in confiscated drugs. It's a Wayne-plays-Kojak film, complete with "funky" soundtrack. The direction throughout is strictly 1970s Movie of the Week caliber. There isn't a lot of strong acting support, either (notable exceptions are Eddie Albert, Clu Gulager, Colleen Dewhurst, and David Huddleston), but even if there had been, it probably wouldn't have helped this turkey.

MAKER OF MEN
Featured actors: Jack Holt, Joan Marsh, and Richard Cromwell
Screenplay by Howard J. Green
Story by Howard J. Green and Edward Sedgwick
Directed by Edward Sedgwick
Produced and distributed by Columbia Pictures
Release date: December 18, 1931

Bob Dudley (Richard Cromwell) makes it onto the Western University varsity football squad, but only because his father (Jack Holt) is the head coach. Bob is actually scared to death of physical contact, and as a result, fumbles the ball in a big game, putting his father's coaching job in jeopardy. The rest of the team thinks Dudley is nothing more than a wimp, so he leaves Western and enrolls at Monroe College, where he joins the football squad. Soon Dudley returns to Western, but this time to play against his former school in a gridiron match. John Wayne has a minor role as Dusty Rhodes, one of the football players at Western U. He has a few inoffensive lines, but nothing memorable. A very young Ward Bond has an unbilled bit part as a teammate.

A MAN BETRAYED
Featured actors: John Wayne, Frances Dee, Edward Ellis, Wallace
Ford, Ward Bond, Harold Huber, Alexander Granach, Barnett Parker,
Ed Stanley (Edwin Stanley), Tim Ryan, Harry Hayden, Russell Hicks,
Pierre Watkin, and Ferris Taylor
Screenplay by Isabel Dawn
Original story by Jack Moffitt
Adaptation by Tom Kilpatrick
Directed by John H. Auer

Produced and distributed by Republic Pictures
Release date: February 27, 1941

Small-town lawyer Lynn Hollister (John Wayne) treks to the Big City
to prove that a young athlete from his hometown didn't commit suicide,
but was murdered. The action centers on the Club Inferno ("40 Beautiful
Girls, 39 Beautiful Costumes"), where the young man had been cheated at
the gambling table before his death. But when Hollister becomes involved
with the behind-the-scenes crime boss and Sabra, his beautiful daughter
(Frances Dee), he begins to lose sight of his noble quest. If he returns to his
goal of solving the crime, he risks losing the love of Sabra, who is fiercely
loyal to her criminal father. It's fun seeing Wayne in a big-city flick wearing double-breasted suits—not his normal milieu, but amusing.

THE MAN FROM MONTEREY
*Featured actors: John Wayne, Duke the Horse, Ruth Hall, Luis
Alberni, Donald Reed, Nena Quartero (Nina Quartero), Francis Ford,
Lafe McKee, Lillian Leighton, and Charles Whitaker (Slim Whitaker)*
Screenplay and dialogue by Lesley Mason (Leslie Mason)
Directed by Mack V. Wright
*Produced by Leon Schlesinger Studios/Warner Bros. (as A Four Star
Western)*
Distributed by Warner Bros. (as Vitagraph, Inc.)
Release date: August 16, 1933

Midwestern actors portraying Spanish ladies and gents in Old California
is only one of several reasons to give this dud a miss. The year is 1848. The
place is California, just as the then-territory prepares for statehood. Ten-
sions run high between the Mexican landowners and the new American
administrators. Enter John Wayne as Captain John Holmes, a U.S. cavalry officer charged with getting the rancheros to register their properties.
Dolores Castanares, the daughter of a large landowner, falls in love with
the handsome cavalry captain. Subterfuge and skullduggery combine to
prevent Dolores's father from registering his rancho—unless Holmes and
his outlaw friend can come to the rescue. Hilarity and hijinks do *not* ensue
in this plodding effort.

THE MAN FROM UTAH
*Featured actors: John Wayne, Polly Ann Young, Anita Compillo (Anita
Campillo), Edward Peil (Edward Peil, Sr.), George Hayes (George
"Gabby" Hayes), Yakima Canutt, and George Cleveland*
Screenplay and story by Lindsley Parsons
Directed by Robert Bradbury (Robert N. Bradbury)
*Produced and distributed by Monogram Pictures (as Lone Star
Productions)*
Release date: May 15, 1934

John Weston (John Wayne) is a lip-synching cowpoke who rides into
town just in time to assist Marshal Higgins (George Hayes) in a gun bat-

tle with a trio of crooks. Higgins immediately deputizes Weston to help clean up the town. Higgins assigns Weston to join the rodeo to unmask a gang of con men who have rigged the otherwise honest rodeo gambling industry. Weston is a straight shooter who might as well be wearing a black suit and white collar as opposed to his Western duds. Speaking of duds, this churn-'em-out stirrups-and-spurs saga is a dud indeed.

THE MAN WHO SHOT LIBERTY VALANCE+

Featured actors: John Wayne, James Stewart, Vera Miles, Lee Marvin, Edmond O'Brien, Andy Devine, Ken Murray, John Carradine, Jeanette Nolan, John Qualen, Willis Bouchey, Carleton Young, Woody Strode, Denver Pyle, Strother Martin, Lee Van Cleef, Robert F. Simon, O. Z. Whitehead, Paul Birch, and Joseph Hoover
Screenplay by James Warner Bellah and Willis Goldbeck
Based on a story by Dorothy M. Johnson
Directed by John Ford
Produced by John Ford Productions
Distributed by Paramount Pictures
Release date: April 11, 1962

Senator Ransom Stoddard (James Stewart) returns by train to Shinbone, the town where he earned his reputation, for the burial of his old friend and benefactor Tom Doniphon (John Wayne). There he recalls his arrival some forty years earlier, bereft of all he owned, apart from a few law books, after being robbed on the incoming stage. The rest of the film is a flashback to the time when Doniphon, an old desert warhorse, instructs the young Stoddard in the art of staying alive. Lee Marvin is exquisite playing the bad guy, Liberty Valance, who focuses all his evil on the young lawyer. Vera Miles is the love interest. Edmond O'Brien does a star turn as the drunken editor of *The Shinbone Star*. *The Man Who Shot Liberty Valance* is one of the finest Westerns ever filmed, and not just because it was the movie in which John Wayne first used the word "pilgrim." True, it's Stewart's movie, but Wayne is superlative as Tom Doniphon. He's at the height of his acting abilities, and brilliant as the film's conscience. His presence looms large even when he's not on-screen. Wayne and Stewart team up with a supporting cast that is mind-numbingly superb, including such ace veterans as Andy Devine, John Carradine, John Qualen, the awesome Woody Strode, Western stalwart Denver Pyle, Lee Van Cleef, Willis Bouchey, and Strother Martin. If Ward Bond had still been alive, he probably would have been there, too.

MEN ARE LIKE THAT
See ARIZONA

MEN WITHOUT WOMEN

Featured actors: Kenneth MacKenna, Frank Albertson, Farrell MacDonald (J. Farrell MacDonald), Warren Hymer, Paul Page, Walter McGrail, Stuart Erwin, George LeGuere, Charles Gerrard

(*Charles K. Gerrard*), *Ben Hendricks, Jr., Harry Tenbrook, and Warner Richmond*
Screenplay and scenario by Dudley Nichols
Titles by Otis C. Freeman
Story by John Ford and James Kevin McGuinness
Directed by John Ford
Produced and distributed by Fox Film Corporation
Release date: January 31, 1930

A desperate submarine crew rests at the bottom of the sea after an accident, but there's little hope of rescue. While a reluctant young ensign assumes command of the terrified submariners, a seasoned chief petty officer attempts to ration the oxygen and calm the men as they wait for uncertain deliverance. John Wayne is an extra in this (mostly) silent movie, but can be seen aboard the British ship searching for the damaged sub. Viewers will find wonderful tension in this sea play, thanks to director John Ford.

MOTHER MACHREE

Featured actors: Belle Bennett, Neil Hamilton, Philippe De Lacy, Pat Somerset, Victor McLaglen, Ted McNamara, John MacSweeney, Eulalie Jensen, Constance Howard, Ethel Clayton, William Platt, Jacques Rollens, Rodney Hildebrand, Joyce Wirard, and Robert Parrish
Titles by Katharine Hilliker (Katherine Hilliker) and H. H. Caldwell
Scenario by Gertrude Orr
Based on a story by Rida Johnson Young
Directed by John Ford (uncredited)
Produced and distributed by Fox Film Corporation
Release date: January 22, 1928

In 1800s Ireland, Ellen McHugh loses her fisherman husband to a storm at sea. Deciding that their future would be improved by emigrating to America, Ellen crosses the Atlantic with her son, Brian, in search of a better life. In the new world, Ellen meets an Irish trio she knew in the old country. They invite her to join a circus sideshow, a job that pays the bills but is far outside the mainstream of society. Soon, her new profession raises questions about her fitness as a parent. Brian is adopted by his school principal and grows into an educated gentleman, believing that the woman who raised him is dead. Will mother and son ever reconnect? John Wayne is supposedly in there, somewhere. This is a lost film.

'NEATH THE ARIZONA SKIES*

Featured actors: John Wayne, Sheila Terry, Shirley Jane Rickert (Shirley Jean Rickert), Jack Rockwell, Yakima Canutt, Weston Edwards, Buffalo Bill, Jr. (Jay Wilsey), and Phil Keefer (Philip Kiefer)
Screenplay and story by Burl Tuttle (Burl R. Tuttle)

Directed by Harry Fraser (Harry L. Fraser)
Produced and distributed by Monogram Pictures (as Lone Star
Productions)
Release date: December 5, 1934

Chris Morrell (John Wayne) is a foster father to a half-Indian girl who is the potential heir to a small fortune from her dead mother's oil lease. Wayne takes the girl in search of her father, who must sign the papers so she can get her money. Meantime, the bad guys are convinced that if they grab the girl, they can get their hands on the dough. The plot is a bit far-fetched, but the acting and dialogue are a huge improvement over Wayne's previous Lone Star efforts. The fact that a new director and scripter (Harry Fraser and Burl Tuttle, respectively) have organized the flick may be a big reason why. George "Gabby" Hayes, Duke's frequent costar in the 1930s, plays a good-hearted old coot, and could hardly be more Gabbyish. Yakima Canutt is back as a bad guy, but as usual, he's too nice 'n' mild to be a believable evildoer.

NEW FRONTIER
Featured actors: John Wayne, Ray Corrigan, Raymond Hatton,
Phylis Isley (Jennifer Jones), Eddy Waller, Sammy McKim, LeRoy
Mason, Harrison Greene, Reginald Barlow, Burr Caruth, Dave
O'Brien, Hal Price, Jack Ingram, Bud Osborne, and Charles Whitaker
(Slim Whitaker)
Screenplay by Betty Burbridge and Luci Ward
Based on characters created by William Colt MacDonald
Directed by George Sherman
Produced and distributed by Republic Pictures
Release date: August 10, 1939

New Frontier is the last of John Wayne's roles in the *Three Mesquiteers* series. Wayne, as Stony Brooke, and his two compañeros, Tucson and Rusty (hey, what the hell happened to Lullaby Joslin from the earlier films in this series?!), find themselves in a war over water. The state wants to condemn the settlement of New Hope Valley to build a reservoir. At first, the local ranchers refuse to give up their homes and are willing to fight to the death. But then the settlers accept an offer from a city slicker to give up their lands in New Hope for twice as much property in . . . Devil's Acres (cue kettledrums). The film has its moments and a fair-to-middlin' plot.

THE NEW FRONTIER*
Featured actors: John Wayne, Muriel Evans, Warner Richmond, Alan
Bridge (Al Bridge), Sam Flint, Murdock MacQuarrie, Allan Cavan,
Mary MaClaren (Mary MacLaren), Theodore Loren (Theodore Lorch),
Glen Strange (Glenn Strange), Phil Keefer (Philip Kieffer), Frank Ball,
and Jack Montgomery

Screenplay and story by Robert Emmett (Robert Emmett Tansey)
Directed by Carl L. Pierson (Carl Pierson)
Produced and distributed by Republic Pictures
Release date: October 5, 1935

Don't confuse this with *New Frontier*, a substandard film. It's 1889 and Oklahoma is up for grabs by presidential decree. Wagon-train guide John Dawson (John Wayne) leaves the former Indian Territory to lead a party of Kansas pilgrims back to the new promised land. Meantime, his father, still in Oklahoma, is murdered by a gunslinger who works for the evil saloon owner. On his return, Wayne agrees to take the sheriff's badge and rid the good citizens of the satanic, murdering bar owner. Curiosity: Pay attention to the splendid snowy mountains of Kansas in the early scenes—mountains of which, in reality, Kansas has . . . none. While not a great John Wayne movie, it's far less hokey than many others from this period, and the underlying (and unexpectedly mature) theme of spiritual redemption adds to its watchability.

THE NIGHT RIDERS

Featured actors: John Wayne, Ray Corrigan, Max Terhune, Doreen McKay, Ruth Rogers, George Douglas, Tom Tyler, Kermit Maynard, Sammy McKim, Walter Wills, Ethan Laidlaw, Edward Peil, Sr., Tom London, Jack Ingram, and William Nestell (Bill Nestell)
Screenplay by Betty Burbridge and Stanley Roberts
Based on characters created by William Colt MacDonald
Directed by George Sherman
Produced and distributed by Republic Pictures
Release date: April 12, 1939

When a forger and a con man partner up to steal three million acres from the region's honest ranchers, the Three Mesquiteers go to work. They form a vigilante group, Los Capaqueros, to take from the bad guys and give to the poor. The evildoers raise a militia to fight the good guys, and the good guys join the militia—in essence, chasing themselves. This egregious equine epic has the boys wearing KKK-like hoods and capes, which is bad enough, but to think that this loser was released after Duke's strong turn in *Stagecoach* is just plain sad.

NOAH'S ARK

Featured actors: Dolores Costello, George O'Brien, Noah Beery, Louise Fazenda, Gwynn Williams (Guinn "Big Boy" Williams), Paul McAllister, Myrna Loy, Anders Randolf, Armand Kaliz, William V. Mong, Malcolm Waite, Nigel De Brulier, Noble Johnson, and Otto Hoffman
Titles by De Leon Anthony
Story by Darryl Francis Zanuck (Darryl F. Zanuck)
Adaptation by Anthony Coldewey (Anthony Coldeway)
Directed by Michael Curtiz

Produced and distributed by Warner Bros.
Release date: November 1, 1928

The Bible story of Noah's Ark is the backdrop of this contemporary tale of World War I. On the eve of the Great War, a group of unlikely individuals (a religious man, a pair of happy-go-lucky Americans, a beautiful German woman, and a mysterious Russian spy) are traveling on the Orient Express when a horrible accident occurs. The Americans, Travis and Al, and the German, Marie, end up in Paris, living the good life before the capital is consumed by the flames of war. Ultimately, Travis marries Marie, both Americans enlist in the Army, and Marie becomes a dancehall floozie showing off her gams in a saloon near the Belgian front. Condemned as a spy, she faces a firing squad that includes (wait for it) Travis, who recognizes her only at the last moment. The comparison of war with the biblical inundation takes the film back to Noah's time and the Flood, which is re-created in frightening detail. John Wayne, among a "cast of thousands," played one of the extras in the flood scene (along with Andy Devine and Ward Bond), which by all accounts resulted in numerous injuries and several deaths. Slow-moving by today's standards, *Noah's Ark* is still a spectacle of interest to cinephiles.

NORTH TO ALASKA
Featured actors: John Wayne, Stewart Granger, Ernie Kovacs,
Fabian, Capucine, Mickey Shaughnessy, Karl Swenson, Joe Sawyer,
Kathleen Freeman, John Qualen, and Stanley Adams
Screenplay by John Lee Mahin, Martin Rackin, and Claude Binyon
Based on a play by Laszlo Fodor (Ladislas Fodor)
From an idea by John Kafka
Directed by Henry Hathaway
Produced and distributed by Twentieth Century–Fox
Release date: November 7, 1960

One of Wayne's "comic" movies—sprawling, with a big setting, yes, but too much of it is played for laughs. Wayne is a prospector in Alaska during the 1898 Gold Rush, with an underused Stewart Granger as his partner, together defending their stake against claim jumpers. The opening includes a bar fight complete with silly sound effects, and, toward the end, a muddy street fight with similar comic sound effects. The scenes are fun, but how are we to take this film seriously?! Wayne is sweet and has a wonderful rapport with his costar, the French actress Capucine. He attempts to set her up with his pal, whose wife has deserted him. But the real love interest is between Wayne and a hooker. Costar Fabian adds little to nothing to the proceedings other than youthful sex appeal.

OPERATION PACIFIC
Featured actors: John Wayne, Patricia Neal, Ward Bond, Scott
Forbes, Philip Carey, Paul Picerni, Bill Campbell (William Campbell),

Kathryn Givney, Martin Milner, Cliff Clark, Jack Pennick, Virginia
Brissac, Vincent Fotre, Lewis Martin, Sam Edwards, and Louis
Mosconi
Screenplay by George Waggner
Directed by George Waggner
Produced and distributed by Warner Bros.
Release date: January 10, 1951

The movie doesn't know what it wants to be—a war drama or a romantic melodrama. John Wayne portrays submarine second-in-command Duke Gifford, wondering why the sub's torpedoes explode short of their mark or fail to explode when they hit their target. Back in Pearl Harbor on shore leave, he woos his ex-wife, Mary Stuart (Patricia Neal), who is falling for the handsome brother (Philip Carey) of Duke's commander (Ward Bond). Between the stock footage and soundstage re-creations, not even the battle scenes elicit much interest. Neal is passionless in the romantic role, Wayne has few if any memorable lines, and the rest of the mostly excellent cast (including Jack Pennick as the Chief) is wasted in this abuse of film stock.

THE OREGON TRAIL

Featured actors: John Wayne, Ann Rutherford, Joe Girard (Joseph W.
Girard), Yakima Canutt, Frank Rice, E. H. Calvert, Ben Hendricks,
Jr., Harry Harvey, Fern Emmett, Jack Rutherford, Marian Ferrell,
Roland Ray, Gino Corrado, Edward LeSaint, and Octavio Giraud
Screenplay by Jack Natteford, Lindsley Parsons, and Robert Emmett
(Robert Emmett Tansey)
Story by Lindsley Parsons and Robert Emmet (Robert Emmett
Tansey)
Directed by Scott Pembroke
Produced and distributed by Republic Pictures
Release date: January 18, 1936

This is a so-called lost film. No known prints exist, only still photographs shot during filming. John Delmont (John Wayne) leads a band of pioneers to California while searching for the man who killed his father. A group of renegade soldiers plot to create a Western empire of their own by attacking incoming wagon trains and stealing their goods. Delmont vows to infiltrate the renegade outpost and make the way safe again for emigrants on the Oregon Trail. Attacking their stronghold, Delmont captures the cannons, turns them on his attackers, and rids the West of the varmints.

OVERLAND STAGE RAIDERS

Featured actors: John Wayne, Ray Corrigan, Max Terhune, Louise
Brooks, Anthony Marsh, Ralph Bowman (John Archer), Gordon
Hart, Roy James, Olin Francis, Fern Emmett, Henry Otho, George

Sherwood, Archie Hall (Arch Hall, Sr.), and Frank La Rue (Frank LaRue)
Screenplay by Luci Ward
Original story by Bernard McConville and Edmond Kelso
Based on characters created by William Colt MacDonald
Directed by George Sherman
Produced and distributed by Republic Pictures
Release date: September 20, 1938

And here it is, the return of the Three Mesquiteers (not that anyone was clamoring for it). The Mesquiteers—Lullaby Joslin (Max Terhune), Tucson Smith (Ray Corrigan), and Stony Brooke (John Wayne)—invest in a fledging airline to help a miner ship his gold by air and thus avoid the robbers on the ground. A highlight is Louise Brooks playing the femme fatale. This horsetail tale is also notable for the clash between eras—in this case, 1870s-style bandidos on horseback robbing a passenger bus carrying the local gold shipment (because, you know, that's how you would ship gold in 1938, right?).

PALS OF THE SADDLE

Featured actors: John Wayne, Ray Corrigan, Max Terhune, Doreen McKay, Josef Forte (Joseph Forte), George Douglas, Frank Milan, Ted Adams, Harry Depp, Dave Weber, Don Orlando, Charles Knight, and Jack Kirk
Screenplay by Stanley Roberts and Betty Burbridge
Based on characters created by William Colt MacDonald
Directed by George Sherman
Produced and distributed by Republic Pictures
Release date: August 2, 1938

Alongside Tucson Smith (Ray Corrigan) and Lullaby Joslin (Max Terhune), John Wayne as Stony Brooke leads the Three Mesquiteers in this sapless saddle scenario from Republic Pictures. Even in the relatively innocent days when this film was made, who would believe that one of the trio (Lullaby) is a ventriloquist who packs his dummy, Elmer, on the boys' adventures? It's . . . just . . . silly. The trio gets mixed up in a government operation to halt the theft of a dangerous chemical called "monium." Stony, playing undercover, gets caught by the bad guys—but can he still thwart the theft of the monium?! Do we care?!

PARADISE CANYON

Featured actors: John Wayne, Marion Burns, Reed Howes, Earle Hodgins, Gino Corrado, Yakima Canutt, Perry Murdock, Gordon Clifford, and Henry Hall
Screenplay by Robert Emmett (Robert Emmett Tansey)
Story by Lindsley Parsons
Directed by Carl L. Pierson (Carl Pierson)

Produced and distributed by Monogram Pictures (as Lone Star Productions)
Release date: July 20, 1935

John Wyatt (John Wayne) is a federal agent attempting to crack a counterfeiting ring in Arizona. Wyatt joins a medicine show to root out the bad guys (who wouldn't?) while falling for the daughter of Doc Carter, the medicine showman. The counterfeiters, we learn, framed Doc Carter for a crime he didn't commit. Part of Carter's mission in operating the medicine show is to track down the counterfeiters and expose them. When Doc Carter & Co. get too close for comfort, the felons vow to do whatever it takes to stop the show. Pretty much as bad as it sounds.

PITTSBURGH
Featured actors: Marlene Dietrich, Randolph Scott, John Wayne, Frank Craven, Louise Allbritton, Shemp Howard, Thomas Gomez, Ludwig Stössel, and Samuel S. Hinds
Screenplay by Kenneth Gamet and Tom Reed
Additional dialogue by John Twist
Original story by George Owen and Tom Reed
Directed by Lewis Seiler
Produced and distributed by Universal Pictures
Release date: November 20, 1942

John Wayne is credited third, after Marlene Dietrich and Randolph Scott, although he has a larger role than you might expect from such billing. Wayne plays "Pittsburgh" Markham, who, along with Cash Evans (Scott), plans to leave the coal mines for a better life. Enter La Dietrich, a glamour puss who, it turns out, is the daughter of a "hunky" (a coal miner). Through sheer chutzpah and a willingness to work hard, Markham and Evans end up big men in the coal game. The trouble, from a fan's point of view, is that Wayne plays a cad, an abusive egomaniac. It's so far off the John Wayne spectrum one hardly knows how to react. A special tip of the Stetson to Shemp Howard of the Three Stooges, who has a minor but memorable part early on as Shorty the tailor.

THE QUIET MAN+
Featured actors: John Wayne, Maureen O'Hara, Barry Fitzgerald, Ward Bond, Victor McLaglen, Mildred Natwick, Francis Ford, Eileen Crowe, May Craig, Arthur Shields, Charles FitzSimons (Charles B. FitzSimons), James Lilburn (James O'Hara), Sean McGlory (Sean McClory), Jack McGowran (Jack MacGowran), Joseph O'Dea, Eric Gorman, Kevin Lawless, and Paddy O'Donnell
Screenplay by Frank S. Nugent
Based on a story by Maurice Walsh
Directed by John Ford

Produced and distributed by Republic Pictures
Release date: August 14, 1952

Sentimental? For sure. A bit too Irish-twilighty? Of course. Superlative? Absolutely! Without putting too fine a point on it, *The Quiet Man* is a highlight of John Wayne's career, one of the best films he ever made, right up there among the best films ever, period. Wayne is Sean "Trooper" Thornton, a prizefighter with a dark secret. To escape his past, he returns to his ancestral home in Ireland, where he meets a stunning (and fiery!) redhead played by Maureen O'Hara, who has never been better. They court, fall in love, and marry, but when O'Hara's brother, played by the fearsome Victor McLaglen, refuses to pay the dowry, Wayne has no choice but to challenge McLaglen to a fight—a sprawling, epic battle that must be one of the greatest duke-outs in filmdom. Not unexpectedly, Wayne's fellow actors get some of the best lines, as when an extra looks at the huge marriage bed of Wayne and O'Hara and says, "A man would have to be a sprinter to catch his wife in a bed like that!" The drop-dead-beautiful Irish countryside should have received an Academy Award for supporting player. All that being said, many of the Irish character portrayals are straight out of a burlesque routine, but it's all done in good fun and with cultural respect.

RAINBOW VALLEY

Featured actors: John Wayne, Lucille Browne (Lucile Brown), George Hayes (George "Gabby" Hayes), LeRoy Mason, Lloyd Ingraham, Buffalo Bill, Jr. (Jay Wilsey), Frank Ball, and Bert Dillard
Story by Lindsley Parsons
Directed by R. N. Bradbury (Robert N. Bradbury)
Produced and distributed by Monogram Pictures (as Lone Star Productions)
Release date: March 12, 1935

The town of Rainbow Valley hires John Martin (John Wayne) to protect road-repair workers from a gang of cutthroats trying to buy out the miners' claims at a cheap price. Martin tries to woo postmistress Eleanor (Lucile Brown), but she finds Martin's he-man attitude a turnoff. Still, there's no one else standing between the town and the villains except Martin. How can Martin do his duty to protect the townsfolk while at the same time win the heart of Eleanor? A flaming bore from beginning to end—except for the always joyful appearance of George "Gabby" Hayes, as the local mailman.

RANDY RIDES ALONE

Featured actors: John Wayne, Alberta Vaughn, George Hayes (George "Gabby" Hayes), Yakima Canutt, Earl Dwire, Arthur Artego (Artie Ortego), and Tex Phelps
Screenplay and story by Lindsley Parsons

Directed by Harry Fraser (Harry L. Fraser)
Produced and distributed by Monogram Pictures (as Lone Star Productions)
Release date: June 15, 1934

Randy Bowers (John Wayne) is arrested and thrown in jail for a brutal crime he didn't commit. The daughter of one of the victims knows that Bowers isn't guilty but has reasons for keeping quiet. How will Bowers ever prove his innocence? After watching this film, viewers might agree that it would have been best just to leave Bowers in the hoosegow. Instead, he is allowed to wander through this cowpoke claptrap, searching desperately for some semblance of a plot. George "Gabby" Hayes, who usually provides some credible acting support in these productions, actually has no speaking role in this film, because he plays a mute. Is there no justice?

THE RANGE FEUD

Featured actors: Buck Jones, John Wayne, Susan Fleming, Ed Le Saint (Edward Le Saint), William Walling (Will Walling), Wallace McDonald (Wallace MacDonald), Harry Woods, and Frank Austin
Dialogue and story by Milton Krims
Directed by D. Ross Lederman
Produced and distributed by Columbia Pictures
Release date: November 22, 1931

This is the third of seven über-dreadful cheapies John Wayne was forced to make under a contract with Columbia (including *Texas Cyclone* and *Two-Fisted Law*, with second-rate cowboy star Tim McCoy, and this one, with the equally inept Buck Jones). Warning: These may be painful to watch. Wayne is cast second to Jones in this no-frills Western. The range war is on between those who want free grazing and those who want fences, the classic cowboy-movie standoff. Clint Turner (Wayne), the son of a prominent rancher, is wrongly accused of murder, attempts to flee, and ends up in the pokey. Will jail prevent him from proving his innocence? Who cares? Not us. This film is the cinematic personification of the old Texas maxim "The bigger the hat, the smaller the spread."

REAP THE WILD WIND

Featured actors: Ray Milland, John Wayne, Paulette Goddard, Raymond Massey, Robert Preston, Susan Hayward, Lynne Overman, Charles Bickford, Walter Hampden, Martha O'Driscoll, Louise Beavers, Elisabeth Risdon, Hedda Hopper, Janet Beecher, and Ben Carter
Screenplay by Alan LeMay, Charles Bennett, and Jesse Lasky, Jr.
Based on a story by Thelma Strabel
Directed by Cecil B. DeMille

Produced and distributed by Paramount Pictures
Release date: March 19, 1942

Duke is in fine company with Ray Milland and Paulette Goddard, but as in many of his early 1940s movies, he simply doesn't have enough to do. Aching to captain a new kind of vessel called a steamship (this is the antebellum South), Wayne woos Goddard, battles shipwreckers, and mans up against his romantic rival Milland. Ultimately, Milland and Wayne must team up to battle the heavies. The film, atmospheric though it is, fails to deliver any real drama. But if you love seafaring action flicks, you might want to stop by and have a look.

RED RIVER+

Featured actors: John Wayne, Montgomery Clift, Joanne Dru, Walter Brennan, Colleen Gray (Coleen Gray), Harry Carey, Sr. (Harry Carey), John Ireland, Noah Beery, Jr., Harry Carey, Jr., Chief Yowlatchie (Chief Yowlachie), Paul Fix, Hank Worden, Mickey Kuhn, Ray Hyke, and Hal Talliaferro (Hal Taliaferro)
Screenplay by Borden Chase and Charles Schnee
Based on a story by Borden Chase
Directed by Howard Hawks
Produced by Monterey Productions
Distributed by United Artists
Release date: September 17, 1948

Thomas Dunson (John Wayne) breaks away from a wagon train in mid-course, despite the wagon master's plea that they need his gun expertise in Indian country. Nevertheless, determined to reach Texas and start a cattle ranch, he sets off with his sidekick (Walter Brennan), only to find out later that the wagon-train pioneers, including his girlfriend, were massacred after his departure. Fast-forward fourteen years to find Dunson leading a cattle drive, the culmination of all his ranching efforts. But the guilt he feels over the wagon train has turned him into a hard and bitter man, one whose determination to succeed at any cost could very well be the source of his failure. The stellar supporting cast couldn't be better, with Harry Carey, Sr., Harry Carey, Jr., Walter Brennan, Noah Beery, Jr., Paul Fix, John Ireland, Hank Worden, Joanne Dru, and Montgomery Clift (in his Hollywood debut). As much as *The Big Trail* and *Stagecoach*, *Red River* marks a pivotal moment in Wayne's career, one that not only sees a more mature approach to his acting, but propels him into the forefront of Hollywood stardom. *Red River* is a major film that every student of John Wayne will want to watch, probably more than once.

RED RIVER RANGE

Featured actors: John Wayne, Ray Corrigan, Max Terhune, Polly Moran, Lorna Gray, Kirby Grant, Sammy McKim, William Royle,

Perry Ivins, Stanley Blystone, Lenore Bushman, Burr Caruth, Roger Williams, Earl Askam, and Olin Francis
Screenplay by Stanley Roberts, Betty Burbridge, and Luci Ward
Original story by Luci Ward
Based on characters created by William Colt MacDonald
Directed by George Sherman
Produced and distributed by Republic Pictures
Release date: December 22, 1938

Stony Brooke (John Wayne) and his two compadres, Tucson Smith (Ray Corrigan) and Lullaby Joslin (Max Terhune), are the Three Mesquiteers, assigned by the attorney general to investigate a gang of cattle rustlers in the Red River range. One of the rancher victims turns out to be the mastermind of the rustlers. As he learns of the Mesquiteers' plans to halt the crimes, he lays plans of his own to put the heroes on ice, permanently. This is Wayne's fourth outing in the *Three Mesquiteers* ongoing series. Pure fluff.

REUNION IN FRANCE
Featured actors: Joan Crawford, John Wayne, Philip Dorn, Reginald Owen, Albert Bassermann, John Carradine, Ann Ayars, J. Edward Bromberg, Moroni Olsen, Henry Daniell, Howard da Silva (Howard Da Silva), Charles Arnt, Morris Ankrum, Edith Evanson, Ernest Dorian (Ernst Deutsch), Margaret Laurence, Odette Myrtil, and Peter Whitney
Screenplay by Jan Lustig, Marvin Borowsky, and Marc Connelly
Based on the original story by Ladislas Bus-Fekete (Leslie Bush-Fekete)
Directed by Jules Dassin
Produced and distributed by Metro-Goldwyn-Mayer (MGM)
Release date: December 2, 1942

At the outbreak of World War II, poor little Parisian rich girl Joan Crawford is in denial about the coming conflagration. But when Paris falls, in June 1940, Nazis commandeer her lavish apartment and rob her of her riches—and suddenly Joan gets patriotic. John Wayne, portraying Pat Talbot, an American pilot in the RAF, doesn't even enter until forty-one minutes into the film. He's on the run from the Germans—and runs right into the arms of Crawford. Wayne has so little screen time, it's almost unfair to even call him a costar, especially with Crawford devouring the set every step of the way.

RIDE HIM, COWBOY
Featured actors: John Wayne, Duke the Horse, Ruth Hall, Henry B. Walthall, Otis Harlan, Harry Gribbon, and Frank Hagney
Dialogue and adaptation by Scott Mason

Based on a novel by Kenneth Perkins
Directed by Fred Allen
Produced by Leon Schlesinger Studios/Warner Bros. (as A Four Star Western)
Distributed by Warner Bros. (as Vitagraph Inc.)
Release date: August 27, 1932

Back in the saddle again as a leading man, John Wayne stars as John Drury, a drifting cowboy. Drury arrives in the Arizona town of Catalo, where he rescues a horse (costar Duke) wrongly accused of being a menace to society. Then he joins the local vigilantes to capture the Hawk, a no-goodnik who has been raiding the region's ranches. Although *Ride Him, Cowboy* is by no means a great (or even very good) film, at least we once again see the John Wayne spark that first captured film audiences in 1930's *The Big Trail.*

RIDERS OF DESTINY

Featured actors: John Wayne, Cecilia Parker, Forrest Taylor, George Hayes (George "Gabby" Hayes), Al St. John, Heinie Conklin, Yakima Canutt, Earl Dwire, Lafe McKee, and Addie Foster
Story by R. N. Bradbury (Robert N. Bradbury)
Directed by Robert N. Bradbury
Produced and distributed by Monogram Pictures (as Lone Star Productions)
Release date: October 10, 1933

John Wayne stars as "Singin' Sandy" Saunders. You say to yourself, "Uh-oh, this can't be good." Well, at least George "Gabby" Hayes and Yakima Canutt are in it, so how bad could it be? You had to ask. . . . The opening scene is particularly cringeworthy, with Wayne riding across the desert on his white steed, holding a guitar, and lip-synching some god-awful melody. You want to say to Singin' Sandy, "What have you done with the real John Wayne?!" Despite it all, there is some semblance of a plot, in which Kincaid, a ruthless landowner, attempts to shut off the water supply to his neighboring ranchers in the hopes they'll sell him their property at a discount. Singin' Sandy to the rescue!

RIO BRAVO+

Featured actors: John Wayne, Dean Martin, Ricky Nelson, Angie Dickinson, Walter Brennan, Ward Bond, John Russell, Pedro Gonzalez-Gonzalez (Pedro Gonzalez Gonzalez), Estelita Rodriguez, Claude Akins, Malcolm Atterbury, and Harry Carey, Jr.
Screenplay by Jules Furthman and Leigh Brackett
Based on a story by B. H. McCampbell
Directed by Howard Hawks
Produced by Armada Productions

Distributed by Warner Bros.
Release date: February 17, 1959

Consider this lineup: John Wayne, Dean Martin, Ricky Nelson, Angie Dickinson, Walter Brennan, and Ward Bond. Music by Dimitri Tiomkin. All under the direction of the notable Howard Hawks. Well, well, this sounds promising! And indeed it is, with dramatic tension, memorable dialogue, and fine acting by all involved. Dean Martin is very good as Dude, the pathetic drunk who once held respect as a lawman but is now too shaky even to light a cigarette. Wayne is at his best as a small-town Western sheriff, John T. Chance, a tough-as-nails Texas lawman with a soft spot for his old buddy. Even young, handsome Ricky Nelson holds his own, though the teen idol was never much of an actor. Sheriff Chance arrests a tough hombre on murder charges, but the man's brother, a wealthy rancher, threatens to bust into the calaboose to break his brother out. The bad guys have a slew of gunslingers on the payroll; Wayne has only Dude, crippled old Stumpy (Brennan), and a young pistolero called Colorado (Nelson). In that sense, the plot is pretty straightforward, very *High Noon*–esque, the men in white hats versus the men in black. But this is also a story of redemption—particularly, Dude's redemption, physical, emotional, and spiritual. Even though Dean Martin is second-billed, this is a movie about his character. With plenty of action, honest suspense, and superb supporting players, this is a Top 10 John Wayne movie. Also in the supporting cast are John Russell (TV's *The Lawman*), Claude Akins, and the amusing Pedro Gonzalez Gonzalez.

RIO GRANDE+

Featured actors: John Wayne, Maureen O'Hara, Ben Johnson, Claude Jarman, Jr., Harry Carey, Jr., Chill Wills, J. Carrol Naish, Victor McLaglen, Grant Withers, Sons of the Pioneers, Peter Ortiz, Steve Pendleton, Karolyn Grimes, Alberto Morin, Stan Jones, and Fred Kennedy
Screenplay by James Kevin McGuinness
Based on a story by James Warner Bellah
Directed by John Ford
Produced and distributed by Republic Pictures
Release date: November 2, 1950

A mustachioed John Wayne, as cavalry post commander Kirby Yorke, has an easy air of leadership and maturity that belies Wayne's real age (forty-three years old). When a batch of recruits arrives at Fort Stark, Colonel Yorke is conflicted to find that one of them is his son, from whom he has been estranged for fifteen years. Putting on a stern face and warning the young man to expect no favoritism, Wayne is nonetheless a proud voyeur of his son's progress from raw recruit to fine soldier. At the same time, he fears that his reckless offspring will put himself in unnecessary danger as the fort braces for an Indian uprising. When Wayne's ex-wife and the mother of their son (Maureen O'Hara) arrives unexpectedly, the family drama nearly rivals the all-too-real dangers that lie outside the fort's stockade walls. Like the previous two films in the so-called Cavalry Trilogy, *Rio Grande* is directed by John Ford and set in the 1870s American Southwest. The exceptional cast includes Victor McLaglen, Grant Withers, Harry Carey, Jr., J. Carrol Naish, Chill Wills, and Ben Johnson, the last of whom was an authentic ranch hand and rodeo performer who supported Wayne in six films between 1944 and 1973. Wayne, O'Hara, and McLaglen would go on to form the principal cast in the 1952 classic *The Quiet Man,* also directed by Ford.

RIO LOBO*

Featured actors: John Wayne, Jorge Rivero, Jennifer O'Neill, Jack Elam, Christopher Mitchum, Victor French, Susana Dosamantes, Sherry Lansing, David Huddleston, Mike Henry, Bill Williams, Jim Davis, Dean Smith, Robert Donner, George Plimpton, Edward Faulkner, and Peter Jason
Screenplay by Burton Wohl and Leigh Brackett
Story by Burton Wohl
Directed by Howard Hawks
Produced by Cinema Center Films/Malabar
Distributed by National General Pictures
Release date: December 16, 1970

When rebel troops steal a gold shipment under the protection of Union colonel Cord McNally (John Wayne), McNally vows to get it back at any cost. The situation takes a desperate turn when the Confederates capture McNally and force him to lead them back south. Fast-forward to the war's end: Wayne reconnects with his former captors, who have ended up as prisoners of war. Wayne appeals to them for the identity of the Union trooper who betrayed his fellow soldiers and sold the gold information to the rebs. They form an unlikely partnership to find the traitor. Midway through the movie, Wayne dons his iconic pink shirt. This is Wayne's last military role. As a coherent film, it doesn't work, because it seems like the director is trying to cram two different movies into one (including a latter-half plotline that mimics *El Dorado* and *Rio Bravo,* both of which were written or cowritten by this film's cowriter, Leigh Brackett). But as an enjoyable John Wayne Western, it's all good. Also before the camera are stunning Jennifer O'Neill, googly-eyed Jack Elam, Christopher (Robert's son) Mitchum, Jim Davis, Edward Faulkner (in the last of his five John Wayne films), Hank Worden (uncredited), and author-editor George Plimpton in a bit part. Plus, good ol' Yakima Canutt is back with Duke—this time as second-unit director—along with his sons Joe and Tap Canutt as stuntmen.

ROOSTER COGBURN+

Featured actors: John Wayne, Katharine Hepburn, Anthony Zerbe, Richard Jordan, John McIntire, Richard Romancito, Paul Koslo, Jack Colvin, Jon Lormer, Lane Smith, Tommy Lee, Warren Vanders, and Strother Martin
Screenplay by Martin Julien (Martha Hyer)
Based on the character from the novel True Grit *by Charles Portis*
Directed by Stuart Millar
Produced by Hal Wallis Productions
Distributed by Universal Pictures
Release date: October 17, 1975

Irascible lawman Rooster Cogburn (John Wayne) returns in this sequel to *True Grit*. This time, Cogburn is commissioned to find the men who stole a wagonload of U.S. government nitroglycerine before they can use it to rob a federal gold shipment. But barely has Rooster started on his mission than he is confronted by the fearsome presence of Eula Goodnight (Katharine Hepburn), whose father has just been murdered by the ruffians. A more unlikely duo of justice-seekers has rarely been seen, but watching Miss Goodnight and ol' Rooster traipse through the gorgeous Western scenery in search of the villains is a treat at every turn. And by the way, to the list of tough old birds who can go toe-to-toe with Duke, add the name of Kate Hepburn, who, as always, is superb in her role. While *Rooster Cogburn* can't quite measure up to its source, the movie is a pleaser in almost every way a Wayne fan could hope for. Costumes by Edith Head. With Anthony Zerbe, Richard Jordan, John McIntire, and Strother Martin.

ROUGH ROMANCE

Featured actors: George O'Brien, Antonio Moreno, Helen Chandler, Noel Francis, David Hartford, Roy Stewart, Eddie Borden, and Harry Cording
Dialogue by Donald Davis
Scenario by Elliott Lester
Story by Kenneth B. Clarke
Directed by A. F. Erickson and Benjamin Stoloff (both uncredited)
Produced and distributed by Fox Film Corporation
Release date: June 22, 1930

Felonious loggers attempt to steal the pelts from lone trappers in the snowy Northwest. Who will win? John Wayne, as an extra, portrays a lumberjack. He's best identified during the raucous dance-hall scene, playing cards with a con man, at about twenty-five minutes into the film, with one line of dialogue ("Sure, why not? If neither of those two cards is a jack, Phil wins"). Despite the grand and adventurous setting, the film is stilted and slow-going throughout. The sole exception is the final scene, in the river full of logs, which is highly dramatic.

SAGEBRUSH TRAIL
Featured actors: John Wayne, Nancy Shubert, Lane Chandler, Yakima
Canutt, Henry Hall, Wally Wales, Art Mix, and Bob Burns
Story by Lindsley Parsons
Directed by Armand Schaefer
Produced and distributed by Monogram Pictures (as Lone Star
Productions)
Release date: December 15, 1933

The film starts with a promising chase scene as wanted criminal John Brant (John Wayne) leaps from a train, steals a horse, and romps through the desert while the sheriff gives chase. After eluding the law, he hooks up with a gang of robbers in hope of finding the despicable hombre who set him up for a crime he didn't commit. Turns out, the man who incriminated him, Joseph Conlon, didn't frame Brant on purpose. During a gun battle with the gang, Conlon takes a bullet for Brant. Not nearly as good as it sounds.

SALUTE
Featured actors: George O'Brien, Helen Chandler, William Janney,
Stepin Fetchit, Frank Albertson, Joyce Compton, David Butler,
Lumsden Hare, Clifford Dempsey, and Ward Bond
Screenplay by John Stone
Dialogue by James Kevin McGuinness
Story by Tristram Tupper
Directed by David Butler and John Ford (both uncredited)
Produced and distributed by Fox Film Corporation
Release date: September 1, 1929

Older brother John Randall (George O'Brien) is an Army cadet at West Point, and Paul (William Janney), the younger, is a midshipman at the Naval Academy. Learning that Paul has fallen for a lovely maiden, John attempts to help, but Paul takes his brother's assistance the wrong way. Ultimately, the two brothers must duke it out on opposite sides of the Army-Navy football game. John Wayne appears in a handful of scenes as one of Paul's fellow middies, but has only a couple of token lines. Ward Bond also has a bit part.

SANDS OF IWO JIMA+
Featured actors: John Wayne, John Agar, Adele Mara, Forrest Tucker,
Wally Cassell, James Brown, Richard Webb, Arthur Franz, Julie
Bishop, James Holden, Peter Coe, Richard Jaeckel, Bill Murphy
(William Murphy), George Tyne, Hal Fieberling (Hal Baylor), John
McGuire, Martin Milner, Leonard Gumley, William Self, Col. D. M.
Shoup, Lt. Col. H. P. Crowe, Capt. Harold G. Schrier, Pfc. Rene A.
Gagnon, Pfc. Ira H. Hayes, and PM3/C John H. Bradley
Screenplay by Harry Brown and James Edward Grant

Story by Harry Brown
Directed by Allan Dwan
Produced and distributed by Republic Pictures
Release date: December 14, 1949

A Marine rifle squad, fresh from the hell of Guadalcanal, is pulled out of action for rest, refitting, and retraining in New Zealand. Joined by straight-out-of-boot-camp troops, the squad prepares for its next assignment: the fight for the Japanese-held island of Iwo Jima, one of the most infamous, desperately fought, and bloodiest conflicts of World War II. Assigned to lead them is battle-hardened Sergeant John M. Stryker (John Wayne), the tough but fair noncom who vows to see them through the horrors that lie ahead. Wayne is pitch-perfect in the role, the battle scenes (including authentic footage shot during the actual engagement) are epic, and the ending is a stunner. The film's sterling supporting troupe includes Forrest Tucker, John Agar, Richard Jaeckel, and a ridiculously young Martin Milner, later the costar of TV's *Route 66* and *Adam-12*.

SANTA FE STAMPEDE

Featured actors: John Wayne, Ray Corrigan, Max Terhune, June
Martel, William Farnum, Le Roy Mason (LeRoy Mason), Martin
Spellman, Genee Hall, Walter Wills, Ferris Taylor, Tom London, Dick
Rush, and John F. Cassidy (James Cassidy)
Screenplay by Luci Ward and Betty Burbridge
Original story by Luci Ward
Based on characters created by William Colt MacDonald
Directed by George Sherman
Produced and distributed by Republic Pictures
Release date: November 18, 1938

Republic Pictures must have had high hopes for the *Three Mesquiteers* series, because they just kept churning them out. And yet Hollywood—and John Wayne—survived this particular cockamamie cactus chronicle as they did the previous ones. The greedy mayor of Santa Fe Junction and his band of thugs terrorize the populace and attempt to jump a claim from a law-abiding miner. The Three Mesquiteers ride into the midst of the mayhem and try to bring law and justice back to the forefront. But can they get their petition to the territorial governor before they're bushwhacked by the mayor's desperadoes? Aw, take your knuckles out of your mouth, snowflake, because Stony, Tucson, and Lullaby are on the case!

THE SEA CHASE*

Featured actors: John Wayne, Lana Turner, David Farrar, Lyle
Bettger, Tab Hunter, James Arness, Dick Davalos (Richard Davalos),
John Qualen, Paul Fix, Lowell Gilmore, Luis Van Rooten, Alan Hale
(Alan Hale, Jr.), Wilton Graff, Peter Whitney, Claude Akin (Claude
Akins), John Doucette, and Alan Lee

Screenplay by James Warner Bellah and John Twist
Based on a novel by Andrew Geer
Directed by John Farrow
Produced and distributed by Warner Bros.
Release date: May 12, 1955

What a strange plot! File under: Questionable Career Moves. John Wayne is Karl Ehrlich, a German freighter captain in Australia at the outbreak of World War II. He's anti-Nazi but pro-Germany, therefore reluctant to turn against his homeland. Viewers may find difficulty in building up much sympathy, considering. Chased by the Royal Navy (in real life, the Royal Canadian Navy) across the South Pacific, Wayne and his crew attempt to zigzag their way to safety, hoping to reach the Fatherland. Bizarre casting: Lana Turner (hair dyed Germanic blond) as a pouty-faced Nazi intelligence officer?! The producers, it seems, weren't aiming for credibility. Still, there's good tension and drama, and Wayne is extremely Wayneish, so there's that. The other costars include Claude Akins (listed as Claude Akin, with hair dyed Germanic blond), James Arness (hair dyed Germanic blond), Tab Hunter (hair naturally Germanic blond), John Qualen, Paul Fix, and Alan Hale, Jr. (credited as Alan Hale), who later played the Skipper on TV's *Gilligan's Island.*

SEA SPOILERS

Featured actors: John Wayne, Nan Grey, William Bakewell, Fuzzy Knight, Russell Hicks, George Irving, Lotus Long, Harry Worth, Ernest Hilliard, George Humbert, Ethan Laidlaw, Chester Gan, Cy Kendall, and Harrison Greene
Screenplay by George Waggoner (George Waggner)
Original story by Dorrell McGowan and Stuart E. McGowan
Directed by Frank Strayer (Frank R. Strayer)
Produced and distributed by Universal Pictures
Release date: September 20, 1936

Bos'n Bob Randall (John Wayne) is the number two to a seasick captain on the Coast Guard patrol boat *Niobe* after having been passed over for promotion. Randall sucks up the professional insult and carries on with his duties as best he can. When Randall's entertainer-girlfriend is kidnapped by seal poachers in Alaska, the fearful captain finds himself out of his depth. It's up to Randall to devise a plan and put the Coast Guard into action. Yet the ineffective captain continues to hobble Randall every step of the way. Notable for not much, apart from being one of the few 1930s films in which Wayne's character is not, remarkably, named "John."

THE SEARCHERS+

Featured actors: John Wayne, Jeffrey Hunter, Vera Miles, Ward Bond, Natalie Wood, John Qualen, Olive Carey, Henry Brandon, Ken Curtis,

Harry Carey, Jr., Antonio Moreno, Hank Worden, Beulah Archuletta,
Walter Coy, Dorothy Jordan, Pippa Scott, Pat Wayne (Patrick Wayne),
and Lana Wood
Screenplay by Frank S. Nugent
Based on a novel by Alan Le May
Directed by John Ford
Produced by C. V. Whitney Pictures
Distributed by Warner Bros.
Release date: May 26, 1956

It's difficult not to think of this as a reverse *Les Misérables,* with the story told from Javert's point of view. Noticeably stouter than in previous outings, John Wayne (now nearly fifty years old) stars in what is arguably the best film of his career—in terms of his acting, the setting, the cinematography, the cast, and the inimitable direction by John Ford. Wayne is Ethan Edwards, just returned to Texas following the Civil War, where he moves in with his brother and family on their remote homestead. Dragooned into a posse to scout out Indian trouble, Edwards returns to his brother's ranch only to find the family slaughtered, except for his niece (Natalie Wood), who has been stolen by the Comanche raiders. Determined to avenge his family and recover his kidnapped niece, he sets out on his vengeful mission with the family's foster son (Jeffrey Hunter), whom Edwards had discovered in the wake of an Indian massacre some twenty years earlier. Wayne's Ethan Edwards has numerous admirable qualities—ruggedness, endurance, determination, focus. But he's also a man full of hate, vitriol, unattractive cussedness, and unapologetic violence. It's a complex role, a mature role, and among the best of the best in Wayne's filmography. With Vera Miles, Ward Bond, Hank Worden, John Qualen, Harry Carey, Jr., Ken Curtis (Festus from TV's *Gunsmoke*), and a young Patrick Wayne (billed as Pat Wayne). A must-see.

SEEING STARS
Featured actors: George Davis, Molly Moran (Molly Malone), Jack
Lloyd, Phil Dunham, Jack Miller, and Ray Turner
Directed by Stephen Roberts
Produced by Mermaid Comedies (Jack White)
Distributed by Educational Film Exchanges
Release date: October 16, 1927

By all accounts, this short comedy, in which John Wayne plays the unbilled role of "Tall Boy," no longer exists. A lost film.

SEVEN SINNERS*
Featured actors: Marlene Dietrich, John Wayne, Albert Dekker,
Broderick Crawford, Anna Lee, Mischa Auer, Billy Gilbert, Richard
Carle, Samuel S. Hinds, and Oscar Homolka (Oskar Homolka)
Screenplay by John Meehan and Harry Tugend

Original story by Ladislas Fodor and Laslo Vadnai (László Vadnay)
Directed by Tay Garnett
Produced and distributed by Universal Pictures
Release date: October 25, 1940

You know something's going on here when Marlene Dietrich is listed above the title on the movie posters and "with John Wayne" is far below. Our hero doesn't even enter the film until eighteen minutes into it. This is a glam vehicle for La Dietrich all the way, and everyone else is secondary. Dietrich plays Bijou Blanche, a gin-palace chanteuse who excites men to such a degree of lust and violence that she keeps getting deported from one exotic locale to another. That's how she ends up singing in the notorious Seven Sinners dive on the fictional South China Sea isle of Boni-Komba. Like every other male within pheromone-smelling distance of Bijou, Navy lieutenant Dan Brent (Wayne) falls head over epaulets in puppy-panting love with the sexy singer. But is he so far gone that he's willing to risk his future in the Navy? The film has high-quality production values and excellent acting (Broderick Crawford, Billy Gilbert, and Mischa Auer provide fine comic relief throughout), but a thin plot. Still, it's a highly enjoyable outing.

THE SHADOW OF THE EAGLE

Featured actors: John Wayne, Dorothy Gulliver, Edward Hearn, Richard Tucker, Lloyd Whitlock, Walter Miller, Edmund Burns, Pat O'Malley, Kenneth Harlan, Little Billy, Ivan Linow, James Bradbury, Jr., Ernie S. Adams, Roy D'Arcy, Bud Osborne, Yakima Canutt, Billy West, and Monty Montague
Story by Ford Beebe and Colbert Clark
Directed by Ford Beebe
Produced and distributed by Mascot Pictures
Release date: February 1, 1932

John Wayne's first serial—a movie told in episodic fashion in discrete installments and popular with juvenile Saturday matinee-goers—finds him as a stunt pilot in a roving carnival. For those whose hearts were warmed by Wayne's starring debut two years earlier in *The Big Trail*, Duke's fall from leading man to this . . . this . . . *drivel*, as a juvenile lead, will be disappointing. Cinema buff alert: Look for the scene (at 28:50 in my copy) that well may have inspired Hitchcock to shoot the airplane scene from *North by Northwest* a quarter century later.

SHE WORE A YELLOW RIBBON+

Featured actors: John Wayne, Joanne Dru, John Agar, Ben Johnson, Harry Carey, Jr., Victor McLaglen, Mildred Natwick, George O'Brien, Arthur Shields, Michael Dugan, Chief John Big Tree, Fred Graham, Chief Sky Eagle (George Sky Eagle), Tom Tyler, and Noble Johnson

Screenplay by Frank Nugent (Frank S. Nugent) and Laurence Stallings
Story by James Warner Bellah
Directed by John Ford
Produced by Argosy Pictures
Distributed by RKO Radio Pictures
Release date: July 28, 1949

John Wayne's Captain Nathan Brittles takes his cavalry patrol on one last mission, this time to escort two ladies to a stagecoach station in the wake of Custer's Last Stand. This may be the movie that truly established Wayne's enduring on-screen persona—reserved, in charge, opinionated, a true man of the West. With Ben Johnson and Victor McLaglen as his costars, he could hardly have gone wrong. One of the earliest examples of Wayne wearing his trademark pink (his long johns, seen especially in the very last scenes). The final fight scene with Victor McLaglen and the soldiers captures some of the most joyous filmed fisticuffs in all Hollywood!

THE SHEPHERD OF THE HILLS*
Featured actors: John Wayne, Betty Field, Harry Carey, Beulah Bondi, James Barton, Samuel S. Hinds, Marjorie Main, Ward Bond, Marc Lawrence, John Qualen, and Fuzzy Knight
Screenplay by Grover Jones and Stuart Anthony
Based on a novel by Harold Bell Wright
Directed by Henry Hathaway
Produced and distributed by Paramount Pictures
Release date: June 10, 1941

In his first movie in color, John Wayne plays Young Matt Matthews, Ozarks moonshiner, bound and determined to kill the father who abandoned the family. Harry Carey is rock solid (as always) as the stranger who moves in among the backwoods distillers. The film offers a look into the lives of people who live on the fringes of society—a life that is as simple and pure as it is backward and ignorant. Beautifully filmed, superbly directed, and egregiously sentimental, *Shepherd* is a class act all the way. It is not, however, a prime John Wayne vehicle, as he plays a secondary role, despite his star billing. Worth watching—just not "a John Wayne film."

THE SHOOTIST+
Featured actors: John Wayne, Lauren Bacall, Ron Howard, Bill McKinney, James Stewart, Richard Boone, John Carradine, Scatman Crothers, Richard Lenz (Rick Lenz), Harry Morgan, Sheree North, and Hugh O'Brian
Screenplay by Miles Hood Swarthout and Scott Hale
Based on a novel by Glendon Swarthout
Directed by Don Siegel

Produced by the Dino De Laurentiis Company and Paramount
Pictures
Distributed by Paramount Pictures
Release date: July 19, 1976

There must have been a line out the casting director's door when shooting for this film was announced, because the list of stars is long indeed: James Stewart (John Wayne's costar in *The Man Who Shot Liberty Valance*), Lauren Bacall (whose last appearance with Wayne was two decades earlier, in 1955's *Blood Alley*), Ron Howard, John Carradine, Hugh O'Brian, Harry Morgan, Scatman Crothers, Sheree North, and big bad Richard Boone. This is the movie that one could only dream would be Duke's swan song. Poignantly, this film about an aging gunslinger dying of cancer was released only three years before Wayne himself succumbed to the disease. If you were to sit down and watch every John Wayne movie, this moving film is the one you would want to watch last. The plot begins in Carson City, Nevada, in 1901. The Old West of story and myth is on its decline, and so, as it turns out, is our hero, former lawman and notorious gunman J. B. Books. The old shootist learns from his doctor (Stewart) that he has a terminal disease, and not long to live. Books's only wish is to run out his final days with dignity and, ideally, as little pain as possible. But a man who lives by the gun rarely is allowed to die in bed, so when word gets out that Books is near the end, the bad guys come out to claim the famous pistolero as a notch on their gun belt. Say what you will about any imperfections in production, casting, story line, or continuity (not that a close viewer would find much to criticize anyway), this is the way Duke wanted to go out, even though his loyal fans hate to see him leave. You don't have to wait until you've watched every other John Wayne film before you watch this one. But after you've viewed all the others, watch *The Shootist* once again, and say a final adiós to the legend. Duke, our trails fork here, old compañero.

SOMEWHERE IN SONORA

Featured actors: John Wayne, Duke the Horse, Henry B. Walthall,
Shirley Palmer, Ann Faye (Ann Fay), J. P. McGowan, Paul Fix, Ralph
Lewis, Frank Rice, and Billy Franey
Dialogue and adaptation by Joe Roach
Based on a story by Will Levington Comfort
Directed by Mack V. Wright
Produced by Leon Schlesinger Studios/Warner Bros. (as A Four Star
Western)
Distributed by Warner Bros. (as Vitagraph, Inc.)
Release date: June 7, 1933

John Bishop (John Wayne) is a top hand at an Arizona ranch who stands accused of rigging a stagecoach race. Fleeing misguided justice, Bishop heads south of the border, down Mexico way, where he finds himself up against a gang of desperate bandits. Duke the Horse comes to the rescue without a second to spare. Although Wayne is as gangly as a colt, he continues to fine-tune his leading-man chops by wooing a city gal. And yes, that's Paul Fix (a character actor best known as Marshal Micah Torrance on TV's *The Rifleman*) in one of his early film roles.

THE SONS OF KATIE ELDER*
Featured actors: John Wayne, Dean Martin, Martha Hyer, Michael Anderson, Jr., Earl Holliman, Jeremy Slate, James Gregory, Paul Fix, George Kennedy, Dennis Hopper, Sheldon Allman, John Litel, John Doucette, James Westerfield, Rhys Williams, John Qualen, Rodolfo Acosta, and Strother Martin
Screenplay by William H. Wright, Allan Weiss, and Harry Essex
Based on a story by Talbot Jennings
Directed by Henry Hathaway
Produced by Hal Wallis Productions
Distributed by Paramount Pictures
Release date: July 1, 1965

John Wayne reteams with Dean Martin and director Henry Hathaway in this whodunit take on an old-school Western. The Elder boys gather in their hometown of Clearwater for the first time in years to attend the burial of their ma, Katie. When the eldest son, notorious gunslinger John Elder (John Wayne), and his brothers (Dean Martin, Earl Holliman, and Michael Anderson, Jr.) learn that their father was murdered six months earlier after losing the family farm in a card game, trouble rears its ugly cowboy hat. The boys set out to find their pa's killer and reclaim the farm. As the plot progresses, the sons learn more about their mother from the local townsfolk than they ever knew, and find that Katie Elder was a complex, generous person beloved by people the sons had never even met before. Some good action here and there, but the plot is strangely slow-moving overall. A "comical" fistfight among the brothers, a seemingly obligatory fixture of Wayne's later movies, does nothing to improve this otherwise decent film. Secondary actors include George Kennedy as the heavy, Paul Fix, Dennis Hopper (who credits John Wayne with salvaging his career with this film), Strother Martin, James Gregory, Percy Helton, John Doucette, and John Qualen.

SPEAKEASY
Featured actors: Paul Page, Lola Lane, Henry B. Walthall, Helen Ware, Sharon Lynn, Warren Hymer, Stuart Erwin, James Guilfoyle, Erville Alderson, Joseph Cawthorn, Ivan Linow, Marjorie Beebe, Sailor Vincent, and Helen Lynch
Dialogue by Edwin Burke (Edwin J. Burke)
Scenario by Frederick Hazlitt Brennan and Edwin Burke (Edwin J. Burke)
Based on a play by Edward Knoblock and George Rosener

Directed by Benjamin Stoloff
Produced and distributed by Fox Film Corporation
Release date: March 13, 1929

This is one of a handful of so-called lost films in which Wayne played a small role. No known copies exist. But based on contemporary reviews, the plot goes like this: A female reporter tries to profile a boxer who has just lost a championship bout. In the speakeasy where the fighter spends most of his time outside the ring, the reporter fails again to get her story. Instead of admitting failure, she writes a fake-news article saying the boxer is planning a comeback. After proving that his manager is a crook, the boxer does indeed fight again, and this time regains his middleweight crown. John Wayne was an extra.

THE SPOILERS*
Featured actors: Marlene Dietrich, Randolph Scott, John Wayne, Margaret Lindsay, Harry Carey, Richard Barthelmess, George Cleveland, and Samuel S. Hinds
Screenplay by Lawrence Hazard and Tom Reed
Based on a novel by Rex Beach
Directed by Ray Enright
Produced and distributed by Universal Pictures
Release date: April 10, 1942

Set in Nome in 1900, during the Alaska gold rush, the film begins with tons of promise. The muddy streets of Nome are clogged with dogsleds, fleabag hotels, mustachioed miners, dance-hall gals, and more. If it weren't for the fact that John Wayne was billed third, below Marlene Dietrich and Randolph Scott, we'd probably feel a lot more excited. Wayne once again plays against type as a roguish law-skirter. His higher-billed costar Scott has connived with the local judge to wrest the mining claims from the hard-bitten sourdoughs. But Wayne (and his always superb costar Harry Carey) are bound and determined to stand up for their rights. Interestingly, this may be the film in which John Wayne starts to talk in the classic, iconic, almost comical Waynespeak that impressionists have copied for decades. Watch, and see if you don't agree. Having Wayne show up in blackface (ugh, ugh, ugh), though, elevates the disagreeableness of this film. Yeah, don't judge a 1942 movie by current standards and all that, but this is pretty egregious.

STAGECOACH+
Featured actors: Claire Trevor, John Wayne, Andy Devine, John Carradine, Thomas Mitchell, Louise Platt, George Bancroft, Donald Meek, Berton Churchill, and Tim Holt
Screenplay by Dudley Nichols
Original story by Ernest Haycox
Directed by John Ford

Produced by Walter Wanger Productions
Distributed by United Artists
Release date: February 15, 1939

This is the film that rebranded John Wayne from a B-movie cowboy to a full-blown film star. Duke went on to make a number of losers after this smash, but *Stagecoach* will forever be remembered as the flick that well and truly introduced the world to the John Wayne best remembered today. Wayne's first entrance is one of Hollywood's great moments—thanks to director John Ford, who would reteam with Wayne again and again over the years. The costars are phenomenal, from screechy-voiced Andy Devine, to the elegant Claire Trevor as the prostitute with the heart of gold, to the drunken doctor Thomas Mitchell, to the immortal John Carradine as the notorious gambler. Duke was elevated into an entirely different level of filmdom in this picture. The plot is blah-blah-blah, but the cinematography, the acting, the staging, and the glorious Monument Valley setting combine in a way that results in world-class moviemaking.

THE STAR PACKER
*Featured actors: John Wayne, Verna Hillie, George Hayes
(George "Gabby" Hayes), Yakima Canutt, Billy Franey, Ed
Parker (Eddie Parker), Earl Dwire, and Tom Lingham (Thomas G.
Lingham)*
Screenplay and story by R. N. Bradbury (Robert N. Bradbury)
Directed by R. N. Bradbury (Robert N. Bradbury)
*Produced and distributed by Monogram Pictures (as Lone Star
Productions)*
Release date: July 30, 1934

The would-be sheriff is killed by a person or persons unknown, so John Travers (John Wayne) volunteers to take his place. Why? Because there wouldn't be a movie, otherwise. Also, because, you know, why wouldn't you?! Get ready for unseen bad guys and nonsensical plotlines. Hey, it's a movie, go ahead and do whatever the heck you want. You sometimes wonder if these moviemakers were on acid or something. "Cover my trail, Yak, I'm going back for the money bags" is this movie's height of cinematic discourse. Yeesh.

STRONG BOY
*Featured actors: Victor McLaglen, Leatrice Joy, Farrell MacDonald,
and Clyde Cook*
Titles by Malcolm Stuart Boylan
*Scenario by James Kevin McGuinness, Andrew Bennison, and Jon
McLain*
Story by Frederick Hazlitt Brennan
Directed by John Ford

Produced and distributed by Fox Film Corporation
Release date: March 3, 1929

A railroad baggage handler (Victor McLaglen) earns a bare existence in the Lost and Found department, largely thanks to the largesse of his friends. Thanks to his supposed efficiency there, he's promoted to fireman on a train carrying a visiting queen. Robbers have targeted the queen's visit to grab her valuables, but McLaglen breaks up the attempted robbery. Now a hero, he marries the boss's daughter. John Wayne is an extra and a prop man, and Ward Bond has a bit part. There apparently are no public prints in circulation, although a fifty-three-second trailer can be found online.

TALL IN THE SADDLE*

Featured actors: John Wayne, Ella Raines, Ward Bond, George "Gabby" Hayes, Audrey Long, Elisabeth Risdon, Don Douglas (Donald Douglas), Paul Fix, Russell Wade, Emory Parnell, Raymond Hatton, and Harry Woods
Screenplay by Michael Hogan and Paul P. Fix (Paul Fix)
Original story by Gordon Ray Young
Directed by Edwin L. Marin
Produced and distributed by RKO Radio Pictures
Release date: September 29, 1944

A John Wayne Western with both Ward Bond (as a bad guy) and Gabby Hayes? What could go wrong? Not much, as it turns out. John Wayne is "Rock" Rocklin, a ranch hand who arrives by stagecoach in Santa Inez only to discover that the rancher who hired him via letter has been killed. In no time flat, Rocklin gets involved in an ugly poker dispute, a grievance with the new owners of the ranch, and a near gunfight with the brother of a man whose hand he broke when he drew on him. And he hasn't even been in town twenty-four hours yet! As it turns out, a despicable lawyer (Bond) is in cahoots with the aunt of the charming young miss who has inherited the ranch (and who has fallen head over hoopskirt for Rocklin), while at the same time Rocklin is being pursued by the pulchritudinous cowgal who owns the neighboring ranch. A fine cast, a pretty darn good plot, and Wayne being a first-rate Wayne make this a well-worth-watching picture.

THE TELEGRAPH TRAIL

Featured actors: John Wayne, Duke the Horse, Frank McHugh, Marceline Day, Otis Harlan, Albert J. Smith, Yakima Canutt, and Lafe McKee
Screenplay and dialogue by Kurt Kempler
Directed by Tenny Wright
Produced by Leon Schlesinger Studios/Warner Bros. (as A Four Star Western)

Distributed by Warner Bros. (as Vitagraph, Inc.)
Release date: March 18, 1933

Gus Lynch wants to keep the telegraph out of his territory to protect his monopoly on supply deliveries to the frontier. Next thing you know, telegraph crews are being wiped out by Indians in the pay of Lynch. Enter John Trent (John Wayne), cavalry scout, who sets out to stop Lynch and get vengeance for the murder of his linemen friends. Indians are induced to join Lynch's team for one final assault, but Trent learns of the ambush in the nick of time. Trent is promoted to captain, and Alice, who has loved him from afar, swoons and falls into his arms. Audience yawns, goes to sleep.

TEXAS CYCLONE
Featured actors: Tim McCoy, Shirley Grey, John Wayne, Wheeler Oakman, Wallace MacDonald, Vernon Dent, Mary Gordon, and Walter Brenan (Walter Brennan)
Dialogue and adaptation by Randall Faye
Story by William Colt MacDonald
Directed by D. Ross Lederman
Produced and distributed by Columbia Pictures
Release date: July 8, 1932

Western star Tim McCoy plays Texas Grant, a footloose cowboy mistaken for a long-missing rancher. When Grant learns that the rancher's wife has been losing cattle to a rustling operation, he adopts the new identity to stop the thieves. John Wayne is a reliable ranch hand who offers to help. Only later do we find that Texas Grant is indeed the missing rancher after all, and has been suffering from amnesia. McCoy earned $800 to star; after watching this movie, you may feel he was overpaid. This picture is notable if only because it marks the first time Duke shared the screen with Walter Brennan, one of Hollywood's greatest character actors and an occasional costar in Wayne's later films.

TEXAS TERROR
Featured actors: John Wayne, Lucille Browne (Lucile Brown), Leroy Mason (LeRoy Mason), Fern Emmett, George Hayes (George "Gabby" Hayes), Buffalo Bill, Jr. (Jay Wilsey), John Ince, Henry Roguemore (Henry Roquemore), and Jack Duffy
Story by R. N. Bradbury (Robert N. Bradbury)
Directed by R. N. Bradbury (Robert N. Bradbury)
Produced and distributed by Monogram Pictures (as Lone Star Productions)
Release date: February 1, 1935

John Wayne portrays John Higgins, a sheriff who blames himself for a friend's death then does penance as a desert rat. When a stage is attacked, the hermit-like Higgins comes to the rescue. A beautiful female passenger turns out to be the daughter of Higgins's dead friend. He takes a job at her ranch, but can't bring himself to declare his love for her because of the guilt he carries. *Texas Terror* is worth taking a peek at if only for a young John Wayne wearing a beard. An early appearance by George "Gabby" Hayes eases the pain of watching this slow-moving oater.

THAT'S MY BOY
Featured actors: Richard Cromwell, Dorothy Jordan, Mae Marsh, Arthur Stone, Douglass Dumbrille, Lucien Littlefield, Leon Waycoff (Leon Ames), Russell Saunders, Sumner Getchell, Otis Harlan, and Oscar "Dutch" Hendrian
Screenplay by Norman Krasna
Based on a novel by Francis Wallace
Directed by Roy William Neill
Produced and distributed by Columbia Pictures
Release date: November 17, 1932

Tommy Scott (Richard Cromwell) goes to a New England college to become a physician, but the fact that he can toss a football like nobody's business leads him to spend more time on the gridiron than in Anatomy 101. Things go south from there—not for Tommy, but for the audience. Tommy gets involved with a shady accountant who uses the footballer's fame to lure investors into a gambling scheme. When the scam goes bust, Tommy's reputation is ruined. Can he repay the investors and win the big game against Harvard? As was common in college football dramas like this, John Wayne is unbilled, though he appears in several scenes on the playing field.

THEY WERE EXPENDABLE
Featured actors: Robert Montgomery, John Wayne, Donna Reed, Jack Holt, and Ward Bond
Screenplay by Frank Wead
Based on a book by William L. White
Directed by John Ford
Produced and distributed by Metro-Goldwyn-Mayer (MGM)
Release date: November 23, 1945

John Wayne is Rusty Ryan, a Navy lieutenant in a group of PT boats in the Philippines at the outbreak of World War II. It's up to Wayne and his buddy John "Brick" Brickley (Robert Montgomery) to prove to the Navy that PT boats can outmaneuver anything the Japanese can throw at them and succeed as a fast-moving group of floating fighters. But as the title of the movie implies, the Navy brass has its own ideas of how to use the PT boats. Not a bad war flick (nothing with John Wayne directed by John Ford could possibly be bad), but Duke plays second fiddle to Montgomery, who gets lead billing in this film, so Wayne's presence on-screen is never fully felt. Lots of action, but light on snappy patter.

THREE FACES WEST*
Featured actors: John Wayne, Sigrid Gurie, Charles Coburn, Spencer Charters, Helen MacKellar, Roland Varno, Sonny Bupp, Wade Boteler, Trevor Bardette, Russell Simpson, Charles Waldron, and Wendell Niles
Screenplay by F. Hugh Herbert, Joseph Moncure March, and Samuel Ornitz
Directed by Bernard Vorhaus
Produced and distributed by Republic Pictures
Release date: July 12, 1940

Even in the earliest scenes of this Republic effort, John Wayne clearly shows evidence of a new maturity and increased confidence. Here Wayne plays John Phillips, a civic-minded citizen of Asheville Forks, North Dakota, who invites a war-refugee doctor (Charles Coburn) and his lovely daughter Leni (Sigrid Gurie) to take up residence in the dust bowl town that otherwise would have no medical man. Despite Leni's initial reluctance, especially after getting her first glimpse of the dust-covered house Phillips has found for them, the dutiful doctor tries his best against overwhelming odds to help the locals. At the same time, Phillips leads the local farmers in their battle against crop failure, with contour farming, windbreaks, and other useless ploys against the all-powerful climate. Over time, and while facing crushing obstacles, Phillips and Leni fall in love and plan to marry. But first, the community agrees to abandon their fields and caravan west to Oregon, where the government has offered them new lands—and hope. Leni then learns from a telegram that her former fiancé, who was thought dead at the outbreak of the European war, is not only alive but on his way to San Francisco to pick up where he and Leni left off. The plot then moves into some intriguing and far more serious themes, with anti-fascist sentiments, Moses-like overtones, and a strong sense of we're-all-in-this-together. Highly worth watching. Charles Coburn, the doctor, is especially good as the film's steady conscience.

THREE GIRLS LOST
Featured actors: Loretta Young, Lew Cody, John Wayne, Joan Marsh, and Joyce Compton
Screenplay and dialogue by Bradley King
Story by Robert D. Andrews (Robert Hardy)
Directed by Sidney Lanfield
Produced and distributed by Fox Film Corporation
Release date: April 19, 1931

Three young women from America's hinterlands join forces to find an apartment, build their careers, and nab a husband in Depression-era

Chicago. Handsome young architect Gordon Wales (John Wayne) helps one of the new neighbors when she's locked out of her flat. They quickly become an item, but then she dumps him for a wealthy beer baron. When she winds up dead, Wales is tagged as a disgruntled ex-boyfriend and arrested for her murder. Later, he falls for the dead woman's friend, who helps clear him of the murder. Ward Bond and Paul Fix also appear, in unbilled bit parts, but they're not on-screen long enough to help this humdrum movie. Fluff and nonsense.

3 GODFATHERS*
Featured actors: John Wayne, Pedro Armendariz (Pedro Armendáriz), Harry Carey, Jr., Ward Bond, Mae Marsh, Mildred Natwick, Jane Darwell, Guy Kibbee, Dorothy Ford, Ben Johnson, Charles Halton, Hank Worden, Jack Pennick, Fred Libby, Michael Dugan, and Don Summers
Screenplay by Laurence Stallings and Frank S. Nugent
Based on a story by Peter B. Kyne
Directed by John Ford
Produced by Argosy Pictures
Distributed by Metro-Goldwyn-Mayer (MGM)
Release date: December 1, 1948

Three troublemakers rob a bank, only to find themselves chased into the Arizona desert by the law, but with no water. John Wayne is Bob Hightower, a roving bank robber in the company of two other charming lawbreakers. As a wanton felon, Wayne is out of character, of course, but his antihero posturing, mixed with an unexpected sentimentality, is appealing nonetheless. The scene in which the robbers come upon a pioneer woman about to give birth is powerful, dramatic, and touching. And it is the impetus for one of Duke's longest speeches in his career.

THE THREE MUSKETEERS
Also titled DESERT COMMAND
Featured actors: Jack Mulhall, Raymond Hatton, Francis X. Bushman, Jr., John Wayne, Ruth Hall, Creighton Chaney (Lon Chaney, Jr.), Hooper Atchley, Gordon De Main, Robert Frazer, Noah Beery, Jr., Al Ferguson, Edward Piel (Edward Piel, Sr.), William Desmond, George Magrill, and Robert Warwick
Story by Norman Hall, Colbert Clark, Ben Cohn, and Wyndham Gittens
Based on a novel by Alexandre Dumas
Directed by Armand Schaeffer and Colbert Clark
Produced and distributed by Mascot Pictures
Release date: April 7, 1933

Tom Wayne (John Wayne) is a desperate character in the deserts of Arabia who bands together with his three pals in the French Foreign Legion to stop the Devil's Circle and its leader, the evil El Shaitan, from collecting an arms shipment that will lead to an Arab rebellion. Wayne sneaks into a meeting of the Devil's Circle in hope of discovering El Shaitan's true identity. All the while, Wayne must be on the lookout for his own personal Javert, an agent of the U.S. Secret Service, who pursues him relentlessly. It's another cheapie Mascot serial, so don't expect much of anything from this clunker.

THREE TEXAS STEERS
Featured actors: John Wayne, Ray Corrigan, Max Terhune, Carole Landis, Ralph Graves, Rosco Ates (Roscoe Ates), Collette Lyons, Billy Curtis, Ted Adams, Stanley Blystone, David Sharpe, Ethan Laidlaw, Lew Kelly, and Naba
Screenplay by Betty Burbridge and Stanley Roberts
Based on characters created by William Colt MacDonald
Directed by George Sherman
Produced and distributed by Republic Pictures
Release date: May 12, 1939

The Three Mesquiteers could never pass a damsel in distress, so they go to work when Nancy Evans (Carole Landis) arrives in Mesquite County to reclaim an abandoned ranch left to her in a will. A nefarious former business partner will stop at nothing to get the ranch into his own hands (obviously, he knows something we don't), including . . . murder! As with other films in the *Three Mesquiteers* series, the setting blends elements of the 1930s with the 1880s, so you never know quite where you are, timewise. The circus background at the start of the plot could have made this into a truly interesting film, but the introduction of an "ape" (just as you'd expect, an obvious actor in a second-rate monkey suit) spoils everything. The ape may have been played by Ray "Crash" Corrigan, one of the Three Mesquiteers actors, who owned an ape suit and got extra work in many 1930s and '40s movies as a result.

THE TRAIL BEYOND*
Featured actors: John Wayne, Verna Hillie, Noah Beery, Sr. (Noah Beery), Noah Beery, Jr., Robert Frazer, Iris Lancaster, James Marcus (James A. Marcus), Eddie Parker, and Earl Dwire
Screenplay by Lindsley Parsons
Based on a story by James Oliver Curwood
Directed by Robert Bradbury (Robert N. Bradbury)
Produced and distributed by Monogram Pictures (as Lone Star Productions)
Release date: October 22, 1934

Rod Drew (John Wayne) goes to Canada in search of the niece of his father's best friend. Fun to see both Noah Beery and Noah Beery, Jr., together in this action-packed film, and the scenery of California's Kings

Canyon National Park is a picturesque costar. Wicked good horse chases, lots of long leaps into rivers (at least four), and plenty of hard-knocking fistfights combine to make this one of Duke's best early efforts. The plot is typical of Wayne's Depression-era Westerns, but somewhat more enjoyable, as Wayne continues to find his footing and comfort zone as an actor.

THE TRAIN ROBBERS*
Featured actors: John Wayne, Ann-Margret, Rod Taylor, Ben Johnson, Christopher George, Bobby Vinton, Jerry Gatlin, and Ricardo Montalban
Screenplay by Burt Kennedy
Directed by Burt Kennedy
Produced by Batjac Productions
Distributed by Warner Bros.
Release date: January 17, 1973

A six-gun veteran named Lane (John Wayne) and his hardened crew of nothing-to-lose hombres head to Mexico in search of the men who stole a half million dollars in gold, in hope of earning a $50,000 reward. Unbeknownst to them, they're being followed by a mysterious band of horsemen who threaten their mission. Ann-Margret is the movie's eye candy. The dry and dusty Southwest setting is beautifully photographed. Despite some inconsistencies, the acting and action are commendable, if not stellar, and Duke is at his manly best. A nighttime shoot-out in a saloon is a fitting climax. Acting alongside Wayne are such capable players as Ricardo Montalban, Ben Johnson, Rod Taylor, and Christopher George.

TROUBLE ALONG THE WAY*
Featured actors: John Wayne, Donna Reed, Charles Coburn, Tom Tully, Sherry Jackson, Marie Windsor, Tom Helmore, Dabbs Greer, Leif Erickson, Douglas Spencer, Lester Matthews, and Chuck Connors
Screenplay by Melville Shavelson and Jack Rose
Story by Douglas Morrow and Robert Hardy Andrews
Directed by Michael Curtiz
Produced and distributed by Warner Bros.
Release date: April 4, 1953

A good old-fashioned college football movie! Steven Aloysius Williams is a disgraced, down-on-his-luck former football coach trying single-handedly to raise his precocious daughter in a New York City tenement. Family Services arrives in the form of the stern Alice Singleton (Donna Reed) to investigate his parenting skills—and possibly remove the child from the premises. At the same time, the rector of St. Anthony's College (Charles Coburn, so good in the role that it hurts) offers Wayne the chance to build a successful football program for the college in hope of staving off bankruptcy. Wayne is charming as all get-out, although the hard-drinking, gambling, womanizing part he plays runs counter to Duke's wholesome image. Yes, it's full of schmaltz, but in the best tradition of 1950s feel-good movies. On the other hand, what's up with that ending?! So what happened to the kid?! With Chuck "The Rifleman" Connors in a minor role.

TRUE GRIT+

Featured actors: John Wayne, Glen Campbell, Kim Darby, Jeremy Slate, Robert Duvall, Dennis Hopper, Alfred Ryder, Strother Martin, Jeff Corey, Ron Soble, James Westerfield, John Fiedler, John Doucette, Donald Woods, Edith Atwater, and Carlos Rivas
Screenplay by Marguerite Roberts
Based on a novel by Charles Portis
Directed by Henry Hathaway
Produced by Hal Wallis Productions
Distributed by Paramount Pictures
Release date: June 12, 1969

From its opening sequence to the very last scene, *True Grit* is one of John Wayne's finest Westerns ever. It's rife with humor, pathos, cold-blooded killing, cowboy justice, authentic staging, and dialogue that sings. *True Grit* also gives us one of Wayne's most memorable characters, Rooster Cogburn, the one-eyed, hard-drinking, seen-it-all bounty hunter whose good-vs.-evil code of honor continually clashes with the vagaries of womenfolk, whippersnappers, courthouse law, and the advance of "civilization." In 1880 Arkansas, young Mattie Ross (Kim Darby) wants to avenge the murder of her father, but the killer has absconded to the Indian Territory, where only federal marshals have jurisdiction. Traveling to Fort Smith, Arkansas, Mattie is referred to Cogburn, a vagabond marshal who agrees to find the killer in exchange for a hefty bounty. At the same time, a sergeant in the Texas Rangers (Glen Campbell) arrives in town intending to catch the killer—but for a different murder, not that of Mattie's father. When he proposes that he and Cogburn team up, Mattie objects, saying she doesn't want the murderer hanged in Texas for someone else's death, but in Fort Smith for her father's. The unlikely trio sets out into uncharted territory, where the challenges of the wilderness, cutthroats, and evildoers stymie them at every turn. The casting is impressive indeed, with Robert Duvall, Dennis Hopper, Strother Martin, John Doucette, and, in uncredited roles, Jay "Tonto" Silverheels, Wilford Brimley, and Hank Worden. *True Grit* is a film worth watching on multiple occasions, and a highlight of John Wayne's career.

TWO-FISTED LAW

Featured actors: Tim McCoy, John Wayne, Walter Brennan, Tully Marshall, Alice Day, Wheeler Oakman, Wallace MacDonald, and Richard Alexander

Story by William Colt McDonald (William Colt MacDonald)
Directed by D. Ross Lederman
Produced and distributed by Columbia Pictures
Release date: August 30, 1932

Once again in the shadow of Tim McCoy (as in *Texas Cyclone*), and with an underutilized Walter Brennan in a bit part, John Wayne plays second fiddle as a ranch hand who stands by his boss (McCoy) when their spread is taken over by an evil mortgage lender. Other ranchers in the town of Eagle Pass are facing the same fate, because their cattle are being stolen before they can pay off their loans. It doesn't take Sherlock Holmes to figure out what's going on. The film is about what you'd expect, and notable only because it is the first film in which Wayne's character is named Duke.

TYCOON
Featured actors: John Wayne, Laraine Day, Sir Cedric Hardwicke (Cedric Hardwicke), Judith Anderson, James Gleason, Anthony Quinn, Grant Withers, Paul Fix, Fernando Alvarado, Harry Woods, Michael Harvey, Charles Trowbridge, and Martin Garralaga
Screenplay by Borden Chase and John Twist
Based on a novel by C. E. Scoggins
Directed by Richard Wallace
Produced and distributed by RKO Radio Pictures
Release date: December 3, 1947

Engineer Johnny Munroe (John Wayne) finds himself in the Andes building a railroad to his employer's tin mine. While on drunken leave with his buddies in the nearby town of Tenango, he gets an eyeful of the beautiful but snooty Maura Alexander, the daughter of the railroad tycoon. They meet cute in church, then they're off to the races, except for one thing: the big boss, Mr. Alexander himself, wants Johnny nowhere near his daughter. Sir Cedric Hardwicke, Anthony Quinn, and James Gleason round out a strong support team. In the end, though, this is a sticky, overblown (and overly long) romance, without the grit and drama of the best John Wayne movies.

THE UNDEFEATED*
Featured actors: John Wayne, Rock Hudson, Tony Aguilar (Antonio Aguilar), Roman Gabriel, Marian McCargo, Lee Meriwether, Merlin Olsen, Melissa Newman, Bruce Cabot, Michael Vincent (Jan-Michael Vincent), Ben Johnson, Edward Faulkner, Harry Carey, Jr., Paul Fix, Royal Dano, Richard Mulligan, Carlos Rivas, John Agar, Guy Raymond, Don Collier, Big John Hamilton, Dub Taylor, Henry Beckman, Victor Junco, Robert Donner, Pedro Armendariz, Jr. (Pedro Armendáriz, Jr.), James Dobson, Rudy Diaz, Richard Angarola, James McEachin, Gregg Palmer, and Juan Garcia

Screenplay by James Lee Barrett
Based on a story by Stanley L. Hough (Stanley Hough)
Directed by Andrew V. McLaglen
Produced and distributed by Twentieth Century–Fox
Release date: October 4, 1969

Wayne is back in full gallop as Union colonel John Henry Thomas at the end of the Civil War. With what's left of his cavalry unit, he resigns his commission and heads to the Southwest, where the men hope to round up wild horses for a living and sell them to the Army. At the same time, Confederate colonel James Langdon (Rock Hudson) bids farewell to his plantation and his tearful slaves and takes the remnants of his Johnny Reb unit and their families on a two-thousand-mile trek to Mexico, where he hopes to find employment with Emperor Maximilian. If you didn't expect a clash between Wayne and Hudson, you haven't been paying attention. But the two former enemies develop a bond as they both trudge south to Mexico, each with his separate goal, while bands of evildoers prepare to swoop down on them all. Great fun (although the comical brawl seems pro forma). Wayne is superb, and Hudson is at his finest. The bourbon-drinking scene is priceless! It's also fun to see former Los Angeles Rams Roman Gabriel and Merlin Olsen, though neither adds much to the goings-on. Supporter Bruce Cabot is back once again, along with other second-tier players such as Jan-Michael Vincent (as Michael Vincent), the never-ending Paul Fix, Lee Meriwether, Ben Johnson, the hardworking character actor Dub Taylor, Richard Mulligan, John Agar, and Harry Carey, Jr.

THE VOICE OF HOLLYWOOD
Featured actors: Farina (Allen "Farina" Hoskins), John Wayne,
Thelma Todd, George Bancroft, El Brendel, Jackie Cooper, Lupe Velez,
Gary Cooper, Eddie Quillan, Jack Dempsey, and Estelle Taylor
Directed by Mack D'Agostino
Produced by Tec-Art Studios
Distributed by Tiffany Productions
Release date: January 17, 1932

This is the last in a series of shorts under the same title in which a revolving cast of mostly B-list stars is seen briefly in publicity appearances or performing a song or a skit. The goal is clear and unabashed: to promote the stars and their studios and to slake the public's thirst for "the real person" behind the actors' façades. Today these one-reelers are mere curiosities. In this installment, John Wayne is an announcer at mythical radio station STAR, providing transitions from one PR clip to the next.

WAKE OF THE RED WITCH
Featured actors: John Wayne, Gail Russell, Gig Young, Adele
Mara, Luther Adler, Eduard Franz, Grant Withers, Henry Daniell,

*Paul Fix, Dennis Hoey, Jeff Corey, Erskine Sanford, and Duke
Kahanamoku*
Screenplay by Harry Brown and Kenneth Gamet
Based on a novel by Garland Roark
Directed by Edward Ludwig
Produced and distributed by Republic Pictures
Release date: December 31, 1948

The year is 1860. The setting is the South Seas. Merchant vessels ply the
waters to trade for valuables with the Pacific Islanders. Among them is
the bark *Red Witch*, flagship of the Batjak Line, captained by a mysterious old salt called Ralls (John Wayne). Wayne once again plays against
type—this time, a violent, vengeance-seeking sea dog with a dodgy past,
the sort of role choice that never sits easy with Wayne fans. Among the
supporting cast (including a Walter Brennan–like Paul Fix, a mustachioed Gig Young, Luther Adler, and Grant Withers) is the fabled Hawaiian surf god, Duke Kahanamoku. If you can overlook the cheesy
giant octopus, place a star next to the movie's title. Interesting side note:
The ship Wayne captains is part of fictional Batjak Ltd., a trading firm.
A few years later, Wayne would use Batjac (a secretary misspelled it on
the incorporation papers) as the trademark for his own production company.

WAR OF THE WILDCATS
See IN OLD OKLAHOMA

THE WAR WAGON
*Featured actors: John Wayne, Kirk Douglas, Howard Keel, Robert
Walker (Robert Walker, Jr.), Keenan Wynn, Bruce Cabot, Joanna
Barnes, Valora Noland, Bruce Dern, Gene Evans, Terry Wilson,
Don Collier, Sheb Wooley, Ann McCrea, Emilio Fernandez (Emilio
Fernández), Frank McGrath, Chuck Roberson, Red Morgan (Boyd
"Red" Morgan), Hal Needham, Marco Antonio, and Perla Walters
(Perla Walter)*
Screenplay by Clair Huffaker
Based on a novel by Clair Huffaker
Directed by Burt Kennedy
*Produced by Universal Pictures, Batjac Productions, and Marvin
Schwartz Productions*
Distributed by Universal Pictures
Release date: May 23, 1967

Taw Jackson (John Wayne) plans to take revenge on Frank Pierce (Bruce
Cabot), who stole his ranch and fortune. Jackson assembles a crew to rob
Pierce's armor-plated "war wagon," used to carry gold from a mine to the
railhead. Another loser, with a mostly monosyllabic Wayne offering little
in the way of action or bons mots, and costar Kirk Douglas seemingly

too interested in showing off his slim fifty-year-old physique via stretchy pants and formfitting vests to offer any interest. Another semi-comical barroom brawl doesn't brighten things much.

WEST OF THE DIVIDE

Featured actors: John Wayne, Virginia Faire Brown (Virginia Brown Faire), George Hayes (George "Gabby" Hayes), Loyd Whitlock (Lloyd Whitlock), Yakima Canutt, Lafe McKee, Billie O'Brien (Billy O'Brien), Dick Dickinson, and Earl Dwire
Screenplay by Robert N. Bradbury
Directed by Robert N. Bradbury
Produced and distributed by Monogram Pictures (as Lone Star Productions)
Release date: February 15, 1934

Ted Hayden (John Wayne) and his saddle pal Dusty Rhodes (George Hayes) find a dying outlaw at a poisoned water hole. The villain, Gatt Ganns, is carrying a letter from the man who killed Hayden's father and stole the family ranch. Hayden assumes the identity of Ganns in the hope of exposing the man who orchestrated his father's murder. At the same time, he searches valiantly for his kid brother, who has been missing ever since the family lost the ranch, twelve years earlier. Ham-fisted storytelling requires Wayne and costar George "Gabby" Hayes to describe the events of the previous few years to put the audience in the picture. Typical of Duke's early 1930s Westerns.

WESTWARD HO

Featured actors: John Wayne, Sheila Mannors (Sheila Bromley), Frank McGlynn, Jr., James Farley (Jim Farley), Jack Curtis, Bradley Metcalfe, Dickie Jones, Mary MacLaren, Yakima Canutt, Hank Bell, Glenn Strange, and the Singing Riders
Screenplay by Robert Emmett (Robert Emmett Tansey) and Lindsley Parsons
Directed by R. N. Bradbury (Robert N. Bradbury)
Produced and distributed by Republic Pictures
Release date: August 19, 1935

John Wyatt (John Wayne) is out to get the men who killed his parents and kidnapped Jim, his younger brother. As it turns out, Jim has fallen into the clutches of the bad guys and become one of the evildoers. Meanwhile, men wearing dark shirts and white neckerchiefs while riding white horses cavort through the West, singing, to get rid of the bad guys. Perhaps the most ludicrous film ever made. Nonetheless, the stunning cinematography of the deserts and mountains makes this a visually pleasing film. This was the first of thirty-three Republic films starring Wayne.

WINDS OF THE WASTELAND

Featured actors: John Wayne, Phyllis Fraser, Lew Kelly, Douglas Cosgrove, Lane Chandler, Sam Flint, Robert Kortman (Bob Kortman), Ed Cassidy, Charles Locher (Jon Hall), W. M. McCormick (Merrill McCormick), Chris Franke (Christian J. Frank), Jack Rockwell, Arthur Millett, and Tracy Layne
Screenplay and original story by Joseph Poland (Joseph F. Poland)
Directed by Mack V. Wright
Produced and distributed by Republic Pictures
Release date: July 6, 1936

John Blair (John Wayne) and his buddy Larry are forced out of the Pony Express by the newfangled telegraph. They decide to buy a stagecoach business but only too late discover that one end of the line, Crescent City, is a nearly deserted town that has little need of stage service. Our heroes then plan to enter a competition for a government contract to deliver mail, which would allow their nascent stage business to thrive. But to win the contest, they must grapple with the no-account villain who sold them the useless stage franchise in the first place and who now is competing against them for the government contract. Who will win? Who do you think?

THE WINGS OF EAGLES

Featured actors: John Wayne, Dan Dailey, Maureen O'Hara, Ward Bond, Ken Curtis, Edmund Lowe, Kenneth Tobey, James Todd, Barry Kelley, Sig Ruman, Henry O'Neill, Willis Bouchey, and Dorothy Jordan
Screenplay by Frank Fenton and William Wister Haines
Based on the life and writings of Commander Frank W. "Spig" Wead, USN
Directed by John Ford
Produced and distributed by Metro-Goldwyn-Mayer (MGM)
Release date: January 31, 1957

A biopic dramedy, with broad slapstick (note the Army-Navy banquet fight scenes) mixed with doses of deep drama (the death of a child), this film would set the tone for many of Wayne's films in later years, including *North to Alaska, The War Wagon,* and *Donovan's Reef.* John Wayne is Navy flyboy "Spig" Wead, an ardent aviation advocate whose passion is often at odds with his young family's well-being. Meantime, Spig does battle with the bureaucracy while risking his own life to prove that Navy fliers can compete with the best of what the Army has to offer. A debilitating injury risks his chances of ever walking again, but determination and hard work ultimately get him back on his feet. *Wings* is notable for Duke's obvious balding in the latter parts of the film. Maureen O'Hara as Wayne's wife is underutilized. Supporting players include a chipper Dan Dailey, Ward Bond (who, unfortunately, doesn't even enter the screen until more than an hour after the opening credits), Ken Curtis, veteran character actor Kenneth Tobey, and uncredited walk-ons by Louis Jean Heydt and Tige Andrews (the latter of TV's *The Mod Squad*).

WITHOUT RESERVATIONS*

Featured actors: Claudette Colbert, John Wayne, Don DeFore, Anne Triola, Phil Brown, Frank Puglia, Thurston Hall, Dona Drake, Fernando Alvarado, Charles Arnt, and Miss Louella Parsons (Louella Parsons)
Screenplay by Andrew Solt
Based on a novel by Jane Allen and Mae Livingston
Directed by Mervyn LeRoy
Produced and distributed by RKO Radio Pictures
Release date: May 13, 1946

Christopher "Kit" Madden (Claudette Colbert, as effervescent as always) heads from New York to Hollywood, where she is contracted to adapt her bestselling novel for the big screen. On the train to the Coast, Kit is captivated by Marine flyer Rusty Thomas (John Wayne), who is completely unaware of Kit's reputation or her book's worldwide fame. Charming, handsome, and well able to fill out a uniform, could Rusty be the "unknown" the studio is hoping to find for the lead role in Kit's movie? Don DeFore as Rusty's Marine buddy is a delight. Madcap mayhem? Nah. The movie lacks the wit to be a screwball comedy. And Colbert, billed above Wayne in the credits, has more screen time and good lines than Duke does. It's not a total loss, though, and is worth 1:40:52 of your time, if you have nothing pressing on the calendar. Plus, there are cameos from Jack Benny and Cary Grant! Sidebar: Take note of the pro-immigrant theme two-thirds of the way through the film, when Wayne, Colbert, and DeFore end up at the Ortega Rancho en route to California.

WORDS AND MUSIC

Featured actors: Lois Moran, Tom Patricola, David Percy, Helen Twelvetrees, Frank Albertson, Elizabeth Patterson, Duke Morrison (John Wayne), William Orlamond, Biltmore Quartette, Collier Sisters, Bubbles Crowell, Vina Gale, Muriel Gardner, Harriet Griffith, John Griffith, Charles Huff, Helen Hunt, Dorothy Jordan, Richard Keene, Helen Parrish, Arthur Springer, Jack Wade, and Dorothy Ward
Scenario by Andrew Bennison
Story by Frederick Hazlitt Brennan and Jack McEdwards
Directed by James Tinling
Produced and distributed by Fox Film Corporation
Release date: September 15, 1929

Another so-called lost film. College students (including Ward Bond as an extra) compete for best song (and prettiest girl) in a contest. John Wayne as frat boy Pete Donahue wants Mary Brown to perform his number in the annual revue. Trouble is, his musical fraternity brother Phil Denning has the same idea. Mary, who is fond of both boys, agrees to perform each of their numbers. At the last minute, though, Phil gives his song to Dorothy, the campus Jezebel. Only at the last minute does Mary realize that Dorothy has blackmailed Phil into giving the song to her. Apparently, audiences in the 1920s loved this sort of stuff. The film marks John Wayne's first screen credit, albeit as "Duke Morrison."

WYOMING OUTLAW

Featured actors: John Wayne, Ray Corrigan, Raymond Hatton, Donald Barry (Don "Red" Barry), Adele Pearce (Pamela Blake), LeRoy Mason, Charles Middleton, Katherine Kenworthy, Elmo Lincoln, Jack Ingram, David Sharpe, Jack Kenney, and Yakima Canutt
Screenplay by Jack Natteford and Betty Burbridge
Based on characters created by William Colt MacDonald
Directed by George Sherman
Produced and distributed by Republic Pictures
Release date: June 27, 1939

Who could go six months without a Three Mesquiteers movie? This time, however, we've got Raymond Hatton subbing for Max Terhune (and his puppet, Elmer), but without explanation as to why Lullaby Joslin has been replaced by Rusty Joslin. Trust me, if you'd been watching all these movies, you'd be asking the same question. Cool note: Yakima Canutt is in here (true to form, playing a henchman), as is Elmo Lincoln (as U.S. Marshal Gregg), the first actor to portray Tarzan, back in 1918. The subtle socialist message is interesting for a John Wayne oater—that Depression-era corruption was preventing the good folks from getting enough to eat—but otherwise, the film is typical of the *Three Mesquiteers* series.

APPENDIX B

All Films in Chronological Order

Note: Films are listed in order of their U.S. premiere and/or general release dates. International release dates may differ. The numbers of the films below correspond to the footnotes in the book's quotations.

1. *Brown of Harvard* (1926)
2. *Bardelys the Magnificent* (1926)
3. *The Great K & A Train Robbery* (1926)
4. *The Draw-Back* (1927)
5. *Annie Laurie* (1927)
6. *The Drop Kick* (1927)
7. *Seeing Stars* (1927)
8. *Mother Machree* (1928)
9. *Four Sons* (1928)
10. *Hangman's House* (1928)
11. *A Home-Made Man* (1928)
12. *Noah's Ark* (1928)
13. *Strong Boy* (1929)
14. *Speakeasy* (1929)
15. *The Black Watch* (1929)
16. *Salute* (1929)
17. *Words and Music* (1929)
18. *The Forward Pass* (1929)
19. *The Lone Star Ranger* (1930)
20. *Men Without Women* (1930)
21. *Born Reckless* (1930)
22. *Rough Romance* (1930)
23. *Cheer Up and Smile* (1930)
24. *The Big Trail* (1930)
25. *Girls Demand Excitement* (1931)
26. *Three Girls Lost* (1931)
27. *Arizona* (also titled *Men Are Like That*) (1931)
28. *The Deceiver* (1931)
29. *The Range Feud* (1931)
30. *Maker of Men* (1931)
31. *The Voice of Hollywood* (1932)
32. *The Shadow of the Eagle* (1932)
33. *Texas Cyclone* (1932)
34. *Lady and Gent* (1932)
35. *The Hurricane Express* (1932)
36. *Ride Him, Cowboy* (1932)
37. *Two-Fisted Law* (1932)
38. *The Big Stampede* (1932)
39. *That's My Boy* (1932)
40. *Haunted Gold* (1932)
41. *The Telegraph Trail* (1933)
42. *Central Airport* (1933)
43. *The Three Musketeers* (also titled *Desert Command*) (1933)
44. *Somewhere in Sonora* (1933)
45. *His Private Secretary* (1933)
46. *The Life of Jimmy Dolan* (1933)

47. *Baby Face* (1933)

48. *The Man from Monterey* (1933)

49. *Riders of Destiny* (1933)

50. *College Coach* (1933)

51. *Sagebrush Trail* (1933)

52. *The Lucky Texan* (1934)

53. *West of the Divide* (1934)

54. *Blue Steel* (1934)

55. *The Man from Utah* (1934)

56. *Randy Rides Alone* (1934)

57. *The Star Packer* (1934)

58. *The Trail Beyond* (1934)

59. *The Lawless Frontier* (1934)

60. *'Neath the Arizona Skies* (1934)

61. *Texas Terror* (1935)

62. *Rainbow Valley* (1935)

63. *The Desert Trail* (1935)

64. *The Dawn Rider* (1935)

65. *Paradise Canyon* (1935)

66. *Westward Ho* (1935)

67. *The New Frontier* (1935)

68. *Lawless Range* (1935)

69. *The Oregon Trail* (1936)

70. *The Lawless Nineties* (1936)

71. *King of the Pecos* (1936)

72. *The Lonely Trail* (1936)

73. *Winds of the Wasteland* (1936)

74. *Sea Spoilers* (1936)

75. *Conflict* (1936)

76. *California Straight Ahead!* (1937)

77. *I Cover the War!* (1937)

78. *Idol of the Crowds* (1937)

79. *Adventure's End* (1937)

80. *Born to the West* (also titled *Hell Town*) (1937)

81. *Pals of the Saddle* (1938)

82. *Overland Stage Raiders* (1938)

83. *Santa Fe Stampede* (1938)

84. *Red River Range* (1938)

85. *Stagecoach* (1939)

86. *The Night Riders* (1939)

87. *Three Texas Steers* (1939)

88. *Wyoming Outlaw* (1939)

89. *New Frontier* (1939)

90. *Allegheny Uprising* (1939)

91. *Dark Command* (1940)

92. *Three Faces West* (1940)

93. *The Long Voyage Home* (1940)

94. *Seven Sinners* (1940)

95. *A Man Betrayed* (1941)

96. *Lady from Louisiana* (1941)

97. *The Shepherd of the Hills* (1941)

98. *Lady for a Night* (1942)

99. *Reap the Wild Wind* (1942)

100. *The Spoilers* (1942)

101. *In Old California* (1942)

102. *Flying Tigers* (1942)

103. *Pittsburgh* (1942)

104. *Reunion in France* (1942)

105. *A Lady Takes a Chance* (1943)

106. *In Old Oklahoma* (also titled *War of the Wildcats*) (1943)

107. *The Fighting Seabees* (1944)

108. *Tall in the Saddle* (1944)

109. *Flame of Barbary Coast* (1945)

110. *Back to Bataan* (1945)

111. *Dakota* (1945)

112. *They Were Expendable* (1945)

113. *Without Reservations* (1946)

114. *Angel and the Badman* (1947)

115. *Tycoon* (1947)

116. *Fort Apache* (1948)

117. *Red River* (1948)

118. *3 Godfathers* (1948)

119. *Wake of the Red Witch* (1948)

120. *She Wore a Yellow Ribbon* (1949)

121. *The Fighting Kentuckian* (1949)

122. *Sands of Iwo Jima* (1949)

123. *Rio Grande* (1950)

124. *Operation Pacific* (1951)

125. *Flying Leathernecks* (1951)

126. *The Quiet Man* (1952)

127. *Big Jim McLain* (1952)

128. *Trouble Along the Way* (1953)

129. *Island in the Sky* (1953)

130. *Hondo* (1953)

131. *The High and the Mighty* (1954)

132. *The Sea Chase* (1955)

133. *Blood Alley* (1955)

134. *The Conqueror* (1956)

135. *The Searchers* (1956)

136. *The Wings of Eagles* (1957)

137. *Jet Pilot* (1957)

138. *Legend of the Lost* (1957)

139. *I Married a Woman* (1958)

140. *The Barbarian and the Geisha* (1958)

141. *Rio Bravo* (1959)

142. *The Horse Soldiers* (1959)

143. *The Alamo* (1960)

144. *North to Alaska* (1960)

145. *The Comancheros* (1961)

146. *The Man Who Shot Liberty Valance* (1962)

147. *Hatari!* (1962)

148. *The Longest Day* (1962)

149. *How the West Was Won* (1962)

150. *Donovan's Reef* (1963)

151. *McLintock!* (1963)

152. *Circus World* (1964)

153. *The Greatest Story Ever Told* (1965)

154. *In Harm's Way* (1965)

155. *The Sons of Katie Elder* (1965)

156. *Cast a Giant Shadow* (1966)

157. *The War Wagon* (1967)

158. *El Dorado* (1967)

159. *The Green Berets* (1968)

160. *Hellfighters* (1968)

161. *True Grit* (1969)

162. *The Undefeated* (1969)

163. *Chisum* (1970)

164. *Rio Lobo* (1970)

165. *Big Jake* (1971)

166. *The Cowboys* (1972)

167. *Cancel My Reservation* (1972)

168. *The Train Robbers* (1973)

169. *Cahill, United States Marshal* (1973)

170. *McQ* (1974)

171. *Brannigan* (1975)

172. *Rooster Cogburn* (1975)

173. *The Shootist* (1976)

APPENDIX C

The Best John Wayne Movies of All Time

The Essentials

These twenty movies, listed in chronological order, should be on every John Wayne fan's must-watch list.

1. *The Big Trail* (1930)
2. *Stagecoach* (1939)
3. *Angel and the Badman* (1947)
4. *Fort Apache* (1948)
5. *Red River* (1948)
6. *3 Godfathers* (1948)
7. *She Wore a Yellow Ribbon* (1949)
8. *Sands of Iwo Jima* (1949)
9. *Rio Grande* (1950)
10. *The Quiet Man* (1952)
11. *Hondo* (1953)
12. *The Searchers* (1956)
13. *Rio Bravo* (1959)
14. *The Alamo* (1960)
15. *The Man Who Shot Liberty Valance* (1962)
16. *McLintock!* (1963)
17. *True Grit* (1969)
18. *Big Jake* (1971)
19. *The Cowboys* (1972)
20. *The Shootist* (1976)

The Eminently Watchable

These thirty-five films may not rate among the best of the best Wayne movies, but they are fun, well acted, written with verve, and directed by pros.

1. *The Trail Beyond* (1934)
2. *'Neath the Arizona Skies* (1934)
3. *The New Frontier* (1935) (not to be confused with *New Frontier* from 1939)
4. *Three Faces West* (1940)
5. *The Long Voyage Home* (1940)
6. *Seven Sinners* (1940)
7. *The Shepherd of the Hills* (1941)
8. *The Spoilers* (1942)
9. *Flying Tigers* (1942)
10. *A Lady Takes a Chance* (1943)
11. *In Old Oklahoma* (1943)
12. *The Fighting Seabees* (1944)
13. *Tall in the Saddle* (1944)
14. *Dakota* (1945)

15. *Without Reservations* (1946)
16. *Flying Leathernecks* (1951)
17. *Trouble Along the Way* (1953)
18. *Island in the Sky* (1953)
19. *The High and the Mighty* (1954)
20. *The Sea Chase* (1955)
21. *Blood Alley* (1955)
22. *Legend of the Lost* (1957)
23. *The Horse Soldiers* (1959)
24. *The Comancheros* (1961)
25. *The Longest Day* (1962)
26. *How the West Was Won* (1962)
27. *Donovan's Reef* (1963)
28. *The Sons of Katie Elder* (1965)
29. *Cast a Giant Shadow* (1966)
30. *El Dorado* (1967)
31. *The Green Berets* (1968)
32. *The Undefeated* (1969)
33. *Rio Lobo* (1970)
34. *The Train Robbers* (1973)
35. *Rooster Cogburn* (1975)

APPENDIX D

Just for Fun—by the Numbers

37

Wayne characters named "John"

Roles named John account for 21 percent of all Wayne's films. In the first instance, he was "John Drury" in *Ride Him, Cowboy* (1932), and, for the last time, "John Bernard Books" in *The Shootist* (1976), his farewell film appearance.

5

Wayne characters named "Duke"

He was plain old "Duke" in *Two-Fisted Law* (1932), "Duke Slade" in *Adventure's End* (1937), "Duke Hudkins" in *A Lady Takes a Chance* (1943), "Duke Fergus" in *Flame of Barbary Coast* (1944), and "Duke Gifford" in *Operation Pacific* (1951).

6

Wayne's horses named "Duke"

Actually, it was the same horse (apparently) in six Warner Bros. Four Star Westerns, 1932–33, identified by the "AH" brand. Sometimes referred to as Duke the Miracle Horse, this handsome white stallion comes off as smarter than some of the villains in Wayne's early Westerns.

18

Wayne's age in his first film appearance

As a member of the popular USC football squad, Wayne and a number of his teammates were sometimes given part-time jobs on studio lots. During the filming of *Brown of Harvard* (1926), Wayne was offered the chance to stand in for star Francis X. Bushman in a football scene.

22

Wayne's age in his first starring role

Director Raoul Walsh was casting for *The Big Trail* (1930) when he noticed the strapping young Wayne on the lot. Walsh thought the young Duke looked right for the lead role of trail scout Breck Coleman. When John Ford, who had previously directed Wayne as an extra, vouched for the young actor, Walsh hired him, despite Duke's lack of experience as a featured player.

69
Wayne's age when his final film was released

The Shootist (1976) wasn't made to be Duke's swan song; it just turned out that way. Wayne's health was deteriorating by the time *The Shootist* was filmed, and even though he appeared several times on television afterward, he never again made a movie. He died less than three years later, at age seventy-two.

24
Directed (all or in part) by John Ford

The total includes *Hondo* and *The Alamo,* in which Ford was not the primary director but did oversee some second-unit scenes. Ford also directed Wayne three times on television: *Screen Directors Playhouse* (episode "Rookie of the Year," 1955), *Wagon Train* (episode "The Colter Craven Story," 1960), and *Alcoa Premiere* (episode "Flashing Spikes," with Wayne billed as Marion Morrison, 1962).

82
Non-Western films

Wayne has portrayed football players and football coaches, boxers and bus drivers, playboys, plowboys, and pilots galore, not to mention servicemen in thirteen films set during World War II. He even played himself— twice: once in a George Gobel comedy and again in a Bob Hope comedy.

91
Western films

Depending on how you define the genre (the number above includes those movies set in cowboy days, frontier America, the Alaskan gold rush, and the post–Civil War South), Westerns formed the majority of works in Wayne's career.

2
Films in which Wayne calls someone "pilgrim"

In *The Man Who Shot Liberty Valance,* Wayne famously calls newly arrived lawyer Ransom Stoddard (James Stewart) "pilgrim" two dozen times throughout the plot. He also uses the term the following year in *McLintock!* just before punching a recent settler. "Pilgrim" was sometimes used by Westerners to refer to new arrivals from back East, who were often perceived to be weak, timid, and religious.

40
Times Orson Welles watched *Stagecoach* before filming *Citizen Kane*

In tribute to the cinematic brilliance of director John Ford, Welles called *Stagecoach* a "textbook" of filmmaking. That's quite a compliment, considering that *Citizen Kane* is cited in numerous polls as the greatest film of all time.

197
Length (in minutes) of Wayne's longest film

The Alamo was three hours and seventeen minutes long when it premiered in Los Angeles in the fall of 1960. It was immediately cut by thirty-five minutes for general release, which makes his next-longest film—appropriately titled *The Longest Day* (1962), at 178 minutes—the technical winner, followed by *In Harm's Way* at 167 minutes. The edited version of *The Alamo*, at 162 minutes, is the show horse in that cinematic trifecta.

3
Oscar nominations

Wayne never had the full respect of the Academy, despite his powerful box-office appeal and his genial off-screen manner. He was nominated for Best Actor in *Sands of Iwo Jima* (1949) and *True Grit* (1969) and for Producer of *The Alamo* (1960).

1
Oscar win

John Wayne's lone Academy Award was given to him in 1970 for Best Actor for his portrayal of eye-patch-wearing Rooster Cogburn in *True Grit,* released the previous year. His heartfelt acceptance speech is almost Lincolnesque in its brevity and sincerity: "Wow! If I'd've known that, I'd've put that patch on thirty-five years earlier. Ladies and gentlemen, I'm no stranger to this podium. I've come up here and picked up these beautiful golden men before—but always for friends. One night I picked up two: one for Admiral John Ford and one for our beloved Gary Cooper. I was very clever and witty that night, the envy of even Bob Hope. But tonight I don't feel very clever or very witty. I feel very grateful, very humble, and all thanks to many, many people. I want to thank the members of the Academy. To all you people who are watching on television, thank you for taking such a warm interest in our glorious industry. Good night."

ACKNOWLEDGMENTS

I gratefully recognize the scores of talented writers of John Wayne's screenplays and the source material on which they are based. Without their words, this book (and possibly "John Wayne") would not exist. They are:

Goodman Ace, Jane Allen, Robert Hardy Andrews, Stuart Anthony, Robert Ardrey, Gladys Atwater, James Lee Barrett, Ben Barzman, James Bassett, Rex Beach, Ford Beebe, James Warner Bellah, Edmund Beloin, Charles Bennett, Ted Berkman, Claude Binyon, David Boehm, John Hunter Booth, Marvin Borowsky, Herman Boxer, Leigh Brackett, Robert N. Bradbury, J. Robert Bren, Harry Brown, Adele Buffington, Betty Burbridge, W. R. Burnett, Thomson Burtis, Niven Busch, Leslie Bush-Fekete, Michael Butler, Vera Caspary, Prescott Chaplin, Borden Chase, Colbert Clark, Donald Henderson Clarke, Kenneth B. Clarke, Ben Cohn, Lewis D. Collins, Will Levington Comfort, Richard Edward Connell, Marc Connelly, Harry Crane, James Oliver Curwood, Scott Darling, Donald Davis, Isabel Dawn, Boyce Degaw, Henry Denker, Beulah Marie Dix, Alexandre Dumas, Guy Endore, Richard English, Harry Essex, Howard Estabrook, Hal G. Evarts, Francis Edward Faragoh, Randall Faye, Andrew J. Fenady, Frank Fenton, Harry Julian Fink, Rita M. Fink, Bob Fisher, Paul Fix, A. S. Fleischman, Ladislas Fodor, John Ford, Carl Foreman, Garrett Fort, Jan Fortune, Harriet Frank, Jr., Jules Furthman, Kenneth Gamet, Ernest K. Gann, Romain Gary, Andrew Geer, Erwin Gelsey, Wyndham Gittens, Willis Goldbeck, Bernard Gordon, William Gordon, James Edward Grant, Charles Grayson, Howard J. Green, Zane Grey, Eleanore Griffin, William Wister Haines, Scott Hale, Norman Hall, Robert Hardy, Ernest Haycox, Lawrence Hazard, Ben Hecht, F. Hugh Herbert, Ethel Hill, Michael Hogan, Stanley Hough, Lionel Houser, Clair Huffaker, Martha Hyer, Frances Hyland, Marion Jackson, Edward James, Rian James, Talbot Jennings, William Dale Jennings, Dorothy M. Johnson, Grover Jones, James Jones, John Kafka, Edmond Kelso, Kurt Kempler, Burt Kennedy, Paul W. Keyes, Tom Kilpatrick, Bradley King, Ben Grauman Kohn, Norman Krasna, Milton Krims, Harry Kurnitz, Peter B. Kyne, Louis L'Amour, Richard H. Landau, Sidney Lanfield, Jesse Lasky, Jr., Alan LeMay, Elliott Lester, Mae Livingston, Jack London, Jan Lustig, William Colt MacDonald, Aeneas MacKenzie, B. H. McCampbell, Bernard McConville, William P. McGivern, Dorrell McGowan, J. P. McGowan, Stuart E. McGowan, James Kevin

McGuinness, Williams Slavens McNutt, John Lee Mahin, Joseph Moncure March, Gene Markey, Arthur Marx, Leslie Mason, Scott Mason, Wendell Mayes, John Meehan, James A. Michener, Bertram Milhauser, Oscar Millard, Seton I. Miller, Jack Moffitt, Robin Moore, George Morgan, Douglas Morrow, Jack Natteford, William W. Norton, Lloyd Nosler, Frank S. Nugent, Bob O'Brien, Eugene O'Neill, Samuel Ornitz, Fulton Oursler, George Owen, Lindsley Parsons, Scott Pembroke, Kenneth Perkins, Joseph F. Poland, Charles Portis, Robert Presnell, Jr., Gertrude Purcell, David Pursall, Martin Rackin, Irving Ravetch, Nicholas Ray, Tom Reed, Robert Riskin, Joe Roach, Garland Roark, Marguerite Roberts, Stanley Roberts, Lawrence Roman, Jack Rose, Cornelius Ryan, Ellis St. Joseph, Barney A. Sarecky, Charles Schnee, C. E. Scoggins, Kathryn Scola, Jack Seddon, Edward Sedgwick, Manuel Seff, James Seymour, Melville Shavelson, Harold Sinclair, Barney Slater, Andrew Solt, Laurence Stallings, George Stevens, John Stone, Thelma Strabel, Sidney Sutherland, Neil H. Swanson, Glendon Swarthout, Miles Hood Swarthout, Jo Swerling, Robert Emmett Tansey, Norman Taurog, Eric Taylor, Augustus Thomas, Harlan Thompson, Barry Trivers, Christopher Trumbo, Harry Tugend, Tristram Tupper, Burl R. Tuttle, John Twist, László Vadnay, George Waggner, Francis Wallace, Maurice Walsh, Luci Ward, Commander Frank W. "Spig" Wead, James R. Webb, Walter Weems, Allan Weiss, Paul I. Wellman, William L. White, Phil Whitman, Ben Ames Williams, Burton Wohl, P. J. Wolfson, Harold Bell Wright, William H. Wright, Philip Yordan, Robert Yost, Gordon Ray Young, Darryl F. Zanuck, and Julian Zimet.

My thanks also go to my agent, Jeffrey Herman; George Witte, editor in chief of St. Martin's Press; and Michael Homler, senior editor at St. Martin's Press, all of whom made publication possible.

My children, Caitlin, Gillian, and Rory, are inspirations to me daily. Kathleen Fox, my wife, never begrudged me the thousands of hours I invested in this project, squirreled away in my treetop writing studio. Only occasionally did she roll her eyes in forbearance when my obsession with this book seemed to overtake me. Love you, Kat.